To

....

From

....

Date

....

365 Daily Devotions

FOR WOMEN

ENCOURAGEMENT FOR EVERY DAY

BARBOUR BOOKS
An Imprint of Barbour Publishing, Inc.

© 2020 by Barbour Publishing, Inc.

Compiled and edited by Linda Hang.

ISBN 978-1-64352-304-0

Devotions previously appeared in *Daily Wisdom for Women: 2013 Devotional Collection*, *Daily Wisdom for Women: 2014 Devotional Collection*, *Daily Wisdom for Women: 2015 Devotional Collection*, *365 Encouraging Verses of the Bible for Women*, *365 Daily Devotions from the Psalms*.

All scripture quotations are taken from the King James Version of the Bible.

Published by Barbour Books, an imprint of Barbour Publishing, Inc., 1810 Barbour Drive, Uhrichsville, Ohio 44683, www.barbourbooks.com

Our mission is to inspire the world with the life-changing message of the Bible.

Member of the
Evangelical Christian
Publishers Association

Printed in China.

INTRODUCTION

More than 400 years after its first publication, the King James Version remains one of the most popular Bible translations available. The beautiful phrasing and cadence of the King James Version have stood the test of time, providing for a moving and powerful reading experience. Believed by many to be one of the most literal and accurate translations of the original Bible languages, the King James Version has changed countless lives over four centuries.

Here, in 365 daily readings, you'll find encouragement from God's Word for an entire year. Spend quiet time immersed in the wisdom only the living and active Word of the Creator of the Universe can offer you, and be blessed!

The Publisher

Day 1

HIS JOY

The LORD thy God in the midst of thee is mighty;
he will save, he will rejoice over thee with joy; he will
rest in his love, he will joy over thee with singing.
ZEPHANIAH 3:17

Joy. What a wonderful word! The connotations of delight and gladness. You are usually joyful when something has pleased you. Maybe it's an energizing run, the chatter of a child, or simply a quiet, starry night that soothes your senses and fills your heart with satisfaction.

Scripture tells us the Lord will rejoice over us with singing. Imagine that! The Mighty Warrior of the universe relishing His creation. And that creation is you. It's hard to imagine when we have our dirty faces or are out of sorts that He could care for us at all. But it's true. Our God saves and loves. Our God is truth and mercy.

Take a deep breath and carve out some time to appreciate and bask in the truth of the Bible. God loves *you* and He rejoices in *you*. You are the apple of His eye. Reach out a hand to Him this day, knowing full well He will interlace His fingers with yours and never let go.

Father God, how we love You. We do not understand
the depth and breadth of Your love for us,
but we are ever so grateful. Amen.

Day 2
REJECTED!

*The stone which the builders refused is
become the head stone of the corner.*
PSALM 118:22

———————— ✺ ————————

When Jesus walked on the earth, it was not the common people, but
those who should have known better, that rejected Him. The learned
men of the day, who had studied long and hard, knew that the Messiah
was to come, but they were unwilling to accept the carpenter's son from
Galilee as the Chosen One. They rejected Him and masterminded His
death on a cross, but that was not enough to thwart the holy plans of
God. Christ was, is, and always will be the one true Son of God. Those
who reject Him build their faith with faulty materials. Only Christ is the
true cornerstone of faith. Upon that stone alone can true faith be built.

———————— ✺ ————————

*Provide the foundation for my faith, Oh God,
and help me to construct a fortress that will withstand
all assaults. Protect me with Your love. Amen.*

Day 3

PRAY FOR OTHERS

I exhort therefore, that, first of all, supplications, prayers, intercessions, and giving of thanks, be made for all men.
1 Timothy 2:1

After Moses received the Ten Commandments from God on Mount Sinai, he called the Israelites together and said to them, "The Lord talked with you face to face in the mount out of the midst of the fire, (I stood between the Lord and you at that time, to shew you the word of the Lord: for ye were afraid by reason of the fire, and went not up into the mount)" (Deuteronomy 5:4–5). Moses often was the intermediary between God and His people. He interceded on their behalf.

Intercessory prayer is a divine act of love and service. It requires persistence, patience, and faith in God. Christians should intercede for family and friends, their country, government leaders, their pastors, the Church, the poor, the sick, the community in which they live, their enemies, and especially for those who are not saved. Wherever there is a need, Christians should pray.

The Bible holds many examples of intercessory prayer. Look for them as you read the scriptures. Discover how God's people prayed and the great changes those prayers made.

Intercessory prayer is just as important today as it was in Moses' time. It draws believers nearer to God and provides them with a powerful way to help others. Whom will you pray for today?

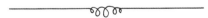

Heavenly Father, guide me as I pray for others. Help me to pray for them faithfully, patiently, and persistently. Amen.

GIVE IT ALL

Then Jesus beholding him loved him, and said unto him,
One thing thou lackest: go thy way, sell whatsoever thou hast,
and give to the poor, and thou shalt have treasure in heaven: and
come, take up the cross, and follow me. And he was sad at that
saying, and went away grieved: for he had great possessions.
MARK 10:21–22

———————— ✿ ————————

It wasn't the response the rich young ruler wanted to hear. Things usually went his way. His position and prestige afforded him that.

But these straightforward, piercing words, blended with the love in Jesus' eyes, troubled the man's soul. It just was too much. He understood just what was being asked of him—everything! The pain in his heart was reflected on his face and in his posture as he slumped away. The truth was, this ruler was not ready to relinquish his all for Jesus.

What has Christ asked *you* to let go of? What are you holding tightly to? Most of us don't have great wealth (we might wish for that kind of "problem"), but are we willing to give up what we *do* have to serve Him?

Outwardly, we may look fine. But inwardly? Are our motives pure? Do we have an "underground" thought life? Is there anger bubbling beneath our calm surface?

Today let's face the truth of exactly who we are and give up those things that prevent us from wholeheartedly serving Jesus.

———————— ✿ ————————

Lord, show me what I need to relinquish to You. Help me to
abandon everything to freely and joyfully serve You. Amen.

Day 5

A NEW DAY

O LORD, be gracious unto us; we have waited for thee: be thou their arm every morning, our salvation also in the time of trouble.

ISAIAH 33:2

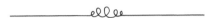

There are days that start off wrong and finish worse. Days in which we feel out of sorts, like a tire out of balance, clumsy and inefficient. We say things we shouldn't say, using a voice that is too harsh, too loud. We experience days full of failure, tinged by sin. Wouldn't it be great to redo our bad days?

We have that opportunity. It's called *tomorrow*. Lamentations 3:22–23 tells us that by God's mercies, He gives us a fresh canvas every twenty-four hours. Anger, grudges, irritations, and pain don't have to be part of it. No matter how stormy the day before, each new day starts fresh. And He is there for us first thing in the morning and every step of the way in our day, even if things begin to go wrong—again.

Every day is a new day, a new beginning, a new chance to enjoy our lives—because each day is a new day with God. We can focus on the things that matter most: worshipping Him, listening to Him, and being in His presence. No matter what happened the day before, we have a fresh start to enjoy a deeper relationship with Him. A fresh canvas, every twenty-four hours.

Before I get out of bed in the morning, let me say these words and mean them: "This is the day which the LORD hath made; we will rejoice and be glad in it" (Psalm 118:24). Amen.

Day 6

WHEN BAD THINGS HAPPEN

If the foundations be destroyed, what can the righteous do?
The LORD is in his holy temple, the LORD's throne is in heaven:
his eyes behold, his eyelids try, the children of men.
PSALM 11:3–4

What does daily life look like when an earthquake rocks a third-world country, killing hundreds of thousands and leaving an already desolate nation in ruins? When a tsunami sweeps away entire villages? When a hurricane flattens everything within a one-hundred-mile radius of the shore?

Law and order collapse when natural disasters strike. The struggle for basic survival eclipses all else. All too often, corrupt or inept governments are unable to meet the needs of their citizens when a catastrophe strikes.

Where is God when it hurts? Where is God in the midst of injustice? Does God care? These timeless questions never lose their relevance. The entire book of Job wrestles with these questions. The psalmist also picks up the lament, and only responds that God is still on the throne.

We may never understand why bad things happen or why God seems to be silent. But we can know that regardless of the way things appear, our loving God is still in control—even when things appear to be spiraling out of control. How will you trust God today?

Heavenly Father, I am always increasing my trust in You.
When bad things happen, I learn to trust You without
understanding. It is enough that You are in control. Amen.

Day 7

REJOICE!

Rejoice in the Lord always: and again I say, Rejoice.

PHILIPPIANS 4:4

Paul wrote these words from prison. Considering his circumstances, it doesn't seem like he had much reason to rejoice. Yet, he knew what many of us forget: when we have the Lord on our side, we always have reason to rejoice.

He didn't say, "Rejoice in your circumstances." He told us to rejoice in the Lord. When we're feeling depressed, anxious, or lost in despair, we can think of our Lord. We can remind ourselves that we are so very loved. We are special to God. He adores us, and in His heart, each of us is irreplaceable.

Perhaps the reason we lose our joy sometimes is because we've let the wrong things be the source of our joy. If our joy is in our finances, our jobs, or our relationships, what happens when those things fall through? Our joy is lost.

But when God is the source of our joy, we will never lose that joy. Circumstances may frustrate us and break our hearts. But God is able to supply all our needs. He is able to restore broken relationships. He can give us a new job or help us to succeed at our current job. Through it all, despite it all, we can rejoice in knowing that we are God's, and He loves us.

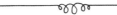

Dear Father, thank You for loving me.
Help me to make You the source of my joy. Amen.

Day 8

STAYING CLOSE

And there was one Anna, a prophetess, the daughter of Phanuel, of the tribe of Aser: she was of a great age, and had lived with an husband seven years from her virginity; and she was a widow of about fourscore and four years, which departed not from the temple, but served God with fastings and prayers night and day. And she coming in that instant gave thanks likewise unto the Lord, and spake of him to all them that looked for redemption in Jerusalem.

LUKE 2:36–38

Talk about commitment. Anna had been widowed since she was a young woman. There's no mention of her having children. Instead of finding another husband, she decided to live out her days serving God.

Anna's years of commitment paid off when she was very old. God made sure that Mary and Joseph brought Jesus to that particular temple so Anna could see Him, hold Him, and declare His presence to all who would listen.

If we want to catch God in His work, in the middle of His most exciting acts, we must stay close to the place He's working. In that day, it was the temple. Today, it might be at church or in the middle of a particular ministry project. But when we put our own schedules and agendas first and disregard God's work, we miss out on His most thrilling exploits.

Like Anna, we should do all we can to serve God and stay close to His work. When we do, we'll witness some amazing feats.

---

*Dear Father, show me where You are working,
and help me to stay close to You. Amen.*

Day 9

SPEAK LIGHT

O send out thy light and thy truth: let them lead me;
let them bring me unto thy holy hill, and to thy tabernacles.
PSALM 43:3

The tiny lighthouse sat out on the rocky shore. Without fail, its bright beacon pierced the night, and its bellowing horn echoed from the rocks, warning ships of dangers and perils. Countless boats strayed off course in dense fog, to be steered from danger by the tiny lighthouse.

True light, sent out through the clouds and darkness, can save lives. A voice speaking the truth of Christ has real power behind it: the power of salvation. Be proud of who you are and all that Christ has done for you. It matters little whether you are big, strong, smart, or powerful. What matters is that you have the truth of Christ to share, and there is no greater force in all creation.

May my light shine in the darkness until all darkness ceases to be.
Let me reflect Your divine light, Lord, clearing away the fog and
helping others come into the safety of Your love. Amen.

Day 10

MEAT OR MUSH?

Whosoever transgresseth, and abideth not in the doctrine of Christ, hath not God. He that abideth in the doctrine of Christ, he hath both the Father and the Son.

2 JOHN 1:9

———— ⁓⁓⁓ ————

Have you had to contend with "smorgasbord Christianity"? Suddenly your minister leaves, and as your congregation seeks a new leader, a succession of preachers fills the pulpit week after week. And every week you're being fed a different kind of spiritual food.

Don't relax and figure you're on a spiritual vacation. This is the time to listen very carefully. You have no idea where these people come from theologically, and it might be easy to be led astray by a deep, mellow voice or empty but high-sounding words.

Spiritual ideas abound, but not all are sound. Sometimes it's easy to assume you're getting good meat when you're actually being served mushy, rotten vegetables.

How can you tell meat from mush? Compare the message to Christ's words. Is the preacher avoiding the Bible's tough commands, preaching ideas that are not biblical, or appealing to non-Christian ideas? Better beware.

Jesus gave us strong doctrines and good teaching to lead us into His truth. Faithful expositors cling to His Word. They offer meat and milk—not rotten teachings.

Eat well!

———— ⁓⁓⁓ ————

Keep me aware of Your truth, Lord.
I want to live on it, not on mush. Amen.

Day 11

ENCOURAGING WORDS

*Let no corrupt communication proceed out of your
mouth, but that which is good to the use of edifying,
that it may minister grace unto the hearers.*

EPHESIANS 4:29

"Sticks and stones may break my bones, but words will never hurt me," goes the old saying. It's not true, however. Words can—and do—hurt. Ask anyone who was bullied as a child. Discouraging, shaming words stay with a person for years, even decades.

As we spend more time texting and giving status updates—and less time talking—we also need to be aware that whatever we "say" online stays online, for good (we can delete things, but others may have captured screen shots or printed our words out). Did you rant on Facebook about a friend or political party? It's out there. That comment belittling a coworker? It's out there. When you left a nasty comment on a blog in a moment of anger? It's out there.

As Ephesians 4:29 says, the words we choose are important. . .especially as the world becomes more disconnected and disinterested in the things of God. The way we talk, both online and off, can either attract people toward Jesus or turn them away from Him. Today, think about the language you use and the tone you're talking with. Are your word choices helpful? Are your phrases kind? Is the tone you're taking sarcastic? Cynical? Bitter? Ask God to help you think before you speak (or post).

*Father, may everything I say be helpful, kind,
and encouraging to others. Thank You for forgiving
me when I mess up, Lord—because I will. Amen.*

Day 12

KNOWING WHO YOU ARE IN CHRIST

Even the righteousness of God which is by faith of Jesus Christ unto all and upon all them that believe: for there is no difference.
ROMANS 3:22

Sometimes we measure our value by "what we do" (our work or our talents), but this should never be. Who you are is more than a name. More than a face. More than the job/work you do. You are uniquely created, a true one of a kind. You are God's kid. His. Loved. Cherished. Blessed.

What does the Bible say about you? You are a new creation. A royal priesthood. A holy nation. The righteousness of God. A holy temple. A member of the body. A citizen of heaven. Saved by faith. Raised up by Him. The aroma of Christ. Filled with heavenly gifts. Delivered from the domain of darkness. Capable of doing all things through Him who strengthens you. On and on the descriptions go.

Wow! When you read all of those things, you begin to see yourself as God sees you. You're not "just" another person. You're a child of the one true King, and He delights in you! Today, take a close look in the mirror. Don't stare at your reflection in the usual way. Get God's perspective. Then begin to see yourself the way He does.

Lord, I needed this reminder that I'm all of the things You say I am. First and foremost, I'm Yours! So, no putting myself down, Father! Give me Your eyes to see myself the way You see me. Amen.

Day 13

UNLOCK THE DOOR

*The eyes of your understanding being enlightened; that ye may
know what is the hope of his calling, and what the riches
of the glory of his inheritance in the saints.*

EPHESIANS 1:18

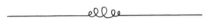

Math is a language all its own. Unfortunately, many students struggle to learn that language. Sometimes they never understand it completely but retain just enough of the language to make it through required courses. In many cases it requires another person who speaks "math" to help struggling students unlock the door to the language barrier.

Your spiritual life is also a different language. God's ways are not the ways of this world. Often His ways of doing things are similar to learning a new language. Prayer can unlock the door to understanding God's Word and His design for your life. As you spend time with God in prayer asking for understanding of His Word, His truth will speak to you in a brand-new way. The Holy Spirit will help you unlock the secrets of His purpose and plan for your life.

Discovering His purpose for your life can be exciting, if you're willing to open the door to a new adventure with Him.

*Heavenly Father, thank You for the Bible. Help me to read it with
understanding and come to know You in a whole new way. Amen.*

Day 14

ONE BIG FAMILY

But he answered and said unto him that told him,
Who is my mother? and who are my brethren?
MATTHEW 12:48

Jesus' family had heard of the crowds of people looking for healings. They were understandably worried. When someone announced their arrival, Jesus asked this question that seemed to deny them. Harsh! Was He having a bad day?

Part of the importance we place on family comes from the fear of strangers, but each "stranger" is beloved by God. Jesus wasn't excluding His mother and brothers—He was expanding the definition of family. He goes on to say, "Whosoever shall do the will of my Father which is in heaven, the same is my brother, and sister, and mother" (v. 50). That's a pretty wide net to cast—but it goes further. Even those who haven't done the will of the Father can join the family if they repent.

The idea of a universal family sounds very "summer of love." The "flower power" generation grasped the concept of loving humanity, but they sometimes put more faith in sex and drugs than in God.

The idea of a family in which we are all God's children is like G. K. Chesterton's description of Christianity. It "has not been tried and found wanting, it has been found difficult and not tried." A true family of Christ is still possible. It begins when we lay aside fear and hold out a hand.

I am honored to be a member of Your family, God. Allow me to see
beyond my own family and to reach out in love to all
my sisters and brothers in Christ. Amen.

Day 15

FOOLPROOF

Answer not a fool according to his folly, lest thou also be like unto him. Answer a fool according to his folly, lest he be wise in his own conceit.

PROVERBS 26:4–5

Skeptics love to point out what they believe are contradictions in the Bible. Well, here's one if ever there was one. The only problem is, of course, that this is no contradiction. Solomon gave these two contrasting pieces of advice, deliberately stating one right after the other, to make it clear that we are to respond differently in different circumstances. Solomon later pointed out, "To every thing there is a season," and, "A wise man's heart discerneth both time and judgment" (Ecclesiastes 3:1; 8:5).

The kind of answer you give a fool (the word here means a "self-confident person") depends on how caught up in his self-confident opinions he is, what the circumstances are, and who's standing around listening. God may lead you to give him a serious answer (in contrast to his proud chatter) or a humorous, foolish answer (to show him how foolishly he's talking).

With a full-blown fool, it's best to bite your tongue and refrain from saying anything at all (Proverbs 23:9). No matter what you say, it won't persuade him.

Dear God, when I don't know how to respond to a foolish opinion, show me. Give me the proper answer, or lead me to keep still. Amen.

Day 16

CHOOSE LIFE

*The thief cometh not, but for to steal, and to kill,
and to destroy: I am come that they might have life,
and that they might have it more abundantly.*
JOHN 10:10

Too often, it seems as if the negatives of life outweigh the positives. The bills are piling up. Your friends and family need your time and attention. So does your boss. You're exhausted and lacking mental focus. Life begins to cave in around you. . . . It's just too much!

God's Word, though, shows us the lie—and the "liar"—behind those defeating thoughts. We have an enemy who delights in our believing such negative things, an enemy who wants only destruction for our souls. But Jesus came to give us life! We only have to choose it, as an act of the will blended with faith.

God is always a gentleman—He's not going to force His life on us. But when we rely on Him alone, He'll enable us to not only survive but *thrive* in our daily routine.

Each day, let's make a conscious decision to take hold of what Christ offers us—life, to the full.

*Loving Lord, help me daily to choose You and the life You
want to give me. Give me the eyes of faith to trust
that You will enable me to thrive. Amen.*

Day 17

SHINING LIGHT

*Ye are the light of the world. A city that
is set on an hill cannot be hid.*

MATTHEW 5:14

———— *eeQ ee* ————

Jesus' disciples knew all about darkness. Centuries before electricity had been harnessed to provide light, people made do with fires and oil lamps. When the sun went down, darkness ruled.

So when Jesus told His followers that they are the light of the world, the image meant a great deal to them. Light that overtakes the darkness—light to illuminate the way to the Savior. What an amazing concept!

Jesus tells us twenty-first-century followers to be light too, boldly and unashamedly flooding the darkness that surrounds us. How do we do it? First, by living the life God calls us to—not sinless, but forgiven. Second, by sprinkling our conversations with evidence of our faith. Did something good happen? Share that blessing with others and give God the credit for it. When someone asks about the peace they see in you, share the joy of Jesus.

Being a light of the world is not about being a Bible thumper or bashing others over the head with religion. It's about living out genuine faith that allows Christ's light to break through our everyday lives. With that goal in mind, shine!

———— *ᵒᏘᏘᏙ* ————

*Jesus, You are my true light. Even though I alone can't shine as
brightly as You, I ask that You shine through me as I seek to
follow after You. I know I won't be perfect, but I also
know that Your grace has me covered. Amen.*

Day 18

TOGETHERNESS

Next unto him repaired Uzziel the son of Harhaiah, of the goldsmiths. Next unto him also repaired Hananiah the son of one of the apothecaries, and they fortified Jerusalem unto the broad wall.

NEHEMIAH 3:8

———————

When Nehemiah started rebuilding the walls of Jerusalem, he used all sorts of people. The perfume makers and goldsmiths may have supplied the means, or they may actually have put stone upon stone. Beside these artisans were merchants and rulers of districts. Men of different tribes worked side by side. Some repaired areas they had a personal interest in. Shallum repaired a section with his daughters. Priests and temple servants labored. Some were less than diligent; others were zealous.

Nehemiah called *all* believers to do the Lord's work. And, working together, they rebuilt the city walls in an amazing fifty-two days! The fact that they were surrounded on all sides by enemies may have been a further incentive.

Faith is in a similar position today. We only have one enemy, but we make him stronger when we treat our brothers and sisters as Satan's reinforcements. By allowing politics and interpretations to divide church from church we only weaken the city of God.

Make the common denominator belief in Him and we will build a wall with all His people on the inside and only Satan left on the outside.

———————

Heavenly Father, lead me to unite with my fellow believers, because when we band together there is nothing that can destroy our love and devotion toward You and Your work. Amen.

Day 19

IN HAND

And he is before all things, and by him all things consist.
COLOSSIANS 1:17

Jesus holds our world together in both the spiritual and the physical realm. It's not that He wraps His arms around our universe to keep it from falling apart. Rather, Jesus fine-tuned our Earth for life and continually preserves those conditions.

Earth's precise distance from the sun is essential to life. If Earth were 5 percent closer, rivers and oceans would evaporate from a strong greenhouse effect. Move 5 percent farther away, both water and carbon dioxide would freeze. Too cold or too hot means no life.

Even our sterile moon makes life possible by stabilizing the tilt of Earth's axis. Without the moon's steady pull, Earth's tilt could randomly swing over a wide range, resulting in temperatures too hot and too cold for life and erratic seasons.

Astronomers are also discovering how other planets in our solar system actually help Earth. For example, the huge planet Jupiter deflects many comets from entering the inner section of the solar system, where they could easily hit Earth with devastating results.

Through science we discover the physical laws Jesus designed for our universe. Through Bible study we unearth the spiritual laws Jesus designed for us. Look to Jesus to hold your life together.

You knit the heavens and Earth together perfectly. You blessed me with spiritual laws to help me live abundantly here on earth and forever with You in heaven. I praise You, Lord! Amen.

Day 20
FOR GOD

And whatsoever ye do, do it heartily,
as to the Lord, and not unto men.
COLOSSIANS 3:23

There are moments, like when we're watching a beautiful sunset or when a loved one strokes an arm in passing, that we don't hesitate to think of as gifts from God. Then there are the times we choose to see life as tedious, like when work is unappreciated or when we are stuck in the company of someone we think is boring. Those times are no less gifts from God. He is beside us always. The only difference is in how we behave, in how grateful we are.

Brother Lawrence, a seventeenth-century lay brother in a Carmelite monastery, practiced "the presence of God." Believing God was always with him, Lawrence turned the washing of the dishes and the repairing of sandals into acts of worship—simple things he would give his best to as a thank-you to the Lord.

It's easy to think you are working for the Lord when you are on some great quest. It's much more difficult to find a purpose in menial chores or to find a child of God in a self-centered bore.

But believe in the presence of God, and there is nothing you can do that can't also be an opportunity to raise a smile upon high.

Jesus, everything You did, You did for God and for me.
You never complained or refused difficult tasks. I want to be
like You—content and willing to do God's work. Amen.

A TIME FOR SADNESS AND A TIME FOR JOY

A time to weep, and a time to laugh;
a time to mourn, and a time to dance.
ECCLESIASTES 3:4

Solomon has been declared the wisest man who ever lived. The third chapter of Ecclesiastes, which Solomon authored, tells us that there is a time for everything.

Do you find yourself in a time of weeping or a joyful time today? You may be mourning a deep loss in your life. You may ache to your very core with disappointment and sorrow. There is a time to be sad. You don't have to put on a show or an artificial happy face. It is okay to grieve. It is appropriate even. There are times in our lives when we must rely on God's grace just to see us through another day. We may need to lean on other believers and let them carry us for a time. But the good news is that there are also joyful occasions. Psalm 30:5 says that weeping may last for a night but that joy comes in the morning. If you are in a sorrowful period, know that joy is just around the corner. You may not be able to imagine it today, but you will smile and even laugh again.

If you are joyful today, know that even when you face sad days, the Lord will be there walking with you. He never leaves us alone.

Thank You, God, for the knowledge that sadness does not last forever. There are highs and lows in life, and as Your Word declares, there is a time for everything. Amen.

Day 22

A PLACE IN HEAVEN

In my Father's house are many mansions: if it were not so,
I would have told you. I go to prepare a place for you.
JOHN 14:2

―――――――― *eeee* ――――――――

At times, heaven seems far, far away. You gaze into the sky and try to imagine it—God on His throne, angels singing, no more tears, only joy, only praise for the Father. But you can't see it. It is not visible to the human eye.

Other times, heaven seems ever so close. Have you said goodbye to a loved one who was a Christian? You simply let them slip away, out of your grasp, from one world to the next, from earth to heaven. Heaven seems close in those moments, just beyond a thin veil, almost reachable, almost visible. If someone you love dearly and who recently talked and laughed with you has gone there suddenly, heaven feels a little closer.

There is much we do not know about heaven, but we know that our Jesus is there preparing a place for us. We are not aware of the exact date or time that we will leave this earth, but God is. The Bible says there is an appointed time for each of us to be born and to die. There is no question for the Christian about what happens after death. We will go instantly into the presence of the Lord. If you know Jesus as your Savior, He is preparing a place in heaven—just for you.

―――――――― *ooOoo* ――――――――

Thank You, Jesus, for preparing a place for me in heaven. . .
with You. . .where I will live eternally. Amen.

Day 23

THE SECRET OF SERENDIPITY

A merry heart maketh a cheerful countenance.
PROVERBS 15:13

Can you remember the last time you laughed in wild abandon? Better yet, when was the last time you did something fun, outrageous, or out of the ordinary? Perhaps it is an activity you haven't done since you were a child, like slip down a waterslide, strap on a pair of ice skates, or pitch a tent and camp overnight.

Adults often become trapped in the cycle of routine, and soon we lose our spontaneity. Children, on the other hand, are innately spontaneous. Giggling, they splash barefoot in rain puddles. Wide-eyed, they watch a kite soar toward the treetops. They make silly faces without inhibition; they see animal shapes in rock formations. In essence, they possess the secret of serendipity.

A happy heart turns life's situations into opportunities for fun. For instance, if a storm snuffs out the electricity, light a candle and play games, tell stories, or just enjoy the quiet. When we seek innocent pleasures, we glean the benefits of a happy heart.

Jesus said, "I am come that they might have life, and that they might have it more abundantly" (John 10:10). God wants us to enjoy life, and when we do, it lightens our load and changes our countenance.

So try a bit of whimsy just for fun. And rediscover the secret of serendipity.

Dear Lord, because of You, I have a happy heart.
Lead me to do something fun and spontaneous today! Amen.

Day 24

A SECOND LOOK

Thou shalt love thy neighbour as thyself.
LEVITICUS 19:18

Most Christians have never actually read the book of Leviticus. As far as they can see from skimming its pages, it contains endless lists of laws and regulations and tedious, outdated instructions on how to sacrifice animals and stay ritually pure. The book of Deuteronomy, they feel, is almost as irrelevant to life in the modern world.

Yet the two greatest commandments in the Old Testament are found in Leviticus and Deuteronomy.

When a Pharisee asked Jesus, "Which is the great commandment in the law?" Jesus didn't quote any of the well-known Ten Commandments that most of us would have repeated. Instead, He quoted Deuteronomy 6:5: "Thou shalt love the LORD thy God with all thy heart." Jesus then stated emphatically, "This is the first and great commandment. And the second is like unto it." He then quoted Leviticus 19:18: "Thou shalt love thy neighbour as thyself" (Matthew 22:35–40).

If the two most important commands in the Law are found in these "dull, dry" books, what *else* might be found there that can inspire and guide us? Stray off the beaten path of your scripture reading and explore the remote corners of your Bible. There are wonderful gems hidden there.

Dear God, I confess that I've found some books of the Bible uninteresting; but I will revisit them! Reveal to me what's hidden there. Open my eyes and my heart. Amen.

Day 25

GOD WILL RESCUE YOU

He brought me forth also into a large place;
he delivered me, because he delighted in me.
PSALM 18:19

God miraculously delivered the Israelites from the waters of the Red Sea. He took them to the Promised Land of Canaan, which was rich and flowing with milk and honey. But He did not do this immediately. The Israelites had lived in Egypt for four-hundred years and had been in bondage for a large part of that time. God heard their cry. He saw their oppression. The Bible tells us that the Lord came down and rescued them. He does the same for us today. It may be that you have been in a hard place for a long time, so long that you have nearly given up on God. You may not believe that He will come for you, that He even wants to rescue you. The Israelites felt this way also. God is still in the business of rescuing His own today. When He saves you out of a depressed and sorrowful situation, He will take you to a new place—from Egypt to Canaan, so to speak. Have you sought God's deliverance? Be diligent in prayer. In His timing, God will answer your plea, just as He did for the Israelites. You are His child. Even while you remain in the desert, He can refresh your soul. Seek Him. He delights in you.

Father, help me to have faith that You know what is best for
me. Hear my cry from my own personal "Egypt" today.
I need to know that You delight in me. Amen.

Day 26

ANSWER ME!

Hear me when I call, O God of my righteousness:
thou hast enlarged me when I was in distress;
have mercy upon me, and hear my prayer.

PSALM 4:1

———————— ℓℓℓℓ ————————

Have you ever felt like God wasn't listening? We've all felt that from time to time. David felt it when he slept in a cold, hard cave night after night, while being pursued by Saul's men. He felt it when his son Absalom turned against him. Time and again in his life, David felt abandoned by God. And yet, David was called a man after God's own heart.

No matter our maturity level, there will be times when we feel abandoned by God. There will be times when our faith wavers and our fortitude wanes. That's okay. It's normal.

But David didn't give up. He kept crying out to God, kept falling to his knees in worship, kept storming God's presence with his pleas. David knew God wouldn't hide His face for long, for he knew what we might sometimes forget: God is love. He loves us without condition and without limit. And He is never far from those He loves.

No matter how distant God may seem, we need to keep talking to Him. Keep praying. Keep pouring out our hearts. We can know, as David knew, that God will answer in His time.

———————— ଜୀ ଜ ————————

Dear Father, thank You for always hearing my prayers.
Help me to trust You, even when You seem distant. Amen.

Day 27

A SMALL DEAL

But let every man prove his own work, and then shall he have rejoicing in himself alone, and not in another.
GALATIANS 6:4

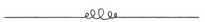

Do you have a tendency to overreact to life's challenges? Do you make a big deal out of things? If so, it's time to accept a challenge. For a full week, make up your mind to "make a small deal" out of your challenges. When you're tempted to panic, take a deep breath, count to ten, and make the smallest possible scenario out of it that you can. Will this be difficult? Absolutely. Is it possible? Definitely.

When you decide to create "big deals" out of everyday situations, you find yourself facing relationship strains, high blood pressure, and other woes. These things morph and grow to crazy proportions when you overreact. When you choose "small deals," you will experience forgiveness, peace, and the ability to bounce back without holding bitterness. It's your choice!

When you opt to make a "small deal" out of things, you will also have the satisfaction of knowing that you are pleasing your heavenly Father's heart. Now, that's a very big deal!

Lord, I don't want to be seen as someone who overreacts to things. I acknowledge that I've done this at times. Please remove this tendency from me so that I can live at peace with others. I want to please Your heart, Father. Amen.

Day 28

A CREATIVE GOD

In the beginning God created the heaven and the earth.
GENESIS 1:1

Did you realize that you are made (designed, created) in the image of a very creative God? It's true! He breathed life into you, after all. It stands to reason that some of His creativity would have spilled over into you, His child.

The same God who created the heavens and the earth—who decided a giraffe's neck should be several feet long and a penguin should waddle around in tuxedo-like attire—designed you, inside and out! And He gifted you with a variety of gifts and abilities, all of which can be used to His glory.

What creative gifts reside inside of you? Have you given them a stir lately? Maybe it's time to ask God which gifts are most usable for this season of your life. He's creative enough to stir the ones that can be used to reach others. He will bring them to the surface and prepare you to use them—much like He did during Creation—to bring beauty out of dark places.

So brace yourself! Your very creative God has big things planned for you!

Lord, thank You for creating me in Your image. I get so excited when I think about the fact that Your creativity lives inside of me. Just as Your Spirit moved across creation in the book of Genesis, I ask You to move across the creative gifts in my life and stir them to life! Amen.

Day 29

IT'S NOT ABOUT THE DOS AND DON'TS

*Who hath saved us, and called us with an holy calling, not according
to our works, but according to his own purpose and grace,
which was given us in Christ Jesus before the world began,
but is now made manifest by the appearing of our Saviour
Jesus Christ, who hath abolished death, and hath brought
life and immortality to light through the gospel.*
2 TIMOTHY 1:9–10

More than six hundred Jewish laws are derived from the Ten Commandments that God gave Moses. Before Jesus the Messiah came, they had to follow a list of rules in order to live a life that pleased God and assured them of His continued blessing in their lives.

Jesus came to the earth, gave His life, and defeated death, hell, and the grave so you could choose eternal life. You are not saved because of a list of dos and don'ts you follow. Instead, it's all about surrendering your heart to God. You are His child by His grace. Once forgiven, He doesn't remember your sins.

Our world is moved by conditional love: I will love you if you do this or that. Thankfully, that has no place in your relationship with God. His love is unconditional. You don't have to work from a list for God to accept you. His grace has already made you lovable and acceptable to Him. There is nothing you can do to make God love you any more or any less.

*Lord Jesus, I surrender my heart to You.
Thank You for the gift of eternal life. Amen.*

GOD IN DISGUISE

*For I was an hungred, and ye gave me meat: I was thirsty,
and ye gave me drink: I was a stranger, and ye took me in. . . .
And the King shall answer and say unto them, Verily I say
unto you, Inasmuch as ye have done it unto one of the
least of these my brethren, ye have done it unto me.*

MATTHEW 25:35, 40

What does it mean to be a missionary? Wholehearted service to God. A heart for others. A desire to lead people to a relationship with Jesus.

A missionary can be anyone—a parent, a teacher, an office worker, an emergency medical technician, a salesperson. God instructs His followers to "go into the world"—across borders—to tell people about Him. But "go" can also mean walking across the street or driving down the road to visit another person.

What is keeping you from your mission field? The details and to-do lists of day-to-day life easily take away time for daily service to others. Sometimes we can become so concerned with serving God that we forget that God is served *when* we serve people. Just as it is possible to have head knowledge *about* God without having a relationship *with* God, so can people interact with others without ever meeting a person's real need.

Jesus met people's immediate needs, but He didn't stop there. He fed and healed people, but He also invited them to accept Him and follow Him. It's all too easy to overlook people. Sometimes they don't even look like they need help. Although we cannot force someone to accept our help, we can make a point to offer it.

Lord, open my eyes to see those who need care. Amen.

Day 31

KING FOREVER

*For God is my King of old, working salvation
in the midst of the earth.*
Psalm 74:12

Sometimes it seems like every part of our lives is affected by change. From the economy and headline news to friendships and family relationships, nothing ever seems to stay the same. Even our leaders are in a constant state of flux. Every election cycle we see politicians come and go. Generation after generation, monarchs succeed their elders to the throne. Ministers move from one church to the next, and bosses get promotions or transfers.

These changes can leave us feeling unsteady in the present and uncertain about the future. With more questions than answers, we wonder how these new leaders will handle their roles.

It's different in God's kingdom. He's the King now, just as He was in the days of Abraham. His reign will continue until the day His Son returns to earth, and then on into eternity. We can rely—absolutely depend on—His unchanging nature. Take comfort in the stability of the King—He's our leader now and forever!

*Almighty King, You are my rock. When my world is in turmoil
and changes swirl around me, You are my anchor and my
center of balance. Thank You for never changing. Amen.*

Day 32

CITIZENS OF HEAVEN

For our conversation is in heaven; from whence
also we look for the Saviour, the Lord Jesus Christ.
PHILIPPIANS 3:20

In this passage, the Greek translation of the word *conversation* is *politeum*, meaning "citizenship." The word is broad in its translation, indicating our citizenship, thoughts, and affections are already in heaven.

For every Christian, heaven is home. From the moment we accept Christ, we are adopted into God's family with the promise of spending eternity with Him and all the saints who have gone before us. We are no longer citizens of this earth; we are born from above, and our names are written in God's celestial register.

Because our citizenship is in heaven, so are our hopes, thoughts, and affections. We are *in* the world, but not *of* it any longer. In the book of Hebrews, we read that Abraham and his descendants "looked for a city which hath foundations, whose builder and maker is God" (Hebrews 11:10). They considered themselves strangers on this earth because "they desire a better country, that is, an heavenly [one]" (Hebrews 11:16).

As heaven's citizens, we will enjoy all the rights and privileges of our heavenly Father. Meanwhile, we look to Jesus and stay steadfast to His Word until He ushers us home.

Heavenly Father, I know that my forever home is there with You.
I cannot imagine how wonderful it is! Thank You for
my road home—Your gift of salvation. Amen.

Day 33

ALL IN

Therefore that disciple whom Jesus loved saith unto Peter,
It is the Lord. Now when Simon Peter heard that it was
the Lord, he girt his fisher's coat unto him, (for he
was naked,) and did cast himself into the sea.

JOHN 21:7

"Now when Simon Peter heard"—in other words, he hadn't actually recognized Jesus Himself at that point. But he didn't need the evidence of his eyes. He only needed the merest possibility.

Peter had been stripped down for work, but he grabbed his coat or robe before launching himself into the water. Why? It wasn't going to help him swim faster. In fact, a heavy woolen garment was more likely to drag him down. So why did he take it with him? Because, there and then, Peter had no notion of ever returning to the boat. He was *all* about getting to his Lord!

After the resurrection the disciples never knew when or where they might meet Jesus—and that's pretty much the situation today. The question of how we respond is still an important one. Will we be hesitant, asking for all kinds of assurances and looking around to see who is watching? Or will we follow Peter's example, casting our so-called dignity to the wind, grabbing our coats, and diving in headfirst?

Jesus, call to me, "Here I am," and I will come to You.
I come in faith, wanting to be near You, wanting to
learn all that You have to teach me. Amen.

Day 34

THE BLAZING FURNACE

If it be so, our God whom we serve is able to deliver us from the burning fiery furnace, and he will deliver us out of thine hand, O king.
DANIEL 3:17

God wouldn't actually let these three godly men, Shadrach, Meshach, and Abednego, be thrown into the furnace, would He? Their bold declaration surely was just an act of defiance to King Nebuchadnezzar's tyrannical order to worship his golden statue. Surely God would provide a way of escape.

But He didn't. Or at least not in the way they had probably hoped. Imagine their thoughts as Nebuchadnezzar's fury was unleashed and he ordered the furnace to be heated seven times hotter than usual. Imagine how they felt as they were bound and carried to the furnace. Imagine the terror they felt as the guards who were ordered to throw them into the furnace perished from its heat!

Had God abandoned Shadrach, Meshach, and Abednego? Hardly!

Nebuchadnezzar looked into the furnace and found the three men walking around, unbound and unharmed, along with a fourth man. Scholars believe this was Jesus, preincarnate.

Too often we think that our faith should keep us out of the furnace: a health crisis, financial worries, conflict in our families. But being in the furnace doesn't mean that God has abandoned us. As promised in Hebrews 13:5, "I will never leave thee, nor forsake thee." He will be right there in the furnace with you.

Lord God, thank You that I can count on You to be with me in every circumstance. Though evil threatens, You hold me in Your loving hands. Amen.

Day 35

HARVESTING APPRECIATION

Sing unto the Lord with thanksgiving; sing praise upon the harp unto our God: who covereth the heaven with clouds, who prepareth rain for the earth, who maketh grass to grow upon the mountains.
PSALM 147:7–8

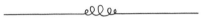

Everything that is seen in nature is a result of the handiwork of God. His power is exhibited in the little mustard seed as well as in the gigantic, blazing sun. He is the one in charge of the seasons and is the impetus for making things grow. And although God's children may plant the seeds and harvest the grain, it is God who waters the crops and the grasslands. He is the one who has engineered the nourishment of wheat and designed the breathtaking beauty of roses.

Even though we are surrounded by the beauty and splendor of God's works, we often go through life with blinders on, watching more traffic than sunrises, eating more processed foodstuffs than naturally whole, and following celebrities instead of glorying in the wonder of the moon and stars.

To show God His handiwork is beyond compare and acknowledge that His works are appreciated, let's stop our frenzied pace for a few moments each day and take in the beauty of God's creation, one cloud, one petal, one planet, one leaf at a time. Would we but "stand still, and consider the wondrous works of God" (Job 37:14), we would grow in admiration and wonder of all God has made for us.

Not only is Your grace amazing, but so is the beauty of Your creation, Lord. I praise You and thank You for all Your wondrous works. Amen.

Day 36

YOU'VE GOT GOD'S ATTENTION

I will bless the LORD, who hath given me counsel: my reins also instruct me in the night seasons. I have set the LORD always before me: because he is at my right hand, I shall not be moved.

PSALM 16:7–8

———————

Phone calls, text messages, someone shouting your name from down the hall—they can all interrupt and completely end a conversation with someone else. Worse yet, once you've regrouped from the distraction, you find that the person you were talking to wasn't even listening in the first place.

Have you ever been in a crowd desperately trying to get someone's attention? Maybe you were telling someone something very important, while they looked over you to see who else was in the room. It can make you feel worthless.

Your heavenly Father would never do that. He loves you and values every moment you are willing to give to Him. You are His focus. His eyes are constantly on you; His ears are tuned to your every word. He's seen every tear you've cried and celebrated every joy of your heart with you.

Even when you feel most alone, you can trust that He is there. He is your constant audience. The more time you spend with Him, the more you will realize that He has a lot to share with you. If you return the favor by giving Him your attention, He will lead you, guide you, and show you things that you'd never discover on your own. He wants to share your life today.

———————

God, thank You for giving me Your undivided attention. Show me the plans You have for me today. Amen.

Day 37

A VERY IMPORTANT PHRASE

And it came to pass. . .
FOUND MORE THAN 400 TIMES IN THE KING JAMES BIBLE

───────── ℓℓℓℓ ─────────

What tremendous words of encouragement! Headaches, toothaches, car troubles, clogged drains, personality conflicts—all come only *to pass*. We can focus on the Lord, and He will bring us through.

There are times in life when we think we can't bear one more day, one more hour, one more minute. But let's not get down—for no matter how bad things seem at the time, they are temporary. The situation will pass; life will go on. Tomorrow will be another day with new victories and challenges—but always with new grace as well.

What's really important is how we handle the opportunities before us today, whether we let our trials defeat us or look for the hand of God in everything. He's giving us more chances to glorify Him in the daily events of our lives.

Every day, week, and year are made up of things that "come to pass"— so even if we fail, we needn't be disheartened. Other opportunities— better days—will come. Let's look past those hard things today and glorify the name of the Lord.

───────── ᵒᵒᵒᵒᵒ ─────────

Lord Jesus, how awesome it is that You send or allow these little things that will pass. May we recognize Your hand in them today and praise You for them. Amen.

Day 38

WORTH REACHING OUT

*He is despised and rejected of men; a man of sorrows, and
acquainted with grief: and we hid as it were our faces from
him; he was despised, and we esteemed him not.*

Isaiah 53:3

Eight hundred years before Christ, the prophet Isaiah predicted that He would take on the sins of the world for our salvation.

His description of a man we would rather not look at, a man bent under the burden of sin, might apply to lots of people in the world today. We probably all know someone we would rather not talk to: nasty people, evil people, or just plain unpleasant people. But they weren't meant to be like that! Sins, theirs and others, have twisted their lives.

They didn't take that burden on board for us, and they certainly didn't do it for our salvation. But that doesn't mean we should look away or walk past. We tend to do so because, if we reach out to them, they might bring us down. People certainly felt the same about Jesus.

But knowing there is a soul God loves in there, knowing that in the least of these the Lord is to be found, our reaching out in His name might just be the saving of them.

*The world is fraught with trouble, and evil people seem to reign;
but God, in each of them there is a soul worth winning.
Show me how I can help. Amen.*

Day 39

DON'T BE SHY

And he began to say unto them,
This day is this scripture fulfilled in your ears.
LUKE 4:21

At the start of a mission that would change the world, Jesus declared Himself the Anointed One in front of a hometown audience. More than a few jaws would have dropped, but the listeners were quite civil about it—until He wouldn't play the game the way they wanted. Then they tried to throw Him off a cliff! These individuals knew Jesus' parents, and they had known Him as a child. Now He was shaking their world.

People who come to faith later in life or Christians who find themselves in a faithless environment (perhaps in the workplace) face the same dilemma. It's difficult to stand up in front of people who know your shortcomings and say, "I am a child of God." Some will think you've flipped; others will poke fun. Who needs the hassle? It's much easier just to do good works and keep quiet, isn't it?

But that isn't what it's all about. God wants to be heard. Jesus spoke up—now God wants us to do the same.

Face others and tell them who you are. It won't be easy, but God will provide the courage. When you proclaim "the acceptable year of the Lord" (v. 19), the scripture is fulfilled in you!

Dear God, take away any shyness I have about sharing
You with my family and friends. You are my Father,
and I am proud to let others know. Amen.

Day 40

FAITHFUL EXAMPLE

Then said Jesus to those Jews which believed on him,
If ye continue in my word, then are ye my disciples indeed.
JOHN 8:31

Jesus taught us how to live in two ways. He spoke words of wisdom, making very clear what God expected of us. But even more importantly, He taught by example. It seems that people say "Jesus did this" or "Jesus did that" more often than "Jesus told us to do this." We remember things best by being shown.

We can *say* anything we want. We can tell everyone we are followers of Jesus, and we can put on quite a show for those around us. All of us have probably known people who attend church and pretend to be Christians on Sunday but seem to be anything but Christians during the rest of the week.

Jesus said, though, that we are truly His followers if we are faithful. That means we continue to be Christians outside of the church. We live the Word of God every day, and although we may have failures, we strive to live as closely to Jesus' teachings as we can. As it is so well said in John 8:31, we must remain faithful. The Lord is certainly faithful to us!

Jesus, Your faithfulness to me is so great. You've set the perfect example for living, and You are so patient with me while I try to be like You. Thank You, Jesus. Amen.

Day 41

REMEMBERING

*Behold, I have graven thee upon the palms
of my hands; thy walls are continually before me.*
ISAIAH 49:16

A phone number, a homework assignment, an item to pick up at the grocery store—we might jot any of these reminders on our hand if a piece of paper isn't available. We know if we write something on our hand we will see it. How can we not? We use our hands all day, every day. They are always in front of us.

When the Lord said He has engraved us on the palms of His hands, He was telling us that He remembers us. All day, every day, He remembers us. We are of utmost importance to Him. We cannot be forgotten. When He submitted Himself to Calvary's cross and allowed nails to be driven through His hands, He was remembering us. Our names are in those scars.

Romans 8:34 says, "It is Christ that died, yea rather, that is risen again, who is even at the right hand of God, who also maketh intercession for us." Jesus is remembering us in constant prayer to the Father. His eyes never close and His memory never fails. God remembers us.

*Father, thank You that through Christ You have brought me to
Yourself, You reign over my life, and You always remember me. Amen.*

Day 42

COMFORTED AND COMFORTING

Blessed be God, even the Father of our Lord Jesus Christ, the Father of mercies, and the God of all comfort; who comforteth us in all our tribulation, that we may be able to comfort them which are in any trouble, by the comfort wherewith we ourselves are comforted of God. For as the sufferings of Christ abound in us, so our consolation also aboundeth by Christ.

2 CORINTHIANS 1:3–5

Young children find comfort in a pacifier or a stuffed animal. Perhaps the most common comfort to them is a special blanket. As we grow older, comfort is harder to find. Certainly, a warm blanket or a hot bath will bring temporary comfort when we are cold. A talk with a friend may soothe your worried heart a bit. But real comfort is found in a relationship with the Lord. No matter what trial or trouble you are facing today, He is there to comfort you. You can rest in Jesus. You can come to Him and lay down your concerns. You can talk with Him, listen to Him, or even just speak His name. There is power and peace to be found in the name of your Savior.

One extra benefit to finding comfort in the Lord is that you are then better equipped to comfort others. You can offer a word of compassion to another who is experiencing a similar hurt to the one you have known. You are ready to comfort because you have been comforted.

Father, please comfort me in that area of my life that troubles me. Equip me to comfort those around me. Amen.

Day 43

LOOK TO THE PROMISE

Let us hold fast the profession of our faith without
wavering; (for he is faithful that promised).
HEBREWS 10:23

———————— ℓℓℓℓ ————————

"I promise to pick up the dry cleaning." "The check is in the mail, I promise." How lightly we use the word *promise*. We toss it around with very little meaning attached. The definition of *promise* is a statement telling someone you will definitely do something, or that something will definitely happen in the future. The use of the word means you can hang your hat on it! This some *thing* is coming. Oh how often we fail to carry through with our word. It's wonderful we can know for sure—definitely—that God's promise is eternal.

God's Word contains promises we can and must depend on. The Bible is a priceless gift, a tool God intends for us to use in our lives. Too often we look away from "The Manual."

Are you tired and discouraged? Fearful? Be comforted in the promises God has made to you through His Word. Experiencing worry or anxiety? Be courageous and call on God. He will protect you and then use you according to His purposes. Are you confused? Listen to the whisper of the Holy Spirit, for our God is not a God of confusion.

Talk to Him, listen to Him, trust Him. Trust His promises. He is steadfast, and He will be by your side. Always.

———————— ∽◯◯◯∾ ————————

Father, how we thank You for Your promises. You are steadfast,
loving, and caring. We cannot praise You enough. Amen.

Day 44

GOD IS IN THE DETAILS

Casting all your care upon him; for he careth for you.
1 Peter 5:7

———————— ✑✑✑ ————————

Do you ever wonder if God cares about the details of your life?

Take a look at nature. God is definitely a God of details. Notice the various patterns, shapes, and sizes of animals. Their life cycles. The noises they make. Their natural defenses. Details!

Have you wandered through the woods? Towering trees. Their scents. The cool refreshment their shade provides. The different types of leaves, and the tiny, life-bearing veins that run through them. How intricate!

What about the weather? It is filled with details from the hand of your God. The Creator sends raindrops—sometimes gentle and kind, other times harsh and pelting. He warms us with the sun, cools us with breezes, and yes—it is true—He fashions each snowflake, each unique, no two alike! The same way He designs His children!

Do you wonder if God cares about that struggle you are facing at work or the argument you had with a loved one? Is He aware of your desire to find that special someone or the difficulty you find in loving your spouse? He cares. Tell Him your concerns. He is not too busy to listen to the details. He wants to show Himself real and alive to you in such a way that you know it must be Him. The details of your life are not *little* to God. If they matter to you, they matter to God.

———————— ✑✑✑ ————————

Thank You, Lord, for caring about the details of my life.
It means so much to know You care. Amen.

Day 45

POWER UP

But if the Spirit of him that raised up Jesus from the dead dwell in you, he that raised up Christ from the dead shall also quicken your mortal bodies by his Spirit that dwelleth in you.

<small>ROMANS 8:11</small>

God is the same yesterday, today, and forever. His strength does not diminish over time. That same mountain-moving power you read about in the lives of people from the Old and New Testaments still exists today. The same power that caused the walls of Jericho to fall, an ax to float, and a dead girl to live again is still available today. The force of God that formed the world, brought the dry land above the waters of the sea, and raised Jesus from the dead is available to work out the details of your life.

It's natural to want to do things on our own. We all want to be independent and strong. When faced with a challenge, the first thing we do is try to work it out in our own skill and ability—within our own power. But there's another way.

We don't have to go it alone. Our heavenly Father wants to help. All we have to do is ask. He has already made His power available to His children. Whatever we face, wherever we go, whatever dreams we have for our lives, take courage and know that anything is possible when we draw on the power of God.

Father, help me to remember that You are always with me, ready to help me do all things. Amen.

Day 46

HYPOCRITE!

If a man say, I love God, and hateth his brother, he is a liar:
for he that loveth not his brother whom he hath seen,
how can he love God whom he hath not seen?
1 JOHN 4:20

This is the verse that risks making hypocrites of us all. Who among us does not know someone we'd cross the road to avoid? That person might be obnoxious, a liar, or have caused all sorts of grief—but is still beloved by God, and He wants that soul brought home.

What about the people begging on the street? There are so many these days, and lots of them are con artists, so we preserve our dignity by walking on by. Well, some of them are in real need, and God values the saving of even a con artist above your dignity. Don't be taken advantage of, but engage with these wayward children of the Lord.

Then there are the people who hurt us, the ones we trusted once and can never forgive for their betrayal. They weren't born cruel and callous. They were hurt, so they inflict hurt. God wants *you* to break that chain, to replace hurt with love.

It's a big task and one we might never be able to live up to, but we will be nearer to God for having tried!

God, sometimes it's hard acting in a Christlike way,
especially toward those who are not my friends. Help me, please,
to love everyone, not just those who love me back. Amen.

Day 47

TRADITION TRUMPED

For laying aside the commandment of God,
ye hold the tradition of men.
MARK 7:8

Despite this warning from Jesus to the Pharisees, very little has changed. Since then the church has been split by traditions of men countless times.

One takes communion while another abhors it. One will ordain women priests, and that causes a walkout elsewhere. Some churches adhere to strict dress and moral codes, while others are open to addicts and criminals in whatever state of dress they can attend. Some prefer guitars; others prefer organs. And who do these divisions help?

Before we pass judgment, we might consider what Moses would make of the average American church service. He actually walked with God! Would he recognize our style of worship as correct?

Let's face it, if Jesus visited our place of worship, He wouldn't stop to see what the minister or priest was wearing. He wouldn't check if the cross was real gold or plate. He, frankly, wouldn't be interested in which prayer book we read from. He would want to know one thing: Do we hold on to the commands of God, loving the Lord our God and our neighbor as ourselves? It's a question that is much more important than any tradition—and one we should be ready to answer at any time.

Lord, are You happy with my church? Is it a place that honors
and promotes You and Your commands? If not, Lord,
show me what to do and where to go. Amen.

Day 48

HE RULES

They that hate me without a cause are more than the hairs of mine head: they that would destroy me, being mine enemies wrongfully, are mighty: then I restored that which I took not away.

PSALM 69:4

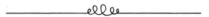

Being king isn't easy. Either people love you or they hate you. The same is true of every position of power and authority. Presidents, deans, prime ministers—the list can go on and on—all these people have to face the passions of the people they lead. Even God Himself has to face such problems. God is not loved by everyone. There are those who, for whatever reason, have chosen to reject God. There are those who curse Him as regularly as Christians praise Him.

We are the subjects of the greatest sovereign in creation. Our Lord rules with justice and love. We might not agree with everything He does or everything He calls us to do, but we owe Him our allegiance and loyalty. Be loyal to the Lord, and He will rule over you justly and with compassion.

It is easy to bow down before a ruler of such love and grace, Lord. In every age, You have ruled fairly. I pray for all those who do not know Your greatness and Your goodness. Break through with Your light into their lives. Amen.

Day 49

PRAYER OR "BREVITY MANIA"?

*For God is my witness, whom I serve with my spirit
in the gospel of his Son, that without ceasing I
make mention of you always in my prayers.*
ROMANS 1:9

Our language is laden with abbreviations, or as one called it, "brevity mania." Organizations are known for their acronyms—MADD, CARE, WAVES—and abbreviations like the AMA, ADA, NRA, and AFT abound. And how about texting—using symbols and letters to translate whole phrases or emotions? Crying equals :'(and FWIW means "for what it's worth."

Although abbreviations are convenient, they can become ineffective—even confusing or frustrating—if used in excess. Likewise, our prayers are often lost in brevity. We love fast food and instant success. All the while we struggle to take the time to utter a few extra syllables to God. We shoot "arrow" prayers while expecting God's response ASAP. We expect the Lord, who knows all, to interpret our every need.

Although arrow prayers are sometimes needed, God asks us to pray *specifically* and often for the person or problem just as Paul did. God made us to fellowship with Him. That includes open communication void of brevity mania!

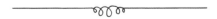

*Lord, forgive me for my abbreviated prayers, void of substance
and heart. Teach me to pray in specifics and less in generalities as
I openly pour out my innermost needs and desires to You. Amen.*

Day 50

STANDING IN THE LIGHT

When I fall, I shall arise; when I sit in darkness,
the Lord shall be a light unto me.
MICAH 7:8

Ever fall so low you think you'll never get up again? We've all been there. Whether it's a job that's fallen through, a bad medical report, or a failed relationship, life has a way of knocking us down. When that happens, we often feel like we'll never stand again.

But with God, we know the low times aren't the end of our story. We may fall down, but He will lift us up. We may feel surrounded by darkness on every side, but He will be our light, guiding the way, showing us which step to take next. No matter where we are, what we've done, or what we're facing, God is our rescuer, our Savior, and our friend.

Satan wants to convince us that we have no hope, no future. But God's children always have a future and a hope. And someday, when death calls our name, even then we will be victorious. For on that day, we will be ready to experience total love and acceptance. We will know once and for all that we are special, we are cherished, and we belong to Him.

Dear Father, thank You for giving me confidence in a future filled with good things. When I'm down, remind me to trust in Your love. Thank You for lifting me out of darkness to stand in Your light. Amen.

Day 51

HOLY, WHOLLY

But as he which hath called you is holy, so be ye holy in all manner of conversation; because it is written, Be ye holy; for I am holy.
1 PETER 1:15–16

———————————

Holiness is one of the most difficult concepts to grasp about God because it is so foreign to us. He is unable to sin, set apart in glorious light. However, we can easily understand why Isaiah fell on his face when he beheld the Lord, feeling his sinfulness weighing heavy upon him (Isaiah 6:5).

Just as the angel cleansed Isaiah's lips, Christ made us His righteous, holy people (1 Peter 2:9). Because Christ has given us His holiness, we don't have to earn it ourselves. For Christians, pursuing holiness isn't fulfilling a set of rules in order to be accepted before God. Instead, it is a heart-deep desire to model our lives after our Savior's perfect example.

Though we are holy in Christ, we still struggle with sin in this life. Where is the Holy Spirit convicting you to practice holiness? Do you have trouble being kind in your words, spoken or unspoken? Are your thoughts filled with peace and thankfulness, or do you struggle with envy? Does the way you treat others, especially those who disagree with you or are different from you, honor Christ?

Don't be discouraged by how you fall short. Our Savior rewards His children who pursue holiness; He will give you grace to learn to practice His ways faithfully.

———————————

Father God, thank You that Christ's holiness covers me.
Show me the sins I've ignored so that I can be
holy in my actions as You are holy. Amen.

Day 52

POWERFUL ONE

*For, lo, he that formeth the mountains, and createth the wind,
and declareth unto man what is his thought, that maketh
the morning darkness, and treadeth upon the high places
of the earth, The Lord, The God of hosts, is his name.*

AMOS 4:13

Ever pondered the power of our Lord God Almighty? Meditating on God's power can soothe our biggest worries and calm our deepest fears.

The Word of God speaks often of His power—we know He created our universe in less than a week. But if that's too much to comprehend, consider the enormity of a single mountain or ocean. Those vast, mighty things came into being simply by God's voice—and they're only a tiny fraction of everything He made. What power!

The Lord opens the morning curtains to reveal the dawn and pulls the sky shades back at night to bring darkness. He plots the course of the wind, arranges for rainfall, and causes grass, crops, and trees to grow. He feeds the gigantic whales of the ocean, and every tiny little bird. If our Lord has enough knowledge and power to handle these jobs, surely He can (and will!) look after us.

Problems that seem insurmountable to us are simply a breath to Him. Let's not be anxious today—God holds each one of us in the palm of His hand.

*Lord God, You are my provider. Thank You for holding such power—
and for choosing me to be Your child. Please give me a greater
understanding of who You are, helping me to remember
that You, the Lord God Almighty, love me. Amen.*

PICK YOUR BATTLES

*As for these four children, God gave them knowledge and
skill in all learning and wisdom: and Daniel had
understanding in all visions and dreams.*
DANIEL 1:17

———————— ✑ℓℓℓℓ ————————

Daniel was one of the first Hebrew exiles taken from Jerusalem into
friendly captivity (if there is such a thing) in Babylon. Separated from his
family, forced into servitude, given a new identity and new gods, Daniel
was probably only a teenager! He was now living in Babylon, the pagan
center of the earth.

Did Daniel completely reject his new lifestyle? Did he argue with
his master and refuse to learn? No! Amazingly, there were only a few
areas where Daniel refused to compromise: he would not bow down
and worship any other god or eat food that had been offered to idols.

We live in a type of Babylon, too. We're surrounded by anti-God
behavior, customs, pop culture. It's easy to be offended by just about. . .
everything. Everyday language is flavored with swear words, television
shows mock our faith, and schools introduce curricula that make us cringe.

Surprisingly, God didn't tackle every single issue in Babylon. He
picked Daniel's battles for him, and Daniel was greatly used in the midst
of a pagan culture. Not indignant or antagonistic, but compassionate
and seeking the best for his captors.

Can we be Daniels in our communities today?

———————— ✑∿∿∿∿∿ ————————

*Lord, show me how to seek Your wisdom and discernment while
picking my battles. Help me to love those who oppose You. Amen.*

Day 54

ALWAYS RELEVANT

For the word of God is quick, and powerful.
HEBREWS 4:12

The Bible is many things. May we never overlook the fact that of all the things that can be said about it, God's Word is an incredible work of art.

The measure of a good work of art is whether it is fresh and relevant each time it is experienced. Is the work powerful and moving? Certainly the Bible is! Each time we read it, we can discover new things relevant to our current position in life. It is new and different each time we read it. It is alive!

How many books can boast such a property? People change, technology changes, schools of thought change. . .but the Word of the Lord will remain as relevant two thousand years from now as it was two thousand years ago!

The Word of God says several things about itself throughout the Bible. As we are reminded in Hebrews 4:12 that God's Word is alive and powerful, we can meditate on just how relevant it continues to be. Even now, we can still communicate with our Lord through prayer and by reading and filling our minds with His words. Let us remember to praise God for this opportunity He has provided us to hear from Him!

*I praise You, Father, for Your Holy Word. I've hidden it in my heart.
It speaks to me night and day, teaching me and
leading me in righteousness. Amen.*

Day 55

AGAINST GOD ALONE

Against thee, thee only, have I sinned, and done this evil in thy sight:
that thou mightest be justified when thou speakest,
and be clear when thou judgest.

PSALM 51:4

Sin is not merely doing what is wrong, but doing what is wrong in the sight of the Lord. God has offered us suggestions for living full and happy lives. Our being disobedient to those suggestions doesn't hurt God; it hurts us. God is saddened by our refusal to be obedient, but He is always willing to hear our petition for forgiveness, and He will show us His mercy. When we sin, it is a private matter between God and ourselves. Take your sins before God, repent for each one, and glory in the grace of God, by which we receive full pardon of all we do wrong.

Forgive me, Lord. Make a new creation out of this old soul.
Prepare me for the kingdom to come, each day of my life. Amen.

Day 56

LIVING BIOGRAPHY

And there are also many other things which Jesus did, the which,
if they should be written every one, I suppose that even the world
itself could not contain the books that should be written.

JOHN 21:25

———————— *elle* ————————

The Bible contains four Gospels, but it doesn't have a single biography of Jesus.

Aren't the Gospels biographies?

Not exactly. Two of the Gospels ignore Jesus' birth completely, and only Luke makes any mention of His childhood years.

Carl Sandberg needed six volumes to write a biography of Abraham Lincoln. The apostle John said that to write a definitive biography of Jesus would require more room than is available in the whole world. So he chose which details of Jesus' life to include—and with great care.

All of the Gospel writers did. They each had a particular purpose in writing their accounts of Jesus' life. John spells his out clearly: "That ye might believe that Jesus is the Christ, the Son of God; and that believing ye might have life through his name" (John 20:31).

Jesus' story continues to be written—in us. May our lives lead others to faith in Him.

———————— *somo* ————————

Jesus, the Gospels inspire me. They make me want to know more
about You. Teach me to become more like You and to
grow nearer to You as I learn. Amen.

Day 57

VOICE OF THE SHEPHERD

My sheep hear my voice, and I know them, and they follow me.
JOHN 10:27

Next time you're around a group of children, watch for this fascinating phenomenon: At Sunday school or the day-care center, even with upwards of thirty kids playing, crying, or quietly looking at books, each child will hear their own mother's voice as soon as she enters the room. As soon as Mom acknowledges the teacher or helper, her child, instantly latching on to her voice, will look up to see her face. None of the other kids stop playing because she's not their mom—her voice doesn't catch their attention. Only a mother's child hears that one special voice above the ruckus.

It should be the same way for us as God's children. We may be engrossed in our day, running around, checking items off our to-do list, working and taking care of ourselves and others—but when our Lord speaks, we should hear Him because we as His children know His voice.

God's voice is distinct—and when we become part of His family, we learn to recognize it. The more we tune in to that distinct voice, the more we'll hear it.

Let's be like a child, eager to hear a parent's loving voice.

Lord, I know I am Your child—yet often I find it difficult to hear Your voice over the noise of my life. Please give me ears to hear Your still, small voice, and the strength and faith to obey what You say to me. Amen.

Day 58

MAKE A CHOICE

Let not your heart be troubled:
ye believe in God, believe also in me.
JOHN 14:1

———————— *elle* ————————

Some days are full of joy and peace; others are not. When we face the inevitable dark days in life, we must choose how we respond. We bring light to the darkest of days when we turn our face to God. Sometimes we must let in trusted friends and family members to help on our journey toward solving our problems.

David knew much distress and discomfort when he cried out, "God is our refuge and strength" (Psalm 46:1). Matthew Henry's commentary says of Psalm 46, "Through Christ, we shall be conquerors. . . . He is a Help, a present Help, a Help found, one whom we have found to be so; a Help at hand, one that is always near; we cannot desire a better, nor shall we ever find the like in any creature."

Knowing that Christ is at the center of our battles—and that we can trust Him—lends peace and stills the weakest of hearts. Rely on Him to lead you through the darkest days.

———————— *oooooo* ————————

Oh Lord, still my troubled heart. Let me learn to rely on You in all
circumstances. Thank You, Father, for Your everlasting love. Amen.

Day 59

WHO ARE YOU?

*He was in the world, and the world was
made by him, and the world knew him not.*
JOHN 1:10

Have you ever seen someone, spoken to them, and the whole time your brain is running through your database—who *is* this person? You can't place them in context. One of life's frustrating moments, until the *aha* moment, and a sigh of relief trickles in. Yes, you do know who it is. Certainly a trusted friend wouldn't require you to frantically scroll through a list, because you have a relationship with that person.

Does your database recognize the One who created you? Do you have a passing acquaintance with God, or do you have a relationship with Jesus? Are you certain or filled with doubts? This unease can be fixed with an open heart and a sincere prayer for salvation.

Only when we move beyond knowing God only as God and instead crown Him Lord in our lives will our doubts flee. Our souls will sigh with relief, recognizing our Savior.

*Dear Jesus, I look to You this day in full surrender.
I choose to have a relationship with You.
Please come into my heart and be my Lord. Amen.*

GOD IS THE BOSS

And whatsoever ye do, do it heartily,
as to the Lord, and not unto men.
Colossians 3:23

————————— ℓℓℓℓ —————————

Over the centuries, many men and women have accomplished amazing things—things that have won them recognition from the world in the form of Nobel prizes, Olympic medals, literary awards, books on the bestseller lists, honorary doctorates, and much more. Most pursue these awards and titles to bring glory to themselves; a few make their accomplishments less known, seeking God's direction, following His leading. Earthly medals and awards, recognition and acclaim only last a few years at best.

Jesus said, "Lay not up for yourselves treasures upon earth, where moth and rust doth corrupt, and where thieves break through and steal: but lay up for yourselves treasures in heaven, where neither moth nor rust doth corrupt, and where thieves do not break through nor steal: for where your treasure is, there will your heart be also" (Matthew 6:19–21).

It's so easy to fall into performance or approval traps, but they usually suck the joy out of the job. When we recognize that we work for the Lord, not for the approval of man, we are freed from man's laws and expectations. We are free to be the people God created, fulfilling the purposes He had in mind for us. Remember something C. T. Studd, British cricketeer and missionary, wrote: "Only one life, 'twill soon be past. Only what's done for Christ will last."

————————— ୧୨୨ଠଠ —————————

Father, help me put aside any desire for man's approval,
but only seek to do those things that will last for eternity. Amen.

Day 61

FULL REDEMPTION AND LOVE

Let Israel hope in the Lord: for with the Lord there is mercy,
and with him is plenteous redemption.
PSALM 130:7

Jesus offers each of us full redemption: complete freedom from sin because of His great love for us. God doesn't want us to carry around our list of sins, being burdened by our past mistakes. He wants us to have a clear conscience, a joy-filled life!

The Bible tells us that God removes our sins as far as the east is from the west (Psalm 103:12) and that He remembers our sin no more (Isaiah 43:25; Hebrews 8:12). It's so important to confess your sins to the Lord as soon as you feel convicted and then turn from them and move in a right direction. There is no reason to hang your head in shame over sins of the past.

Turning from sin is tough. Especially when it has become a bad habit. Find an accountability partner to pray for you and check in with you about your struggles, but don't allow the devil to speak lies into your life. You have full redemption through Jesus Christ!

Dear Jesus, I confess my sin to You. Thank You for blotting out each mistake and not holding anything against me. Help me to make right choices through the power of Your Spirit inside me. Amen.

Day 62

THE SIMPLE THINGS

For our heart shall rejoice in him,
because we have trusted in his holy name.
PSALM 33:21

Think about the simple pleasures in everyday life—that first sip of coffee in the morning, waking up to realize you still have a few more minutes to sleep, or putting on fresh, warm clothes right out of the dryer on a cold winter morning. Perhaps it's a walk along the beach or a hike up the mountains into the blue skies that give you a simple peace.

God knows all the simple pleasures you enjoy—and He created them for your delight. When the simple things that can come only by His hand fill you with contentment, He is pleased. He takes pleasure in you. You are His delight. Giving you peace, comfort, and a sense of knowing that you belong to Him is a simple thing for Him.

Take a moment today and step away from the busyness of life. Take notice and fully experience some of those things you enjoy most. Then share that special joy with Him.

Lord, thank You for the simple things that bring pleasure to my day.
I enjoy each gift You've given me. I invite You to share
those moments with me today. Amen.

Day 63

BLESSABLE

*Love the LORD your God, and. . .serve him with all your heart
and with all your soul, that I will give you the rain
of your land in his due season.*
DEUTERONOMY 11:13–14

———————— *elle* ————————

We all want God's blessings. We want it to rain on our crops; we want the sun to shine on our picnics; we want a gentle breeze to relieve us from summer's scorch. We want job security and bigger paychecks.

Though God allows some blessings to grace every person in the human race, there are some keys to receiving more of God's goodness. If we want God's blessings, we must be blessable. So how do we become blessable? We must love God. And we must serve Him with all our heart.

Loving God is the easy part. But the evidence of that love comes through our service to Him, and that's a little harder. When we love God, we serve Him by loving others. We serve Him by taking the time to mow the widow's lawn or prepare a meal for someone who's ill or provide a coat for someone who's cold. We serve Him by offering a hand of friendship to the friendless or by saying something positive about the victim of gossip.

When we love God and our actions show evidence of that love, we become blessable. That's when God will pour out His goodness on us in ways we could never imagine.

————————  ————————

Dear Father, I love You. Show me ways I can serve You today. Amen.

Day 64

WHEN GOD'S PEOPLE PRAY

Pray for the peace of Jerusalem:
they shall prosper that love thee.
PSALM 122:6

———————— *ello* ————————

When it comes to making a difference in this life, sometimes it's easy to feel helpless. Wars are being fought on the other side of the world. People are starving, suffering, hurting. As much as we'd like to help, there's not much we can do, right?

Except, there is something we can do. It's the most powerful thing anyone can do—we can pray. God, in all His power, has invited us to come alongside Him. He's asked us to join Him in His work by praying for each other.

For centuries, God's people have been treated unfairly and unjustly. Yet we've survived, when other groups haven't. The reason we've survived when so many have sought to silence us is because we have something our enemies don't have. We have the power of God behind us.

When we pray, we call upon every resource available to us as the children of God. We call upon His strength, His compassion, His ferocity, His mercy, His love, and His justice. We have the ability to extend God's reach to the other side of our town or the other side of the world, all because we pray.

———————— *oooo* ————————

Dear Father, thank You for letting me join You in Your work.
Please bless the people who love You, wherever they are in this
world. Allow them to prosper according to their love for You. Amen.

Day 65

OFFENSE

Is not this the carpenter, the son of Mary, the brother of James, and Joses, and of Juda, and Simon? and are not his sisters here with us? And they were offended at him.

MARK 6:3

———————— ✤ ————————

"I'm so offended!" How many times have you felt like crying out these words? Probably more times than you could count. We all go through periods of offense, especially when we feel like there's a target on our back. Some people wear offense like an out-of-season garment. It's always with them, but it's not terribly attractive or appropriate.

Jesus certainly knew what it felt like to be rejected, but He wasn't one for offense. The same couldn't be said about the religious zealots who had it out for Him, though. They took offense at everything! If Jesus healed someone on the Sabbath, they got offended. If He spoke the truth about His deity, they got offended about that too!

You know, there are some people who are just going to be offended. Instead of worrying about hypersensitive people, try turning your focus to God. Make sure your life, your words, your actions aren't offensive to Him. As long as you can answer in good conscience to your heavenly Father, He can take care of the feelings of others. And while you're at it, lay aside any feelings of offense you might be carrying. They will only weigh you down.

———————— ✤ ————————

Father, I choose to lay down my offenses today. Help me forgive those who have offended. And Lord, help me not to tiptoe around those who are easily offended. Deal with their hearts in Your own way and time, Father. They are not mine to fix. Amen.

Day 66

DAVID'S DIARY

Save me, O God; for the waters are come in unto my soul. I sink in deep mire, where there is no standing. . . . I am weary of my crying: my throat is dried: mine eyes fail while I wait for my God.

PSALM 69:1–3

———————— ⤸ ————————

We think of the book of Psalms as poetry, or even a peek into King David's private diary—over half of the psalms are credited to him. But they were originally verses set to music, compiled as a hymnbook for corporate worship in the temple.

There is a psalm to match every emotion and mood experienced by human beings: joy, anger, frustration, discouragement, loneliness, doubt. Thousands of years after they were written, they still speak to our needs and desires.

But the psalms are much more than beautiful words that parallel our emotions: God is their central focus. Psalms often begin as a heart cry of pain from the psalmist—but they invariably end with a focus on God.

The psalm writers had a very real, genuine relationship with God. They sang praises to God, they got angry with God, they felt abandoned by God, they didn't understand God's slow response. . .and yet they continued to live by faith, deeply convicted that God would overcome.

These ancient prayers remind us that nothing can shock God's ears. We can tell Him anything and everything. He won't forsake us—His love endures forever.

———————— ⤸ ————————

Oh Lord, You know the secrets of my heart. Teach me to talk to You through every emotion and every circumstance. My focus belongs on You. Amen.

Day 67

GOD HAS LEFT THE BUILDING

The veil of the temple was rent in the midst.
LUKE 23:45

On the day of Christ's death on the cross, all of creation was affected as the earth shook and the skies turned black. Inside the Jerusalem temple, the thick curtain separating the people from the inner room was split in two by a power unknown to man.

God, who had dwelled in the temple, the Holy of Holies, and had talked to Zechariah there (Luke 1), left the building when the curtain ripped on crucifixion day. He left a man-made structure to go and make a new home inside each individual who would invite Him in.

No longer did people have to physically move to Him to offer sacrifices and pray. Now God came to each individual on a personal level that was never known before. He made Himself accessible to anyone in any country on any continent.

God is an unchanging God who seeks relationship with us just as He did throughout biblical history. But we no longer have to walk the streets of Jerusalem to find God's Spirit. He comes to us and finds us just where we are.

Holy God, I invite You to make Your temple within me. I pledge that all I do will show honor to You and give You praise. Amen.

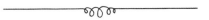

ENCOURAGING THOSE AROUND YOU

*Pleasant words are as an honeycomb,
sweet to the soul, and health to the bones.*
PROVERBS 16:24

Are you an encourager? Are your words pleasant and cheerful when you enter a room? Do you find yourself talking mostly about yourself, or do you focus on the other person in the conversation?

The tongue is a powerful thing. Words can encourage or discourage, build up or tear down. As you go throughout your day today, seek to be one whose words are healing to the body and sweet to the mind as the writer of Proverbs describes. If you are in the workplace, take time to greet your coworkers with a genuine "*Good morning.*" Be sure to truly listen for an answer when you use the phrase "*How are you?*" rather than moving on as if your question were rhetorical. You will find that while kind words encourage the person that receives them, speaking them to others will also bless you. You will feel good knowing that you have lifted someone's spirits or shared in their sorrow. You will begin to focus on others rather than going on and on about your own problems or plans.

It has been said that conversation is an art. Hone your conversation skills this week. Speak words of encouragement, words of life that remind the hearer that they are special to you, and more importantly, to God.

Father, help me to speak life today. May my words be pleasant, sweet, and healing. May my conversations be pleasing to You. Amen.

Day 69

BOLD REQUESTS

And it came to pass, when they were gone over, that Elijah
said unto Elisha, Ask what I shall do for thee, before I be
taken away from thee. And Elisha said, I pray thee,
let a double portion of thy spirit be upon me.
2 KINGS 2:9

What a bold request!

Elijah offered a blessing to Elisha. Elisha responded, "Let a double portion of thy spirit be upon me."

Elijah filled the role of leader, prophet, and miracle worker. Why would Elisha want the heavy responsibilities and difficulties involved in this type of work? Elisha could have asked for wealth, unlimited power, or a life with no problems. Even the ability to live each day in peace was within his reach. Yet Elisha asked for Elijah's spirit. He did not ask to have a larger ministry than Elijah—he was only asking to inherit what Elijah was leaving and to be able to carry it on.

What might God give us if we asked boldly for the impossible? God deeply desires to bless us. If our hearts line up with His will and we stay open to His call, He will surprise us. God takes the ordinary and through His power transforms our prayers into the extraordinary—even double-portion requests.

Bless me, Lord. When my heart aligns with Your will and
when I ask for the impossible, bless me. Show me beyond
my expectations that You are my God. Amen.

Day 70

TRIALS HAVE A PURPOSE

*And Joseph said unto his brethren, Come near to me, I pray you.
And they came near. And he said, I am Joseph your brother,
whom ye sold into Egypt. Now therefore be not grieved,
nor angry with yourselves, that ye sold me hither:
for God did send me before you to preserve life.*

GENESIS 45:4–5

———————— ℓℓℓℓ ————————

How many of us could forgive as Joseph did? His jealous siblings had
kidnapped him, thrown him into a pit, and then allowed him to be sold
into slavery. Yet Joseph trusted that from God's perspective, not his own,
his trials had a purpose.

Joseph walked through his humiliating ordeal with his eyes focused
on the Lord. He continued not only to love his brothers but to find
forgiveness in his heart for them. Studying his life enables us to look
at our own situations differently: God can accomplish miracles in the
midst of trials.

Is there a hurt so deep inside that you have never shared it with
another human being? Perhaps someone in your own family has rejected
or betrayed you. Remember the pain suffered by Joseph; remember
the anguish of Jesus Christ, who was betrayed by one as close as a
brother, Judas Iscariot. God knows your pain, and He is strong enough
to remove any burden.

———————— ⁊⁊⁊⁊ ————————

*Lord, sometimes I want to enjoy my agony awhile longer. Show me
the brilliance of Your forgiveness that I might trust You in the
trial and not miss the outcome You've planned. Amen.*

Day 71

FINANCIAL STRAIN

*No man can serve two masters: for either he will hate the one,
and love the other; or else he will hold to the one, and despise
the other. Ye cannot serve God and mammon.*

MATTHEW 6:24

⁓⁓⁓

Do you ever get nervous when you watch the news and see reports about the stock market? Does your head spin when you see the prices rise at the gas pump? Can you feel your heart race when you look at your bills in comparison to your bank statement? Even though many of our day-to-day activities depend on money, it's important to remember that money is not a provider or sustainer. Only God can provide for you and sustain you. When we begin to focus on and worry about money, then we are telling God that we don't trust Him.

As you feel yourself start to worry about money, stop and change your focus from wealth to God. Thank Him for what He has provided for you and then humbly ask Him to give you wisdom about your financial situation. Be at peace as you remember that you can absolutely trust God to provide for you and to sustain you.

⁓⁓⁓

*Dear God, help me not to worry but to trust that You will provide
for me. Help me to be devoted to You only. Amen.*

Day 72

YOU ARE WHAT YOU CLING TO

Abhor that which is evil; cleave to that which is good.
ROMANS 12:9

The invention of superglue was revolutionary because the glue has the ability to bond immediately with a variety of materials. That is wonderful news if your grandmother's porcelain vase breaks in half. But superglue must be used with extreme caution. Accidents can happen in a split second. If the tiniest drop falls in the wrong place, two items will unintentionally and permanently bond.

What are we cemented to? Bonding takes place as we draw close to something. Choose to cling to what is good and avoid evil at all costs. We should not even flirt with sin, because it can quickly get a foothold in our lives. Like superglue in the wrong place, we could unintentionally find ourselves in bondage by embracing temptation. What may seem innocent at the time could destroy us.

Beware of your temptations. Know your areas of vulnerability and avoid them. If you struggle with unhealthy eating habits, do not buy tempting foods. If overspending is a temptation, cut up those credit cards. If certain websites or books are an issue, stay away from them. Instead, draw close to the Lord. Allow Him to satisfy your deepest longings. When we cling to good, evil loses its grip.

Dear Lord, help me avoid temptation. May I draw close to You so I can cling to good and avoid evil in my life. Amen.

Day 73

OVERCOME WITH LIGHT

And the light shineth in darkness;
and the darkness comprehended it not.
JOHN 1:5

There is a belief that the natural inclination of the universe is to fall apart. The "law of entropy" states that everything ultimately fades and breaks down. Even the stars will go dark, eventually. According to entropy, darkness wins.

The same thing, people say, happens in society—the general trend seems always to be downward. But that's not universally true.

The enemy of darkness is God. He shines His life and light into each of us. With His help, we can banish the darkness from our families, our workplaces, and our neighborhoods. It's up to us to make things better rather than worse.

In space, the Herschel telescope showed that fading stars are actually hurling bits of themselves out into the universe—stardust that coalesces to make new stars. So maybe entropy and darkness don't win after all. Let's make sure they don't here on earth. As we pass through this world, let's spread as much "God dust" as we can so that new Christians will grow and shine—and the darkness will be more confused and confounded than ever!

Lord, I want to be a light in the world. I want to be a light for
the lost and shine my light on the road to heaven. Amen.

Day 74

JUDGE NOT

There is one lawgiver, who is able to save and to destroy:
who art thou that judgest another?
JAMES 4:12

Have you ever "gotten even" with someone over something? Have you ever reacted unkindly to someone else's unkindness? We've all done it. It's our way of passing judgment on others. This is what we think they deserve, so we give it to them.

Does that kind of judgment make us better people? No, never. So what's the alternative? Oh yeah, soppy old love! And we dismiss it as the soft option, the option that gets us taken advantage of, the way that makes us look foolish to others. But how foolish do we look when we lower all our personal standards to get even, when we make ourselves as bad as our enemies because *they* deserve it. That's just a win-win situation for the devil.

Jesus wasn't vague when He told us to love God and one another. It's the answer to every problem, and anyone who dismisses it as the soft option obviously hasn't tried it. Judging others usually only makes us deserving of a harsh judgment in return. Don't judge—love. Then, when it comes our time to face the Lawgiver, His judgment on us will be a love we didn't deserve, either.

Jesus, I am no better than anyone else, so who am I to judge
my neighbors? Help me, Jesus. Help me not to judge
them but to love them instead. Amen.

Day 75

HURT BY OTHERS' CHOICES

And God heard the voice of the lad; and the angel of God called to
Hagar out of heaven, and said unto her, What aileth thee, Hagar?
fear not; for God hath heard the voice of the lad where he is.
GENESIS 21:17

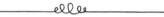

A slave during early biblical times, Hagar had little say in her life decisions—others made them for her. Because of the infertility of her mistress, Sarah, Hagar became the concubine of Sarah's husband, Abraham, and gave birth to Ishmael.

At first, Hagar's hopes soared. Her son would become Abraham's heir, rich and powerful beyond her wildest dreams! However, the surprise appearance of Isaac, the late-life son of Sarah and Abraham, destroyed Hagar's fantasies of a wonderful future. Sarah wanted Hagar and Ishmael out of their lives. Abraham, though upset, loaded Hagar with water and food and told her to take Ishmael into the unforgiving desert.

When their water supply failed, Hagar laid her dehydrated son under a bush and walked away crying because she could not bear to watch Ishmael die. But God showed Hagar a well of water. Quickly she gave her child a drink. Both survived, and "God was with the lad" (Genesis 21:20).

God is also on our side when we suffer because of others' choices. Even when we have lost hope, God's plan provides a way for us and those we love.

Heavenly Father, when my world seems out of control,
please help me love and trust You—even in the deserts of life. Amen.

Day 76

DETERMINED TO WIN

Fear thou not; for I am with thee: be not dismayed; for I am thy God:
I will strengthen thee; yea, I will help thee; yea, I will uphold
thee with the right hand of my righteousness.

ISAIAH 41:10

———————— ℓℓℓℓ ————————

God loves you and desires to bless you; your adversary, the devil, wants to convince you to give up on ever receiving the promises of God.

Think about the last time God showed up and turned your circumstances around. Most likely in the midst of your celebration of the blessing, another challenge or difficulty hit you head on. It's the enemy's attempt to steal what God did for you and even convince you that God wasn't in it.

He wants to bring disappointment in the hope that you'll just give up. When John the Baptist baptized Jesus, God blessed Jesus by declaring Him as His Son. From there Jesus went into the desert to fast and pray for forty days. Immediately the devil came to tempt Jesus, trying to get Him to give up His blessing. Jesus refused to give up. Like Jesus, you can hold tight to the win God has promised you.

Satan, your adversary, wants you to give up and quit. But if you remain determined to win—refusing to let go of God's promise—you will always win.

———————— ⚬⟆⟆⚬⚬ ————————

Heavenly Father, help me to keep my focus on You. I will not
let the enemy talk me out of anything You have for
me. I am determined to win! Amen.

Day 77

NOT FLYING SOLO

For we are his workmanship, created in Christ Jesus unto good works, which God hath before ordained that we should walk in them.
Ephesians 2:10

———— *eeee* ————

Sometimes when we think about doing "God's work," self-doubt can get the better of us. We tell ourselves that we aren't smart or skilled enough; we remember all our skipped prayer times and say, "The Lord wouldn't want to use me since I've been ignoring Him. Besides, my work probably isn't worth that much anyway in the big picture, *if* I don't completely mess up."

In Ephesians 2, Paul emphasizes that we weren't saved because of anything we had to offer, but we received God's gift of salvation through faith. He made us anew in Christ "unto good works." We can't brag about deserving salvation, and we can't brag about our good works being our big idea either! God planned them for us ahead of time to fit in with His perfect plan.

We may fear that our errors will "ruin" what God has going on. Consider that the work itself is a gift—the all-powerful Creator chooses to use us, ordinary believers, to accomplish mighty things. Throughout the Bible, we read stories of unremarkable people doing amazing things for the Lord, because they trusted in His strength to do them. If God has work for us, we can have confidence that He will equip us for the job, no matter the challenges ahead.

———— *∞∫∫∞* ————

Father God, please strengthen me to do the work You have planned for me. Help me to depend on Your ability and strength when I doubt myself. Amen.

PRAISE HIM

And he answered and said unto them, I tell you that, if these should hold their peace, the stones would immediately cry out.
LUKE 19:40

———————— elle ————————

Jesus says that if His people do not praise Him, the rocks will cry out. We serve a God who must be praised. He is worthy of honor and praise. We serve a God who created the universe and everything in it. He is not a small *g* god. He is a capital *G* God. He is a great big God, and He deserves great big praise. How do we praise Him? We praise Him by telling Him of His greatness. When you pray, before you begin asking the Lord for things, try telling Him how wonderful you think He is. Speak scripture back to Him. Tell Him that He is the Great I Am and your provider. He is the Prince of Peace and the King of Kings. He is the Lord of Lords, the Savior, your Abba Father. Praise Him, for you are wonderfully made. Praise Him, for His presence that is always near. Then your heart will be filled with thankfulness and you can move into a time of thanksgiving in your prayers. Certainly it is appropriate to ask God for things that others need or that you yourself desire, but God is honored when you begin with praise.

———————— ⚬⚬⚬ ————————

Lord, I praise You for who You are. You are the Creator of this beautiful world. You are the King of Kings, and yet You became a man and lived on earth. You died for me. I praise You for these things and so much more. Amen.

Day 79

TRUST AND OBEY

*That they might set their hope in God, and not forget
the works of God, but keep his commandments.*
PSALM 78:7

You may remember learning this song as a child: "Trust and obey, for there's no other way to be happy in Jesus than to trust and obey."

It's one thing to talk about trust, another to live it. And here's the problem: if you don't trust God, you probably won't obey His commands. So these two things go hand in hand. Don't believe it? Here's an example: Imagine the Lord asked you to take a huge step of faith, something completely outside your comfort zone. You would likely hesitate. But, would you eventually take the step, even if it made no sense to you? If you trusted God—if you had seen Him work time and time again in your life—you would eventually take the step of faith, even if it made no sense. Why? Because you trust that He's got your best interest at heart. (And you've probably figured out that He has something pretty remarkable up His sleeve!)

God is trustworthy. He won't let you down. Once you settle that issue in your heart once and for all, obedience is a natural response.

*Father, I know I can trust You. Sure, there will be faith journeys ahead.
I know that. But Lord, I want to obey, to step out boldly. When I do,
You take me to new, exciting places I've never been before.
Thank You for leading and guiding, Father! Amen.*

Day 80

CALLED TO BE STORYTELLERS

I will sing of the mercies of the LORD for ever: with my mouth
will I make known thy faithfulness to all generations.
PSALM 89:1

In addition to being prayers and praise songs, some of the psalms also retell portions of Israel's history. The Israelites would sing them together to praise the past deeds of their Deliverer (e.g. Psalm 136). Today's worship songs don't list what He's done for us specifically like the Israelites' songs did, but we should definitely follow their example of remembrance.

Christians often use the word *testimony* to name the story of how they accepted Jesus as their Savior. Salvation is a great proof of God's love, but His work doesn't stop there. He daily fills our lives with His provision, nearness, and loving patience. When we recognize what He has done for us, we can be storytellers of His faithfulness, like the psalmists. We gather strength for the challenges ahead when we recall the victories He granted in the past, and our ongoing testimonies of His faithfulness display His love to those who don't know Him personally.

When you feel troubled, tell yourself *your* stories of His faithfulness. When did you feel His comfort when you called on Him for help? When has He provided for your needs beyond expectation? Just as He did then, your unchanging God will never stop caring for you.

Father, thank You that You've never stopped working in my life.
When I am fearful, help me recall Your goodness and trust You more.
Give me opportunity to tell others what You have done for me
so that they will come to trust You too! Amen.

Day 81

JOY IN THE MORNING

They shall praise the L ORD that seek him: your heart shall live for ever.
P SALM 22:26

How grand God is! He knows how dependent we are on Him for the everyday joy we need to carry on. And every day, He provides us with beauty all around to cheer and help us.

It may come through the beauty of flowers or the bright blue sky—or maybe the white snow covering the trees of a glorious winter wonderland. It may be through the smile of a child or the grateful face of the one we care for. Each and every day, the Lord has a special gift to remind us of whose we are and to generate the joy we need to succeed.

In our own pain and frustration, there are times when our eyes don't see the beauty God sends. But if we'll ask, He'll show us. God is faithful to build us up with everything we need to serve Him with joy. What an awesome God we serve!

Lord God, I thank You for Your joy; I thank You for providing it every day to sustain me. I will be joyful in You. Amen.

Day 82

THY WILL BE DONE

Thy kingdom come, Thy will be done in earth, as it is in heaven.
MATTHEW 6:10

———————— ⟋⟍⟍⟍ ————————

We pray it. We say it. But do we really mean that we want God's will to be done on earth as it is in heaven? Submitting to God's will is difficult. Jesus struggled with submission in the garden of Gethsemane. We wrestle with it most days. Unfortunately, most of us assume that we know best. We want to call the shots and be in control. But following God's path requires trusting Him, not ourselves.

Many times submitting to God's will requires letting go of something we covet. We may be called to walk away from a relationship, a job, or a material possession. At other times God may ask us to journey down a path we would not have chosen. Venturing out of our comfort zone or experiencing hardship is not our desire.

Embracing God's love enables us to submit to His will. God not only loves us immensely, but He desires to bless us abundantly. However, from our human perspective, those spiritual blessings may be disguised. That is why we must cling to truth. We must trust that God's ways are higher than ours. We must believe that His will is perfect. We must hold fast to His love. As we do, He imparts peace to our hearts, and we are able to say with conviction, "Your will be done."

———————— ⟋⟍⟍⟍ ————————

Dear Lord, may I rest secure in Your unconditional love. Enable me to trust You more. May I desire that Your will be done in my life. Amen.

Day 83
LAUGH TODAY!

A merry heart maketh a cheerful countenance:
but by sorrow of the heart the spirit is broken.
PROVERBS 15:13

———————— ✦ ————————

Some researchers say that a positive attitude can actually help you to live longer! Isn't that amazing? Did you know that laughter can do the same thing? Find something to laugh about today. Abraham's wife, Sarah, laughed when she heard God tell Abraham that she would become pregnant at an old age after longing for a baby for so many years. God surprised her when she had given up! Perhaps God has granted you an unexpected blessing. If so, laugh with joy today! If you have trouble with this, read the comics in the newspaper. Watch a humorous YouTube video. Rent a movie that has some good, clean comedy. Read a few entries in a joke book. Do whatever it takes to find some humor in this day. Often, the greatest laughs come when we are free enough to laugh at ourselves. Have you done something really silly lately? Have you made a mistake that left you chuckling? Laughter is good for the soul. The book of Proverbs says that if your heart is happy, your face will show it. Are you going around with a long face? Do people look forward to seeing you, or are you an Eeyore? If you find yourself complaining today, try replacing negative words with cheerful ones. Everyone enjoys being around someone who wears a smile.

———————— ✦ ————————

Father, grant me a happy heart today. Where there is
depression or bitterness within me, replace the
negativity with joy! Thank You, Father. Amen.

Day 84

A PATTERN OF FORGIVENESS

Be it known unto you therefore, men and brethren, that through this man is preached unto you the forgiveness of sins: and by him all that believe are justified from all things.

Acts 13:38–39

Forgiveness means to pardon another who has wronged you. Forgiveness needs to be extended without and released from within so bitterness will not grow and consume you. As Christians we are commanded by scripture to do so. And there is no doubt that this can be difficult.

We often show pity and compassion to others and let a situation go, get over it, apologize. However, all too often we look in the mirror and anger surfaces at ourselves. Forgiving ourselves is the hardest step in the Forgive Pattern. Popular Christian speaker Joyce Meyer stated, "Forgive yourself for past sins and hurts you have caused others. You can't pay people back, so ask God to." It's a choice. When tempted to dredge up the wrongs, the sins, which you have asked the Lord to forgive, make a concerted effort to erase those thoughts. Lay aside all that "stuff." When you are embittered against yourself, forgive! If Jesus doesn't remember it, why should you?

Scripture says you are forgiven from every sin when you ask! So once you've prayed for forgiveness, face yourself in the mirror and say, "I'm free!"

Father God, I choose this day to ask for Your forgiveness for specific sins. And when I've confessed, I ask You to help me forgive myself. Amen.

Day 85

TALKING TO THE FATHER

The effectual fervent prayer of a righteous man availeth much.
JAMES 5:16

———————— *elle* ————————

We have all had those inevitable days when we are exhausted or discouraged and it seems too hard to carry on. We might feel as dry as the desert sand, with nothing left to give. This is a time when we could use nourishment for our souls.

The prophet Zechariah said, "Ask ye of the LORD rain in the time of the latter rain; so the LORD shall make bright clouds, and give them showers of rain" (10:1). Matthew Henry explained this scripture: "Spiritual blessings had been promised. . . . We must in our prayers ask for mercies in their proper time. The Lord would make bright clouds and give showers of rain . . .when we seek the influences of the Holy Spirit in faith and by prayer, through which the blessing held forth in the promises are obtained."

When these times hit, use "knee mail." Don't just "tweet" a short sigh to the Lord, but carve out some time to pray, to praise, and to petition your heavenly Father for strength to carry on. He is faithful to answer our pleas and send refreshment to our hearts. It could be in the form of a restful night's sleep, a friend or relative to exhort and encourage, or a stranger's greeting. We never know how the Lord will answer our petitions, but answer He will. God's inbox is never too full.

———————— *ver* ————————

Dear Lord, how we long for Your presence. Father,
hear our prayers this day; extend Your
hand of mercy to me. Amen.

Day 86

I CAN COUNT ON YOU

It is of the LORD's mercies that we are not consumed,
because his compassions fail not. They are new every
morning: great is thy faithfulness.
LAMENTATIONS 3:22–23

Thomas Chisholm penned words to a hymn that often resounds throughout churches: "Great Is Thy Faithfulness." The words proclaim an eternal truth: God is with us always, through everything. "Pardon for sin and a peace that endureth. . .strength for today and bright hope for tomorrow." Despite any circumstance, we can reach for the hand of our Father and know He is present.

God is faithful to us even when we are not faithful to Him. God keeps His promises even when we stray far from His will. He continues to love us even when we disobey. But God does not force His blessings on us. To experience His love and grace, we must claim them for ourselves. With a conscious choice, we must ask Him to be present in our lives and then tune our hearts to listen to what He says. As His children we show our loyalty and devotion when we walk close to Him, committing our lives to the study of His Word. And as we learn of His promises, we realize we can count on Him.

Whatever our condition, we know for certain our God is faithful and loves us eternally. Be comforted, for God is here.

Dear Lord, how we praise Your name for Your faithfulness.
Forgive us when we fall short of Your will for our lives.
Help us to hear Your whisper. Amen.

SELF-EXAMINATION

Let us search and try our ways, and turn again to the Lord.
LAMENTATIONS 3:40

———————— *elle* ————————

What if you could follow yourself around for the day, carefully examining all that you do? Look at your schedule—your choice of activities, the people you talk to, the things you listen to and watch, the habits being formed, the thoughts you think. Maybe your heart desires intimacy with God, but a real day in your life leaves no time for solitude. God often speaks to us in the stillness and silent spaces. How will we hear Him if we're never still?

Taking time to reflect, to think, and to examine oneself is a necessary step in moving toward intimacy with God. Before we can turn back to Him, we must repent of the things that moved us away from Him in the first place. As we set aside time for solitude and reflection, the Holy Spirit will gently show us these things if we ask. He will show us the sins we need to confess and give us the grace of repentance. Experiencing forgiveness, our fellowship with our heavenly Father is restored.

———————— *oooo* ————————

Lord, help me to still myself before You and be willing to examine my ways. Speak to me through Your Holy Spirit of what is wrong in my life. Give me the gift of repentance and allow me to enjoy the sweetness of Your forgiveness. Amen.

Day 88

PARTNERS ON THE JOURNEY

Plead my cause, O LORD, with them that strive with me.
PSALM 35:1

We need friends and supporters. Jesus sent the disciples out two by two because He knew how important it was to have someone to share with and to support. Standing alone, we feel like our strength is limited; but with someone else by our side, new reserves of strength surface. Psychologically, we need confirmation that what we believe in is true. Just one other person can give us all the confirmation we need.

It is good to remember that our Lord strives along beside us, never leaving us, pleading our cause at every step. He understands us, loves us, and never turns away from us. Because of the mighty love of God, we can be assured that we are never alone.

Lord, be with me this day. Support me in the things I desire to do, and help me to always follow the right path. Amen.

CLIMBING MOUNTAINS

The LORD is my light and my salvation; whom shall I fear?
the LORD is the strength of my life; of whom shall I be afraid?
PSALM 27:1

The Meteora in Greece is a complex of monastic structures high atop a mountain. Access to the structures was deliberately difficult. Some of these "hanging monasteries" were accessible only by baskets lowered by ropes and winches, and to take a trip there required a leap of faith. An old story associated with the monasteries said that the ropes were only replaced "when the Lord let them break."

While the vast majority of us will probably never scale the mountain to visit these monasteries, we often feel that we have many steep mountains of our own to climb. Maybe it's too much month at the end of the money. Or perhaps we are suffering with health or relationship troubles. Whatever the reason we are hurting, angry, or feeling despair or hopelessness, God is ready to help us, and we can place all our hope in He who is faithful.

Lord, I will stay strong in You and will take courage. I can trust and rest in You. Whatever I am feeling now, whatever emotions I have, I give them to You, for You are my hope and salvation. You are good all the time, of which I can be supremely confident. Amen.

Day 90

WATER'S COST

I will give unto him that is athirst of the
fountain of the water of life freely.
REVELATION 21:6

Drinking an ice-cold glass of water on a hot summer day is a wonderful experience. It seems that the thirstier we are, the better water tastes and the more of it we can drink.

Imagine attending a sporting event in the heat of the day. The sun beats down on you, you sweat like crazy, your senses become dull, and an overwhelming desire for a cold bottle of water gradually becomes the only thing you can think about. The players disappear, and the hard bleachers cease to matter; you would pay any amount of money for one sip of water.

Jesus, well aware of basic human needs, likens His message to water, "the fountain of the water of life." Just as we cannot live without water, we cannot live without the Word of God. We are shocked to learn that this life-giving message—one we must have at any price, and one to which we cannot assign value—costs us nothing. Jesus loves us so much that He gave up His life that we might partake of these invigorating waters. So drink up, and leave your money at home; the water of life is free.

Dear Lord, thank You for letting me drink for free from the fountain
of the water of life. Help me to remember Your sacrifice
and Your love for me. Amen.

Day 91

WALK IN LOVE

And this is love, that we walk after his commandments.
This is the commandment, That, as ye have heard
from the beginning, ye should walk in it.
2 JOHN 1:6

———

Walk in love. It sounds so easy, so attractive. So why don't more people do it?

Because it goes against our worst instincts. Let's not forget we were rebels from the start. Eve, encouraged by the serpent, feared God was keeping something from her. So she went her own way—and took Adam with her. They ran from God. You might think we would be wiser, but we're all still doing our own thing—and still getting it wrong.

It's human nature to rebel when someone is keeping you down, taking advantage of you, or playing you for a fool. But this is *God* we're talking about, not some con artist, dodgy politician, or tin-pot dictator. He doesn't have anything to prove, and He doesn't have anything to gain. He made everything, so it's already His. To put it bluntly, we can trust Him.

So put aside those fears. If you must rebel, rebel against rebellion. God's "commands" are simply instructions on how to walk beside Him. Stop going your own way and start going His—and you will know what it's like to truly walk in love.

———

God, You love me. You desire to go with me and lead me.
Why then would I go my own way? Take my hand.
I want us to walk together. Amen.

Day 92
20 / 20 VISION

Turn away mine eyes from beholding vanity;
and quicken thou me in thy way.
PSALM 119:37

How's your spiritual eyesight? Are things in focus, or is your life a little blurry? Are worthless things impeding your vision?

The psalmist recognized that many things in life vie for our attention. Some have little value and take us farther away from God's transformational power—they are "vanity," worthless. Myopic distractions may foster a selfish, nearsighted focus. A farsighted focus can keep us so busily distracted with others that we have no time to reflect and grow in our own lives. Astigmatism reflects the struggle for balance between the two extremes.

But some things bring us closer to God and preserve our life—life that comes through God's Word. To turn away from worthless things, let's focus our eyes on Jesus, "the author and finisher of our faith" (Hebrews 12:2). Let's allow our lives to be changed by the power of His Word as we encounter Him each day.

What are the things in your life that you need to bring into focus in order to restore 20/20 spiritual vision?

Jesus, there are so many distractions in life, things that get
in my way. Help me to make them less important
and to center my focus on You. Amen.

Day 93

HOLY SPIRIT PRAYERS

*Likewise the Spirit also helpeth our infirmities: for we know not
what we should pray for as we ought: but the Spirit itself maketh
intercession for us with groanings which cannot be uttered.
And he that searcheth the hearts knoweth what is the
mind of the Spirit, because he maketh intercession
for the saints according to the will of God.*
ROMANS 8:26–27

Many times the burdens and troubles of our lives are too complicated
to understand. It's difficult for us to put them into words, let alone know
how to pray for what we need. And unless we know someone who has
been through similar circumstances, we can feel isolated and alone.

But we can always take comfort in knowing that the Holy Spirit
knows, understands, and pleads our case before the throne of God the
Father. Our groans become words in the Holy Spirit's mouth, turning our
mute prayers into praise and intercession "according to the will of God."

We can be encouraged, knowing that our deepest longings and
desires, maybe unknown even to us, are presented before the God
who knows us and loves us completely. Our names are engraved on
His heart and hands. He never forgets us; He intervenes in all things for
our good and His glory.

*Father, I thank You for the encouragement these verses bring.
May I always be aware of the Holy Spirit's
interceding on my behalf. Amen.*

Day 94

RACHEL'S SADDLEBAGS

Now Rachel had taken the images, and put them
in the camel's furniture, and sat upon them.
And Laban searched all the tent, but found them not.
GENESIS 31:34

———————— *oll ee* ————————

Why did Rachel feel a compulsion to steal her father's household idols and hide them in her saddlebags? The idols were probably little statues of gods common to the time and culture. She risked the wrath of the true God and jeopardized the safety of her family. Didn't she know better, as the wife of Jacob—the great patriarch of God's nation of Israel?

From our twenty-first-century vantage point, it's easy to wag a finger at Rachel. Living in a western culture, we find such idols strange. But in Rachel's day, those little idols were pervasive, part of the culture. She didn't dismiss Jacob's God—she just added to Him. Naive, ignorant, or sinful, she allowed idols to replace God's primary position in her life.

Household idols probably don't tempt us. But we can all identify with Rachel. Think of the importance we place on material things, financial security, achievement—those ambitions can easily consume us! They can occupy our thought life, fill our spare time, and become our life's focus.

Let's take care to keep God exactly where He belongs, in first place.

———————— *oo* ————————

Lord, clean my house! Open my eyes to the worthless idols
in my life. Teach me to desire only You. Amen.

Day 95

WELL OF SALVATION

Therefore with joy shall ye draw water out of the wells of salvation.
ISAIAH 12:3

In biblical times, wells were of great importance. Digging a well meant you planned to stay at a place. Owning a well meant your family possessed the surrounding countryside. Wells were gathering places and landmarks. People went to the well daily to get water for drinking, cooking, and cleaning. A well was essential to life for man and beast.

Our salvation is also a well. In it is not only our eternal life but also our abundant life while we live on earth. Christ is the living water, continually refreshing and nourishing us, giving life to our bodies and souls. He is strength when we are weak, wisdom when we are foolish, hope when we are despondent, and life when we are dying.

Just as a bucket is lowered into a deep well, what begins as a descent into unknown darkness and depth becomes the means by which we draw up the water of life. Colossians 2:12 says, "Buried with him in baptism, wherein also ye are risen with him through the faith of the operation of God, who hath raised him from the dead." We have died with Christ and now we live, but daily we need to go to the well of our salvation, remembering our need for Jesus' life and drawing out the living water with joy.

Lord, thank You for saving me. Thank You for being the living water, my continual source of peace, comfort, strength, and joy. Cause me to remember that my life is hidden in Yours. Amen.

Day 96

WATER WALKERS

*And he said, Come. And when Peter was come down
out of the ship, he walked on the water, to go to Jesus.*
MATTHEW 14:29

Maybe you've seen the bumper sticker: IF YOU THINK YOU'RE SO PERFECT,
TRY WALKING ON WATER. It refers to those times in the Bible when Jesus,
the perfect Son of God, broke the rules of physics by hiking over the
waves. But there was someone far from perfect who also walked on water.

Earlier, Jesus had told His disciples to get into a boat and go on
without Him to the other side of the lake. He stayed behind to send the
crowds away—and then to pray. Later that evening, the disciples, wrestling
their boat against a contrary wind, saw a ghostly figure approaching.
Jesus assured them it was He, and Peter asked the Lord to command
him to come. Jesus did—and Peter, briefly, walked on water.

What does it take for an ordinary person to walk on water? A
command of God. By the power of God, ordinary men and women,
responding to God's call, have successfully accomplished difficult, even
impossible, tasks.

Don't give up when things seem worst. That's the time to find the
strength of God.

*You are my strength, Oh Lord. Whenever I feel like giving up,
I will turn to You believing that You will give me
the power to carry on. Amen.*

Day 97

HIGHER THAN

For as the heavens are higher than the earth, so are my ways higher than your ways, and my thoughts than your thoughts.
ISAIAH 55:9

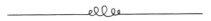

God tells us, "My thoughts are not your thoughts, neither are your ways my ways" (v. 8), and then goes on to describe the vast difference between the way He thinks and the way we mortals think and between the way He operates and the way people try to work things out. God reasons and works on such a higher level that He compares it to the heavens, which are immeasurably higher than the earth.

God has given us intelligence and common sense, and He intends us to use our brains to think through everyday problems and come up with solutions. We are not infinitely smart, however, and sometimes the solution to our problems may be different from anything our minds can envision. A good example is Jesus' command to love our enemies (Matthew 5:44). It runs contrary to normal human logic.

God knows best, and though we may feel certain that God's way won't work or even seems downright foolish, we do well to remember that "the foolishness of God is wiser than men" and that compared to God, "the thoughts of the wise. . .are vain" (1 Corinthians 1:25; 3:20).

Father, sometimes You send me down a path that I view as foolish, and then I discover that it leads to something grand. I praise You for Your perfect wisdom! Amen.

Day 98

SWIFT AND SLOW

Wherefore, my beloved brethren, let every man be swift to hear,
slow to speak, slow to wrath: for the wrath of man
worketh not the righteousness of God.
JAMES 1:19–20

Kindergartners learning traffic signals know that yellow means "slow down." James 1:19–20 also is a yellow light!

Have you wished, after a conversation with a friend, that you had not given that unsolicited advice? Your friend needed a listening ear, but you attempted to fix the problem instead.

Have you raced through a hectic day, only to end it by taking out your frustrations on family members or friends? Or perhaps you have borne the brunt of someone else's anger and reacted in the same manner, thus escalating the situation. Later, when tempers calmed, you found yourself regretting the angry outburst.

Too often words escape before we know what we are saying. Like toothpaste that cannot be put back in the tube, once words are spoken it is impossible to take them back. Words, whether positive or negative, have a lasting impact.

Practice being swift and slow today—swift to listen, slow to speak, slow to become angry.

God, grant me the patience, wisdom, and grace I need to be a good
listener. Remind me also, Father, to use my words today to
lift others up rather than to tear them down. Amen.

Day 99

LIFE COACH

His name shall be called Wonderful, Counsellor.
Isaiah 9:6

—————— ~~~~~ ——————

There's a new title for an old profession: life coach. The phrase was first used in 1986 and refers to an advisor who helps people set and reach goals, deal with problems, and make decisions. Professionals can be trained and receive a certification to be a life coach.

While this is a worthy, fulfilling profession, we need to remember we already have a life coach. God sends His Holy Spirit to anyone who asks, and He guides us. He gives us wisdom. He shows us the best way to live.

The problem is, many of us don't want to listen to His counsel. We want what we want. We want to live the way we think is best, the way that seems easiest or most comfortable for us right here, right now. But God is more concerned with the big picture than our current circumstances. Oh, He will guide us through today, but if we listen to Him carefully and follow His direction, we will end up on the best path for eternity.

Our Wonderful Counselor isn't in it for the paycheck or to build a résumé. He loves us and only wants what is best for us. When we are confused about which way to go, which decision to make, we can go to our Life Coach. We can trust that He will always lead us in the right direction.

—————— ~~~~~ ——————

Dear Father, thank You for being my Life Coach.
Help me to heed Your counsel. Amen.

MUCH LOVE

*Wherefore I say unto thee, Her sins, which are many,
are forgiven; for she loved much.*

LUKE 7:47

Scripture records the story of Jesus dining with Simon the Pharisee. At the dinner, a woman of loose morals came forward, kissed Jesus' feet, and washed them with her tears. Simon was incensed. He felt Jesus should reprimand the woman; after all, she had sinned greatly. Jesus didn't condemn her; He forgave her. Her faith saved her because she poured out everything at His feet.

Often we feel we fall short in our walk with God. We plunge into the trap of measuring ourselves by another's yardstick. This isn't what God wants for us. He desires that we fall at His feet and worship Him—loving Him with an extravagant love. When sin enters our lives, as it will, we confess that sin and turn to His face. He's there in the darkest hours.

Others may know what you've done, but Jesus knows what you can become. Simon the Pharisee saw this woman as a weed, but Jesus saw her as a potential rose and watered it. When you fall in love with Christ, the first thing He opens is your heart. Be transformed by the Father's grace. Love extravagantly.

*Dear heavenly Father, I love You.
Pour Your love into my heart this day. Amen.*

Day 101

WHAT'S YOUR GIFT?

Yea, brother, let me have joy of thee in the Lord:
refresh my bowels in the Lord.
PHILEMON 1:20

Encouragement comes in many forms. A standing ovation and generous applause encourage the performer. Sport teams are uplifted through the cheers of loyal fans. For the Christian, nothing compares to the encouragement we receive from one another through God's love.

The world is full of competition; consequently, words of encouragement are few. Sadly, the body of Christ often does the same, as jealousy blocks the flow of encouragement toward our brothers and sisters in Christ.

Every believer is gifted in different ways. Yet we often covet another's God-given gift. We wish we could sing or recite scriptures or teach like others. Yet God equips every believer with different talents.

Have you found yours? Often the greatest gifts are ones behind the scenes. The intercessors who pray daily for the pastors and leaders are greatly gifted with the power of the Holy Spirit to target and pray for whomever God puts on their hearts. Some possess the gift of giving—not just financially, but of themselves. Others possess God's wisdom and share a word that someone desperately needs. Where would we be without these loving, caring people?

While in prison, Paul wrote to Philemon asking him for a favor, indicating it would be of great encouragement to him. Similarly, God encourages us to encourage too.

Lord, help me encourage others just as You encourage me. Amen.

Day 102

THE RIGHT FOCUS

So that thou incline thine ear unto wisdom, and apply thine heart to understanding; yea, if thou criest after knowledge, and liftest up thy voice for understanding; if thou seekest her as silver, and searchest for her as for hid treasures; then shalt thou understand the fear of the LORD, and find the knowledge of God.

PROVERBS 2:2–5

If you've ever lost something—your keys, your glasses, or an important document—you've no doubt searched everywhere. Sometimes when you finally find it, you realize that, in your haste, you simply overlooked the very thing you were frantically searching for.

It's all about focus! Even when you're looking in the right direction, you can still miss something because your focus is slightly off. This can be the challenge in our relationship with God. We can ask God a question and be really intent on getting the answer, only to find that His response to us was there all along—just not the answer we expected or wanted.

Frustration and stress can keep us from clearly seeing the things that God puts before us. Time spent in prayer and meditation on God's Word can often wash away the dirt and grime of the day-to-day and provide a clear picture of God's intentions for our lives. Step outside the pressure and into His presence, and get the right focus for whatever you're facing today.

*Lord, help me to avoid distractions
and keep my eyes on You. Amen.*

Day 103

ALL ABOUT ME

My substance was not hid from thee, when I was made in secret, and curiously wrought in the lowest parts of the earth. Thine eyes did see my substance, yet being unperfect; and in thy book all my members were written, which in continuance were fashioned, when as yet there was none of them.

Psalm 139:15–16

Have you ever considered how matchless you are in this world? No one is created in exactly the same way. We each have our own personality, gifts, ideas, and dreams. C. S. Lewis wrote, "Why else were individuals created, but that God, loving all infinitely, should love each differently?"

Accepting our individuality is a lifetime lesson since there will be many times we will want to compare ourselves to others. But God has shown His love through the unique manner in which He creates and guides our lives. We are distinct, one from another. His presence in our lives keeps us on a path He created just for us. It's hard to fathom that kind of love.

With that knowledge, we can learn to love ourselves and others with Christlike love and enrich our relationship with Him. Ever-growing, ever-learning, we can trust the heavenly Father to mature us into what He created us to be: "Just ME."

Thank You, Father, for loving me each day.
Keep me on the path You created. Amen.

A GOOD MORSEL

O taste and see that the LORD is good:
blessed is the man that trusteth in him.
PSALM 34:8

Parents sometimes have to encourage children to eat foods they may not even want to try. This may be because of the way a food looks or smells or because they've gotten the notion it's just not going to be tasty. Having more life experience, adults know that it's not only good but also good for them.

The world gives the idea to nonbelievers that God isn't worth a taste. The world emphasizes a self-focus, while the Lord says put others before self and God before all. In reality, walking and talking with God is the best thing you can do for yourself. As you walk with God, learning to pray and lean on Him and operate in His will, you are storing up treasures for yourself in heaven. In the world you are demonstrating the love of Christ and being an influence to get others to taste of the Lord.

Like so many foods that are good for us, all it requires is that first taste, a tiny morsel, which whets the appetite for more of Him. Then you can be open to all the goodness, all the fullness of the Lord.

Lord, fill my cup to overflowing with Your love so that it pours out
of me in a way that makes others want what I have. Amen.

Day 105

TO KNOW HIM IS TO TRUST HIM

And they that know thy name will put their trust in thee:
for thou, LORD, hast not forsaken them that seek thee.
PSALM 9:10

Names often reveal the character of a person. This is true in biblical times, especially when it comes to the names of God. A study of His names often brings a deeper awareness of God and who He is. Isaiah, in predicting the birth of Christ, listed several of His names: "For unto us a child is born, unto us a son is given: and the government shall be upon his shoulder: and his name shall be called Wonderful, Counsellor, The mighty God, The everlasting Father, The Prince of Peace" (9:6).

In other places He is referred to as Lord Jehovah, Almighty God, Shepherd, Priest, King of Kings, and Lord of Lords. He is the God who Sees, the Righteous One, Master, Redeemer, the All-Sufficient One. Each name describes a different attribute. All are perfectly true about Him.

A study of the names of God, Jesus, and the Holy Spirit not only gives us a deeper insight into the nuances of who He is, but it also strengthens our ability to trust Him implicitly with every detail of our lives. He has promised to reveal Himself to those who truly seek Him out, who truly desire to know Him (Philippians 3:10).

Father, reveal Yourself to me through Your names
so I will trust You more. Amen.

Day 106

THANK YOU

But I will hope continually, and will yet praise thee more and more.
My mouth shall shew forth thy righteousness and thy salvation
all the day; for I know not the numbers thereof.
PSALM 71:14–15

Those in the workplace, be it an office or at home, really appreciate a "thanks—well done" every now and then. Kudos can make the day go smoother. And when others brag on us a tad, it perks up the attitude. Think then how our heavenly Father loves to hear a hearty "thank You" from His kids.

Our lives should be filled with praise to the living Lord and King of Kings. He is a mighty God who created us and watches over us. We ought to tell others of the deeds He has done in our lives, for the power of our testimony is great. Tell how He is our Savior and our hope. The psalmist exhorts us to hope continually because we know even in the darkest days that He has given us a promise to never leave our sides.

Synonyms for praise include: *admire, extol, honor, glorify, honor,* and *worship*. This day take one or two of these words and use them to thank your heavenly Father. Don't take Him for granted. Give Him the praise He deserves.

Father God, how good You are. You have blessed us immeasurably,
and for that we choose to glorify Your name. Let us shout
it from the mountain: Our God is good, forever and ever. Amen.

PEACEMAKER

Peace be within thy walls, and prosperity within thy palaces.
PSALM 122:7

Some people's homes are war zones. Families in conflict abound in our society. So much unhappiness comes from people no longer knowing how to share and give. Too many people are looking out for themselves, and they aren't willing to look out for each other. Mothers fight with daughters, sons with fathers, husbands with wives, brothers with sisters, each feeding the beast of hurt and discord. We are lost without a peacemaker, one who knows our hearts and can pave the way to reconciliation. Luckily, Christians have such a peacemaker. Christ came to unite all God's children, brothers and sisters in the faith. He works in the home to call us to a deep love that is consecrated in blood. If we strive for peace within our walls, then we are one step closer to peace between our nations. God will heal all our wounds, if we will only welcome Him in.

Christ, You have broken down the dividing walls of hostility, and You are waiting to build bridges of love. Begin with me, Lord, and move forth in love. Amen.

Day 108

ANXIOUS ANTICIPATIONS

Not that I speak in respect of want: for I have learned,
in whatsoever state I am, therewith to be content.
PHILIPPIANS 4:11

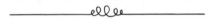

Have you ever been so eager for the future that you forgot to be thankful for the present day?

We anxiously await the weekend, our next vacation, retirement, or some other future event. Maybe we're eager to start a new chapter in our life because we've been frustrated with our current responsibilities.

Humans have a tendency to complain about the problems and irritations of life. It's much less natural to appreciate the good things we have—until they're gone. While it's fine to look forward to the future, let's remember to reflect on all of *today's* blessings—the large and the small—and appreciate all that we do have.

Thank You, Lord, for the beauty of today. Please remind me when
I become preoccupied with the future and forget
to enjoy the present. Amen.

Day 109

CREATING MARGIN

My presence shall go with thee, and I will give thee rest.
EXODUS 33:14

From the very first chapter of Genesis, God teaches us to take rest. He rested on the seventh day of creation and declared it good. Later, as the Israelites entered the Promised Land, God ordered the people to give the *soil* a rest every seven years.

When we short ourselves on rest, illness can result. That's our body's way of saying "Slow down! I can't keep up! If you won't listen to me, then I'm going to force you to."

God believes in rest! But most of us live lives that are packed to the brim with activities and obligations. We're overwhelmed. With such a fragile balance, unexpected occurrences, like a dead car battery, can wreck us emotionally, spiritually, and physically.

That's not the lifestyle God wants us to have. "He giveth his beloved sleep," wrote the psalmist (Psalm 127:2). God wants us to create a margin for the unexpected: a neighbor in need, a family member who requires extra attention, a friend who needs encouragement.

Life is busy. But in God's presence we find rest.

*Help me, Father, to listen to Your instruction
and heed Your words. Amen.*

RADICAL LOVE

*But I say unto you, That ye resist not evil: but whosoever shall
smite thee on thy right cheek, turn to him the other also.*
MATTHEW 5:39

There was one four-letter word Jesus hoped would forever be on the
tip of our tongues: *love.*

The Lord had more to say about love than almost any other topic.
His advice was straightforward: Jesus said we should love God (Matthew
22:36–37), love our neighbors (Matthew 22:39), and love our enemies
(Matthew 5:44)!

Our enemies? Now that's called "pushing the envelope"!

In theory, it sounds wonderful. But in reality, it can feel impossible.
Take the disciple Peter, for example. For years he had heard Jesus'
teachings on love, but when the high priests came to arrest Jesus, Peter
resisted love and defensively cut off the enemy's ear. Jesus corrected
him, saying, "Put your sword away" (see John 18:10–11). Then He healed
the man's ear. (Luke 22:51)

God knows we live in a world where walking away is often judged
spineless. That's why he sent Jesus to really "push the envelope" and
become the definition of love.

Because God extended us His grace, we too can courageously
accept the enemy's strike and turn the other cheek.

*Heavenly Father, when someone does wrong to me, please quiet my
anger and soothe my hurt. Help me to love my enemies
with Your kind of grace. Amen.*

Day 111

WHAT'S LEFT BEHIND

For we brought nothing into this world,
and it is certain we can carry nothing out.
1 Timothy 6:7

Paul preached "you can't take it with you" long before those words became a familiar saying.

In this letter, Paul addressed the issue of falling into the trap of believing that riches brought about a contented life. Paul reminded Timothy that one day people would leave their things behind. In addition, Paul warned that spending their time chasing after wealth was going to lead his flock into temptations that would have a domino effect in their lives. Soon they'd be more dedicated to their money than they would be to their faith.

Jesus also preached about the struggle the wealthy face when it comes to thinking about the kingdom of God (Matthew 19:16–30). The book of Ecclesiastes is full of the despair that comes from seeking after the wrong things.

Though we don't take anything out of the world, we do leave things behind, and not just material items. We leave behind the people whose lives we have touched for better or for worse. We leave behind the words we've spoken, which may or may not have been encouraging.

We also leave behind the comments that others say about us, remarks that can show either our love for possessions or our love for God.

When I leave this world, I want others to remember me as
a disciple of Christ who led others to Him. Help me to
live out that legacy, Lord. Amen.

FISHERS OF MEN

And he saith unto them, Follow me,
and I will make you fishers of men.
Matthew 4:19

Walking beside the glistening blue waters of the Sea of Galilee, Jesus saw two brothers casting their fishing nets. When He spoke the words recorded above, Peter and Andrew must have been intrigued. But Jesus didn't invent the phrase "fishers of men." Philosophers and teachers of that day used this term to describe those who captured men's minds.

The passage goes on to say that Peter and Andrew immediately left their nets and followed Jesus. But this wasn't their first invitation to follow Him. They had gone with Jesus to Capernaum and Galilee and later returned to their trade of fishing. However, this particular invitation was to full-time ministry, and they responded wholeheartedly.

But why did Christ want these fishermen? Peter and Andrew were men of action who knew how to get a job done without quitting or complaining. Their tenacity would be an asset to Christ's ministry of soul winning.

Jesus came not only to save but to teach men and women how to have a true servant's heart. The substance of ministry is service. When the apostles agreed to follow Christ, they accepted the call on His terms, not theirs.

Lord, show me clearly where I can be of service within
my local body of believers. Amen.

Day 113

THE WAY OUT

There hath no temptation taken you but such as is common to man:
but God is faithful, who will not suffer you to be tempted above
that ye are able; but will with the temptation also make
a way to escape, that ye may be able to bear it.
1 Corinthians 10:13

———————— *elle* ————————

Everyone faces temptation. Scripture says that no one escapes it, and all become its victims (Romans 3:23). But don't be discouraged. God provides a way out.

Believers learn to endure and stand up to temptation by God's grace. When they rely on the power that comes from the Holy Spirit, then God provides them with strength to resist. Jesus said that this willpower comes by watchfulness and prayer: "Watch and pray, that ye enter not into temptation: the spirit indeed is willing, but the flesh is weak" (Matthew 26:41).

As hard as people try, temptation sometimes wins. God has a plan for that too. He sent His Son, Jesus, into the world to take the punishment for the sins of everyone who believes in Him. Not only did Jesus suffer the consequences of sin, but also through His sacrifice He provided God with a way to forgive sinfulness and to promise believers eternal life.

Watch and pray today that you don't fall into temptation; but if you do, then remember this: sin might win in the moment, but God's grace and forgiveness are forever.

———————— *roooo* ————————

Dear Lord, lead me not into temptation but deliver me
from evil today and always. Amen.

BE STILL AND LEARN

But his delight is in the law of the LORD;
and in his law doth he meditate day and night.
PSALM 1:2

Do you desire to know God better? To be strengthened by Him? Spending time with the Lord in prayer and Bible reading are the best ways to learn more about His mercy, His kindness, His love, and His peace.

These disciplines are like water on a sponge. They help us understand who God is and what He brings to our lives. In His presence, we become aware of His blessings and the resources He has provided to strengthen us for each day's battles. He will empower us to fulfill His plan for our lives.

It does take discipline to spend time with the Lord, but that simple discipline helps to keep our hope alive, providing light for our paths. When the schedule seems to loom large or the weariness of everyday living tempts you to neglect prayer and Bible study, remember they are your lifeline. They keep you growing in your relationship with the Lover of your soul.

Heavenly Father, I want to know You more. I want to feel Your
presence. Teach me Your ways that I may dwell in
the house of the Lord forever. Amen.

Day 115

LOADED!

Blessed be the Lord, who daily loadeth us with benefits,
even the God of our salvation.
PSALM 68:19

—————————— *elee* ——————————

When we ask God for our daily bread, what do we mean? Is it merely food to nourish our bodies? Is it all the basic necessities of life? Does it include the bread Jesus spoke of: the Word of God? It is all these things and more. Our heavenly Father wants us to have everything we need to affirm His image within us. God never calls His children to tasks they are not ready for, and he will not abandon us without the resources we need to succeed. Our God provides us with everything we need to be the best people we can be. Call upon the Lord to load you daily with benefits. He will do even more than you expect.

—————————— *ᵒᵧᶜᵔ* ——————————

Lord, I do not even know what I need to be better than I am today,
but in Your wisdom, You see my every need. Give me what You
will, in order that I might be an honor and a glory to You. Amen.

Day 116

RENEWING FIRE

For our God is a consuming fire.
HEBREWS 12:29

———————— *ello* ————————

Fire signifies the presence, judgment, and holiness of God. Fire is a powerful image throughout the entire Bible, causing worshippers to approach the throne of the Lord with awe and reverence. An Israelite, ready to make the perfect offering to the Lord, would bring the best lamb to sacrifice on the altar. The holy ritual of spilling blood and burning the fat of the animal in an all-consuming fire symbolized the cleansing of the worshipper's sin.

A consuming fire destroys everything. The massive destruction observed in fierce forest fires at first looks like complete annihilation. But soon signs of rebirth appear with shoots of green growth and the return of life. What was destroyed soon brings forth new life.

God's fire burns away our self-centeredness, ego, and sinful nature when we place our hearts on His altar. His love melts away our selfishness, pride, and anything that blocks His light from shining through our lives. Let the passion of God burn away your old life, allowing His life to be reborn within you.

———————— *ello* ————————

Lord, cleanse me of my sin. Burn away my old ways, and from the ashes redeem me. Create in me a new and more holy life. Amen.

Day 117

MAGNIFYING LIFE

My soul shall make her boast in the LORD: the humble shall hear thereof, and be glad. O magnify the LORD with me, and let us exalt his name together.

PSALM 34:2–3

————————— *elle* —————————

To magnify is to make larger, more visible, more easily seen. When the angel of the Lord appeared to Mary telling her she would be the mother of the Messiah, her response was to quote the psalm, "O magnify the LORD with me." Mary knew she was the object of God's favor and mercy. That knowledge produced humility. The humble soul desires that God be glorified instead of self.

Try as we might, we can't produce this humility in ourselves. It is our natural tendency to be self-promoters, to manage the impressions others have of us, and to better our own reputations. We need the help of the Spirit to remind us that God has favored each of us with His presence. He did not have to come to us in Christ, but He did. He has chosen to set His love on us. His life redeemed ours, and He sanctifies us. We are recipients of the action of His grace.

Does your soul make its boast in the Lord? Does your life make Christ larger and easier for others to see? Maybe you can't honestly say you desire this. Start there. Confess that. Ask Him to remind you of His favor and to work humility into your life, to help you pray like Mary did.

—————————  —————————

Christ Jesus, help me to remember what You have done for me and to desire for others to see and know You. Amen.

Day 118

LIGHT IN THE DARKNESS

And I will bring the blind by a way that they knew not;
I will lead them in paths that they have not known: I will make
darkness light before them, and crooked things straight.
ISAIAH 42:16

In the dim moonlight, we can sometimes find our way in the darkness of our home. In familiar places we know the lay of the land. At best we will make our way around the obstacles through memory and shadowy outline. At worst, we will lightly stumble into an armchair or a piano bench. When all else fails, we know where the light switch is, and, blindly groping in the darkness, we can turn on the light to help us find our way.

But when we walk in the darkness of unfamiliar places, we may feel unsettled. Not sure of our bearings, not knowing where the light switch is, we become overwhelmed, afraid to step forward, afraid even to move. At those times, we need to remember that our God of light is always with us. Although we may not see Him, we can rest easy, knowing He is ever-present in the darkness of unknown places, opportunities, and challenges.

God will never leave us to find our way alone. Realize this truth and arm yourself with the knowledge that no matter what the situation, no matter what the trial, no matter how black the darkness, He is ever there, reaching out for us, helping us find our way. Switch on the truth of His light in your mind and walk forward, knowing He is always within reach.

Lord, be my light. Guard me in the darkness of these days.
Make my way straight and the ground I trod smooth.
And if I do stumble, catch me! In Jesus' name, I pray. Amen.

A POTENT PARADOX

Be not overcome of evil, but overcome evil with good.
ROMANS 12:21

There's an old adage that says "Don't get mad, get even." Unfortunately, that's going expressly against what Romans 12:21 would have Christ followers do. So if revenge is out, what other ways of dealing with evil could we take? Well, we could allow it to taint and dictate everything in our life, or we could run and hide in fear. None of these ways seem very empowering, do they?

Jesus and New Testament writers give Christians many paradoxes. And the above verse is no different. Like the text about turning the other cheek (Matthew 5:39), Romans 12:21 instructs God's people not to bow down to, hide from, or return evil for evil, but to conquer it by doing good. Amazingly enough, it works! And, as a bonus, it will not only stop evil (and evil doers) in its (their) tracks but relieve the flesh-filled human desire of revenge.

What a glorious day it would be if, instead of taking revenge for or hiding from evil, every child of the King faced the dark beast head on. Neither cowering in fear or wallowing in self-pity, God's kids can count on His power to step boldly, repay evil with kindness, and move on. What a paradox! What a godsend!

Lord, it seems natural for me to want to return evil for evil.
But I want to do the supernatural. Help me to conquer
evil by doing something good! Amen.

Day 120
HE GIVES

Therefore take no thought, saying, What shall we eat? or, What shall we drink? or, Wherewithal shall we be clothed? (For after all these things do the Gentiles seek:) for your heavenly Father knoweth that ye have need of all these things.
MATTHEW 6:31–32

What is weighing on your heart? It might be the burgeoning credit card bill from when the car's transmission failed unexpectedly last month. It might be a newly discovered lump—your palms sweaty as you wait for lab results. You might be wondering if your family is going to stay together or worrying about family members who don't love God. Worry can tangle a heart into fearful, anxious knots, cutting off its life.

Jesus tells us that the Creator who cares for the birds and the wildflowers knows our needs intimately (Matthew 6:28–30). The same God who keeps the Earth perfectly tilted and spinning so that the seasons arrive at the right time also cares about medical bills, missing keys, and difficult family relationships.

The antidote to worry is prayer—telling our Father the things we lack, the things that hurt, the things that don't seem to have an answer—because He *listens*. He opens His hand to bless and fill us, to calm and heal us, to extend wisdom and peace. He invites us to seek Him wholly and to lean on His sure and faithful promise to provide for all our needs (Matthew 6:33).

Father God, I want to put You first in my heart. Help me bring all my worries to You and leave them at Your feet. Thank You for how You love me and promise to provide for me. Amen.

COUNT YOUR BLESSINGS

*Every good gift and every perfect gift is from above,
and cometh down from the Father of lights, with whom
is no variableness, neither shadow of turning.*

JAMES 1:17

There is an old hymn that drives the same point home: "Blessings all mine and ten thousand beside."

Whether you stand with hands raised or kneel beside your bed in silent prayer, moved to tears of gratitude, does not matter. Whether your lips utter the words of a hymn or a contemporary chorus is not of any consequence. What matters is that you praise Him. What matters is that you thank Him. Every good and perfect gift that you find in your life has come straight from the hands of God. He withholds nothing good from His children. Even earthly parents know how to love, and they desire to give good gifts to their children. How much more does your heavenly Father love you! How much more does He want to lavish blessings on you! Thank the Lord today for the blessings in your life.

Father, I am so blessed. Why do I grumble and complain? Look at all that You have done in my life! Look at all that You have freely given me! Thank You, Lord, for Your many blessings. Amen.

Day 122

COMMUNE WITH ME

*The cup of blessing which we bless, is it not the communion
of the blood of Christ? The bread which we break,
is it not the communion of the body of Christ?*
1 CORINTHIANS 10:16

———————— ✤ ————————

Oh, what a blessed privilege, to commune with the Lord. To spend time with Him. To break bread together. To remember the work that Jesus did on the cross. Yet how often do we do this without really "remembering" the depth of its meaning?

The night that Jesus was betrayed—the very night before some of His closest followers turned on Him—He sat down for a special meal with them. He took the bread and broke it, then explained that it, symbolically, provided the perfect picture of what was about to happen to His very body on the cross. Then He took the cup of wine and explained that it too had pertinent symbolism, for it represented His blood which was about to be spilled on Calvary.

The disciples surely couldn't comprehend fully what Jesus was talking about, but less than twenty-four hours later, it was abundantly clear. And now, two thousand years later, it's clearer still. And Jesus still bids us to come and commune with Him. He longs for us to remember—to never forget—the price that He paid on the cross that day.

"Commune with Me." Such simple words from God to mankind.

———————— ✤ ————————

*Father, I get it! It's not just about breaking bread together.
It's all about spending time with You. Being with You.
Remembering all You did for me. I long to sit next to
You today, Lord. I choose to commune with You. Amen.*

Day 123

CORPORATE WORSHIP

Praise ye the LORD. Sing unto the LORD a new song,
and his praise in the congregation of saints.
PSALM 149:1

Worship is so powerful in a private, intimate setting, but there's something equally as powerful in corporate worship. There, side-by-side with other Christians, we lift our hearts, our voices, our words of praise in a mighty, thunderous chorus. What bliss! And, what a wonderful way to prepare for heaven, where we will gather around the throne of God and sing, "Holy, holy, holy!" together with all His people.

When we come into the house of God, like-minded and ready to focus on Him, we are a force to be reckoned with! The gates of hell cannot prevail against us. Two or more (in this case, often hundreds) are gathered together in unity. And unity is the key. Like-minded. Together.

When we enter into corporate worship, we aren't focused on self. The problems of the day wash away. We aren't focused on others, though they are surrounding us on every side. We are solely focused on God, the one we adore. Our eyes, our hearts, our thoughts are on Him alone.

Father, I love worshipping with fellow believers. What a blast to stand
alongside my brothers and sisters in Christ to lift my voice in song
and to hear Your Word preached. Whether we're singing,
praying, or hearing a life-changing message,
we do it all for You. Amen.

Day 124

SABBATH REST

Let us therefore fear, lest, a promise being left us of entering into his rest, any of you should seem to come short of it.
HEBREWS 4:1

———————— ℓℓℓℓ ————————

We move at such a rapid pace. Life tugs and pulls at us, and we respond, sprinting toward goal after goal. What overachievers we are!

The Lord never intended for us to go around the clock. He didn't design our bodies to run in "energizer bunny" mode 24-7. We can live like this for a little while, sure, but eventually something's gotta give, and it's usually our health. Or our emotions. Or our relationships. Or—worst of all—our times of intimacy with God.

We are created in the image of God, and He is always on the move! Still, He instigated the Sabbath for a reason, because He knows mankind's tendency to go, go, go. Sure, we have work to do. Yes, we have people to care for and souls to reach. But if we're broken down from lack of sleep or from overextending ourselves, there won't be anything to offer others. So slow down! Take a breather. For that matter, take a nap. And don't apologize for it! Moments of respite are precious.

———————— ༺ༀ༻ ————————

Lord, thank You for the reminder that You want me to rest. It's not always easy. I'm such a go-getter, but I have to confess that taking a break feels really, really good. Draw me away to Your side for a special time of rest, I pray. Amen.

Day 125

DEEP UNDERSTANDING

I have more understanding than all my teachers:
for thy testimonies are my meditation.
PSALM 119:99

―――――――― ༄ ――――――――

Jesus amazed the learned men in the temple when He was just twelve years old. He had never received professional schooling in the history and law of the Hebrew people, and yet He displayed an incredible insight into even the most complex meanings of holy scripture. His understanding far surpassed that of many of the elders present. Where did His incredible knowledge and wisdom come from? God, of course.

True knowledge is not found in books. God has granted us each a measure of common sense and logic. He is willing and able to instruct us in all His ways, if we will take time to contemplate His mysteries. We too can amaze the learned of our age by speaking the truth of God, which surpasses even the most complex knowledge. Like Christ, we can know more than we ought to, through the guidance and counsel of God Himself.

―――――――― ༄ ――――――――

Instruct my mind, heart, and soul in all of Your ways,
Oh Lord. Teach me those things that are truly important,
and enable me to spread what I learn to others. Amen.

THE EXTRA MILE

And whosoever shall compel thee to go a mile, go with him twain.
MATTHEW 5:41

———————— *ello* ————————

Going the extra mile. The Romans adopted the ancient Persian custom of forcing someone to carry their baggage for them while they traveled. Against their will, people were compelled to lug these conquerors' belongings the length of a mile or one thousand paces.

In the book of Matthew, Jesus said in the Sermon on the Mount to surprise your enemies. Don't just go the minimum distance—be willing to double the effort and walk two miles.

God's love exceeds our wildest imagination. He pours out His blessings, forgiveness, and strength on us even in our toughest circumstances. He goes the extra mile.

God calls us to do likewise, and live to a higher standard. We choose not to retaliate when we have been wronged. We volunteer for two shifts when others leave early and don't complete their assignments. We help someone without any thought of what we may get in return. We pray for people others ignore. We strive to love the unlovable.

God expects us to go beyond all expectations and to go the extra mile.

———————— *ellee* ————————

*God, help me to go that extra mile by giving with no thought
of receiving and by loving those most in need
of Your mercy and love. Amen.*

Day 127

YOU ARE AN ANSWER TO PRAYER

Blessed be God, even the Father of our Lord Jesus Christ, the Father of mercies, and the God of all comfort; who comforteth us in all our tribulation, that we may be able to comfort them which are in any trouble, by the comfort wherewith we ourselves are comforted of God.

2 CORINTHIANS 1:3–4

It's part of our maturing process. At some point, as Christians, we should arrive at a place where we are comfortable using our own past experiences and current circumstances as tools to reach out to others in need. Maturing believers are able to look back on the things they have gone through with gratitude, as their purpose in the body of Christ begins to unfold.

For various reasons, it can be difficult to move past that point of being ministered to, in order to minister to others in need. But, according to the apostle Paul, one of the reasons God comforts us is so we can share that comfort with others when they need it.

We might say, "I'm just a new Christian," or "I wouldn't know what to say." But as members of the body of Christ, we are an extension of the Holy Spirit.

So when someone is praying for comfort, be ready—it might just be you God will send to minister to that hurting soul.

Jesus, please help me open my heart and eyes to see the needs around me. Give me the grace and wisdom to comfort others with the comfort You have shown me time and time again. Amen.

Day 128

WIMPS FOR JESUS?

Wherefore lift up the hands which hang down, and the feeble knees;
and make straight paths for your feet, lest that which is lame
be turned out of the way; but let it rather be healed.
HEBREWS 12:12–13

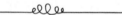

God's discipline sometimes leaves us feeling limp—and not too bright.

"How could I do such a thing? Why didn't I stop to think, read the Bible, and pray about the situation?"

All Christians live through these humbling experiences, because we all make mistakes—sometimes big ones. Washed up and wiped out, we wonder why Jesus bothers with us. We want to give up. Satan would like nothing better. "What's the use?" he whispers. "You've embarrassed yourself and God, and there's no way you will ever hold up your head again." We let our Bibles gather dust and stop going to church. When we see other Christians around town, we hide! We also find ourselves spending time and energy in paths that aggravate our pain rather than heal it.

As always, God presents better solutions for our problems. He disciplines us for the same reason a mother corrects her children: out of love. Ultimately, parents want their kids to lead healthy, productive lives. How can we think God wants any less for us?

Lord Jesus, You gave Your life that I might be healed of my sin
and weakness. Please help me to obey You, trusting that
You know what You're doing in my life. Amen.

LEAD GOOSE

This thing is too heavy for thee;
thou art not able to perform it thyself alone.
EXODUS 18:18

───────── ❧❧❧ ─────────

The V formation of flying geese is a fascinating example of aerodynamics. Each bird flies slightly above the bird in front of it, resulting in a reduction of wind resistance. It also helps to conserve the geese's energy. The farther back a goose is in formation, the less energy it needs in the flight. The birds rotate the lead goose position, falling back when tired. With this instinctive system, geese can fly for a long time before they must stop for rest. This is an example of God's wisdom displayed in the natural world. We often find ourselves as a lead goose. But we have a hard time recognizing signs of exhaustion in ourselves. Even harder is falling back and letting someone else have a chance to develop leadership skills. Deep down we think that no other goose could get the gaggle where it needs to go without getting lost or bashing into treetops. Jethro, Moses' father-in-law, came for a visit as the Israelites camped near the mountain of God. Jethro found Moses to be on the brink of exhaustion. "You will wear yourself out and these people as well," he told Moses. Jethro recommended that Moses delegate responsibilities. Moses listened and implemented everything Jethro suggested, advice that benefited the entire nation of Israel.

─────── ∽∾∾∾ ───────

Dear Lord, help me to know when to fall back and rest,
letting someone else take the lead. Teach me to
serve You in any position. Amen.

Day 130

CLUED IN

This book of the law shall not depart out of thy mouth; but thou shalt meditate therein day and night, that thou mayest observe to do according to all that is written therein: for then thou shalt make thy way prosperous, and then thou shalt have good success.

JOSHUA 1:8

God clues Joshua in on a few things, things he'll need to know now that he's Israel's new leader. The Lord tells Joshua that everywhere he steps, whatever land his foot touches, God has *already* given him (v. 3). It's a done deal! God also tells him that he will not be defeated, that God will be with him no matter what, and that Joshua should never be afraid or discouraged. (God repeats that last one two more times in this chapter alone!)

But then God mentions *success*, a word that appears only once in the King James Version. To have good success and to prosper, Joshua needs to speak, think about, and obey God's Word. After hearing these instructions, Joshua remains true to them and becomes the conquering hero God created him to be!

Believers today can have the same victory! God has *already* given His children all we need to be successful—in whatever roles we fill. Keeping that in mind, as well as God's Word on our tongues and obedience in our actions, we cannot be anything other than prosperous in everything we do!

Thank You, Lord, for the gift—and challenge—of Your Word. I know that as I live, move, and have my being in You, I will have success! Amen.

INFINITE AND PERSONAL

*Am I a God at hand, saith the LORD, and not a God
afar off? . . . Do not I fill heaven and earth?*
JEREMIAH 23:23–24

————————— ✑✑✑ —————————

Back in the 1950s, the Union of Soviet Socialist Republics sent up its first satellite, *Sputnik*. At that time, communism held Russia in its tightfisted grip. Everyone who was anyone in the USSR was a communist and an atheist. Not long after *Sputnik*, the Russian cosmonauts circled planet Earth. After their return to earth, one cosmonaut made this announcement to the world: "I saw no God anywhere."

When US astronauts finally made it into space some months later, one remarked, "I saw God everywhere!"

Our worldview determines the way we see reality. The cosmonaut didn't expect to see God, and he didn't. The astronaut didn't see anything more or less than his Russian counterpart, but he came away with an entirely different response. God says that He is both close at hand and over all there is. The late theologian and philosopher Francis Schaeffer called Him the infinite-personal God.

Whether your day is crumbling around you or is the best day you have ever had, do you see God in it? If the "sky is falling" or the sun is shining, do you still recognize the One who orders all the planets and all your days? Whether we see Him or not, God tells us He is there. And He's here too—in the good times and bad.

————————— ✑✑✑ —————————

Lord, empower me to trust You when it's hard to remember that You are near. And help me to live thankfully when times are good. Amen.

Day 132

MOUNTAIN-MOVING COMPANY

If ye have faith as a grain of mustard seed, ye shall say unto this mountain, Remove hence to yonder place; and it shall remove; and nothing shall be impossible unto you.
Matthew 17:20

We've all made the lament at some point, "If only I had enough faith. . ."

". . .my parent/child/friend/spouse wouldn't have died."

". . .I would have received that job offer."

". . .I would have enough money for everything in my budget and more besides."

Any of those laments for greater faith pale when compared to faith to move a mountain. After all, doesn't Jesus say that all we need is faith the size of a tiny seed?

The problem with that line of thought is that we put the emphasis on ourselves. If *we* have faith, our problems will go away.

Jesus isn't prodding us to show more faith. He is pointing us to the object of our faith—God. However small our faith, God can move mountains. When we drop the seed of our faith into the ground of His will, He will move the mountains out of our way. He will show us the direction He wants us to take. He may move the mountain; or He may carry us over, around, or through it.

The next time a mountain looms ahead, God wants us to apply to His moving company. He will take us to the right destination.

Lord God, You are the God of the impossible. We trust You to move the mountains of our lives and to move us through them. Amen.

Day 133

MORE THAN ENOUGH

And let us not be weary in well doing:
for in due season we shall reap, if we faint not.
GALATIANS 6:9

———————— ✿ ————————

How often do we become impatient and give up? We stand in line at the coffee shop and find ourselves behind an indecisive person. Frustrated and afraid of being late, we give up—but before we get to our car, that person, coffee cup in hand, walks past. If we'd only waited another minute, we too could be sipping a steaming caramel latte.

Or maybe we have a dream that we can't seem to make a reality—and rather than trying "just one more time," we give up. A piece of who we are drifts away like a leaf on the sea.

The Word of God encourages us to keep going, to press on, to fight off weariness and never give up. Jesus Christ has a harvest for each of us, and He eagerly anticipates blessing us with it—but we have to trust Him and refuse to give in to weariness.

We can only imagine what that harvest might be, because we know that God is the God of "exceedingly abundantly above all that we ask or think" (Ephesians 3:20). We can be recipients of His exceeding abundance if we press on in the strength He provides.

When you're tired, keep going—and remember that, in His perfect timing, you will reap an unimaginable harvest.

———————— ✿ ————————

Father, You know that I'm tired and weary in this uphill struggle.
Fill me with Your strength so I can carry on. I long to reap
the harvest You have for me. Amen.

Day 134

OPEN HEARTS

For the eyes of the Lord run to and fro throughout the whole earth,
to shew himself strong in the behalf of them whose
heart is perfect toward him.

2 Chronicles 16:9

———————— ✑✑✑ ————————

God is on a quest. He explores throughout the world and searches in every corner. He is relentless in His pursuit of something.

What is the object of His exploration? He wants people with a particular type of heart condition—hearts fully devoted to Him. God seeks a relationship with those who have open and receiving hearts. He is not looking to condemn or judge but to find hearts committed to knowing Him and learning His way. He desires people who want to talk and listen to Him and who have a deep thirst to serve and please Him.

God gives loyal hearts a gift—His strength. He eagerly pours His spirit into these open hearts in order to draw closer and build an intimate relationship with them.

God looks for us, and the only requirement is for each of us to have a fully devoted heart. We open our hearts and hands to receive Him, and He will find us.

———————— ✑✑✑ ————————

Find me, Lord, draw me near to You. Open up my heart
so that I may fully receive all that You want to pour into it. Amen.

Day 135

WHEN OTHERS DOUBT

And of some have compassion, making a difference.
JUDE 1:22

───────── ✻ ─────────

Jude *wanted* to discuss the joys of salvation but first had to warn his readers of the dangers posed by those who follow a more worldly path.

He cautioned the faithful to be cautious—but he didn't say, "Stay away from those heathens!" Instead, he recommended building ourselves up in "holy faith" (v. 20) because there is work to be done. God doesn't want to lose anyone—and with His help, we might be able to snatch "them out of the fire" (v. 23).

Not all of those faithless ones are intentionally evil or wicked. Many have been fooled into thinking God is for others. Some have doubts and questions and might come to faith if only they could see how it applied to a life like theirs. The world certainly isn't going to show them that—and if we just walk on by, they might never know.

Like Jude, we might want to celebrate our salvation. But, just as he found, there is something more important to concentrate on. Rubbing shoulders with some worldly people might be a risk worth taking if, in the process, a few doubters can be saved.

After all, if Christianity consisted only of those who never doubted, there would be very few going to heaven—and a lot more feeling the heat.

───────── ✻ ─────────

Heavenly Father, Jesus welcomed unbelievers and He led them to You. I want to be like Jesus. Show me how to transform doubt into faith and trust in You. Amen.

Day 136

DO GOOD

Therefore to him that knoweth to do good,
and doeth it not, to him it is sin.
JAMES 4:17

"The road to hell is paved with good intentions." Wouldn't it be interesting to know what the context was when this maxim was written? It sure sounds like an adaptation of James 4:17.

We've all heard anecdotes about how numerous people stood by and ignored cries for help as a heinous crime was committed. Stories abound on the shocking apathy of human nature, just when it matters the most. And as we learn of them, we think, *I would never stand idly by and do nothing in circumstances such as those.*

And yet, how many smaller opportunities slip right past us as we fail to make the connection? How many times do we think, *It would be really nice if I did something for this person*, and then proceed to talk ourselves out of it. *They'll think this is silly*, or, *They won't even notice*, or even, *I don't have time.*

James warns us to stay focused on doing what's right. Regardless of our plans, we never know what the future holds. We never know when we will desperately need the intervention of a good deed from someone else.

Dear God, today make me aware of little ways that I can brighten
the lives of others. Where You see a need, Father,
send me to fill it. Amen.

Day 137

MISPLACED WORSHIP

*And he found a new jawbone of an ass, and put forth his hand,
and took it, and slew a thousand men therewith.*

JUDGES 15:15

God used Samson to provoke and judge the Philistines, who were ruling harshly over Israel. At one point, Samson set their fields on fire, and the Philistines responded by burning his wife. His own people, fearful of further violence, came to arrest Samson and hand him over to the Philistines. He agreed, but at the moment of handoff, the Spirit of God came upon Samson, who grabbed a jawbone of a donkey and wiped out a thousand Philistines.

How could that be? It was certainly the power of God that allowed one man to take down a legion of others. Sadly, though, Samson was dismissive of the things of God. He was a man of the flesh, a womanizer who never rose to his true potential—and he ended up praising his own strength and a lowly jawbone for the victory, rather than the empowering Spirit of God.

That's common for human beings. We'll worship something—either the stuff of this world or the One who gave us this world by His power.

Which will you choose today?

*Holy Spirit, You empower me to make the right choices and
to do well. I worship You above all else! All glory,
praise, and honor belong to You. Amen.*

Day 138

IT'S MORE THAN YOU THINK

For as he thinketh in his heart, so is he.
Proverbs 23:7

———————— ℓℓℓℓ ————————

Some Christians become so desperate for financial success and relief from economic uncertainty that they subscribe to the magical thinking sweeping society today. The "secret" to prosperity is said to be simple: think about the things that you want God (or the universe) to give you, focus on them, repeat to yourself, "They're already mine," and they will be yours.

A verse often quoted by such teachers is "For as he thinketh in his heart, so is he"—as if you only need to think about something to bring it into existence. However, this verse is *actually* talking about dining with a stingy man who says, "Eat and drink. . ." but "his heart is not with thee" (v. 7). He pretends to be generous, but he's actually cringing as you eat up his food. In his heart he's stingy, and as he thinks in his heart, so *is* he.

Certainly God has promised to answer our prayers, and Jesus said, "All things are possible to him that believeth" (Mark 9:23). So yes, we should have more faith, but faith alone is not enough. God's promises are conditional on His will for us, our obedience, etc. (1 John 5:14–15; Isaiah 59:1–2). After all, God is God, not our servant.

———————— ⤜⤛ ————————

God, thank You for Your gracious gifts. Teach me not only to have faith in Your generosity but also to be worthy and accepting of whatever You choose to give me. Amen.

Day 139

I CAN DO IT!

The young lions do lack, and suffer hunger: but they that seek the LORD shall not want any good thing.

PSALM 34:10

———————— ℓℓℓℓ ————————

Remember the prodigal son? He thought he was ready to set out on his own, and it almost led to his ruin. He squandered all his wealth and found he really couldn't make it by himself. He had to humble himself and return home, where his father awaited him with open arms.

We need to learn that being mature and independent does not mean breaking our ties with other people. God did not create us to live apart from others. He gave us each other in order to make our lives more enjoyable. We never need to lack for anything, because we are to take care of one another. The Lord provides for us through the love of our brothers and sisters in Christ. Growing up doesn't mean learning to do everything by yourself, but realizing how wonderful it is to need other people.

———————— ————————

I think I am strong and self-sufficient when I am not. I sometimes act as if I don't need anyone else, but deep inside, I know that I do. Put me in community with others who love You, Lord. Make me stronger through the relationships I develop. Amen.

Day 140

GRIEVING? WORSHIP!

Then Job arose, and rent his mantle, and shaved his head,
and fell down upon the ground, and worshipped.
JOB 1:20

———————— ✿ ————————

Grief expresses itself in different ways. When troubles come, some people spill copious tears, others burst with fits of anger, and a few simply shut down in silent numbness. In Western cultures, black is the color of grief. People wear white in some Asian countries.

How did Job express his grief? He worshipped.

Job followed the traditional ways of mourning in his culture by tearing his clothes and shaving his head.

But Job also *worshipped.*

Despite overwhelming darkness of shock and grief, he turned to God. He lay prostrate on the ground in front of the Lord, submitting his entire self. In his time of overwhelming loss and overpowering helplessness, he opened his heart to the only one who fully understood and could help him in his time of deepest need—God.

When everything in life seems gone, lost, or out of reach, God is waiting. God understands our sorrow and stays with us while we grieve. As we turn our hearts to Him in worship, His healing Spirit will provide comfort.

———————— ✿ ————————

Sadness is a powerful emotion, Lord, but not nearly as
powerful as Your love. I worship You for understanding,
for comforting me, and for sharing my pain. Amen.

Day 141

COMMON GROUND

*Now while Paul waited for them at Athens, his spirit was stirred
in him, when he saw the city wholly given to idolatry.*
ACTS 17:16

While exploring Athens, Paul discovered the appalling truth of a common Roman saying: "It's easier to find a god at Athens than a man."

Burdened for the Athenians, Paul began proclaiming Christ in the Jewish synagogue and every day in the agora (marketplace). As a result, Epicurean and Stoic philosophers met Paul and brought him to Mars Hill to hear his teachings.

Previously, Paul had noticed an Athenian altar to *agnostos theos*, "the unknown god." In his address on Mars Hill, Paul used this unknown god as a bridge from the Athenian idols to God and His Son, Jesus. He also quoted Epimenides and Aratus, poets familiar to the Athenians.

Rather than condemning the people and spouting dire warnings, Paul looked for common ground and built his case for Christ from there. As a result, several men and women believed his message.

Are you around people whose beliefs differ greatly from yours? Do you sometimes feel lost as to how to turn a conversation to Christ? Copy Paul's approach. Look for a shared viewpoint or familiar truth and slowly build from there.

---

*Father, when I encounter people whose opinions differ greatly
from mine, help us to find common ground. Then show
me the way to lead them toward You. Amen.*

Day 142

CALL ME

And call upon me in the day of trouble:
I will deliver thee, and thou shalt glorify me.
PSALM 50:15

———————— ℓℓℓ ————————

"Call me and we'll do lunch."

"Call me and we'll talk more."

"Call me if you need anything."

How many times have we said those words or heard them in return? Those two little words, *call me*, which hold such significance, have become so commonplace we barely think about them.

But when God says He wants us to call Him, He means it. He must lean closer, bending His ear, waiting, longing for the sound of His name coming from our lips. He stands ready to deliver us from our troubles or at least carry us through them safely.

David called on God in his troubles. Some of those troubles were of David's own making, while others were out of his control. It's a good thing God doesn't distinguish between the troubles we deserve and those we don't deserve. As far as He's concerned, we're His children. He loves us, and He wants to help us any way He can.

While He doesn't always choose to fix things with a snap of His fingers, we can be assured that He will see us through to the other side of our troubles by a smoother path than we'd travel without Him. He's waiting to help us. All we have to do is call.

———————— ∽∾∾∾ ————————

Dear Father, I'm so glad I can call on You anytime,
with any kind of trouble. Amen.

Day 143

CHOOSE LOVE

A new commandment I give unto you, That ye love one another;
as I have loved you, that ye also love one another. By this shall all
men know that ye are my disciples, if ye have love one to another.
JOHN 13:34–35

———————— ⁓⁓ ————————

There are people in your life that you can't help but butt heads with—the ones that get under your skin, rub you the wrong way, and push your buttons at a moment's notice. They can cause an eruption of emotion within you just by entering the room—people you work with, go to church with, and, unfortunately, even those within your own family.

So how do you keep the volcano from exploding and causing deep hurts in your relationships? Jesus gave a command to love; and because we love Him, we have the ability to live each day in His love.

The Bible says that "the love of God is shed abroad in our hearts by the Holy Ghost" (Romans 5:5). It's not your love but God's love that responds to those button-pushing moments. Imagine taking your irritations and dropping your emotional reaction into the sea of God's love that flows through your heart. It disappears in the flood, and then you can love out of His overflow of love for others.

———————— ⁓⁓ ————————

Heavenly Father, remind me to take a deep breath and choose
to love no matter the circumstances. Help me to love others
as You do by living out of Your love and responding
to them as You would. Amen.

Day 144

GOD'S RESOURCES

And he said unto me, My grace is sufficient for thee: for my strength is made perfect in weakness. Most gladly therefore will I rather glory in my infirmities, that the power of Christ may rest upon me.

2 CORINTHIANS 12:9

How do you define stress? Perhaps you feel it when the car doesn't start or the toilet backs up or the line is too long at the grocery store. Or maybe your source of stress is a terrible diagnosis, a late-night phone call, a demanding boss, or a broken relationship. It's probably a combination of all of these things. You might be able to cope with one of them, but when several are bearing down at once, stress is the inevitable result.

It has been said that stress results when our perceived demands exceed our perceived resources. When the hours required to meet a deadline at work (demand) exceed the number of hours we have available (resources), we get stressed. The most important word in this definition is *perceived*. When it comes to stress, people have a tendency to do two things. One, they magnify the demand ("I will *never* be able to get this done"), and two, they fail to consider all of their resources. For the child of God, this includes His mighty strength, which remains long after ours is gone.

In an uncertain world, it is difficult to say few things for sure. But no matter what life throws our way, we can be confident of this: our demands will *never* exceed God's vast resources.

Strong and mighty heavenly Father, thank You that in my weakness I can always rely on Your perfect strength. Amen.

Day 145

IN THE IMAGE OF GOD

*And God saw every thing that he had made,
and, behold, it was very good.*
GENESIS 1:31

God started with light, and His finishing touch was mankind. He created the heavens and the earth and everything in them. God was pleased with His creation. After He created the ocean and dry land, the plants and animals, He said that it was all *good*. But then He created man, and He said this was *very* good. Mankind is different from all of the rest of God's creation, we have intellect beyond that of animals. We have souls. We are made in the image of God. He is creative; we have a bit of creativity within us. He is loving; we are capable of love. We are His children, and we are to reflect who He is. Just as children look somewhat like their earthly parents, we bear God's image. We are to look like our heavenly Father. When others listen to you, do they know that you are a child of the King of kings? When they look at how you carry yourself, do they see humility and yet confidence? You are a child of the Creator of the universe. Made in His image, you represent Him on this earth.

Father, I am created in Your image. I am Your child. Help me to live like it today. Help me to reflect Your light in a dark world. Amen.

Day 146

THE COMPARISON TRAP

*But let every man prove his own work, and then shall he
have rejoicing in himself alone, and not in another.
For every man shall bear his own burden.*
GALATIANS 6:4–5

In John 21, the apostle John records a conversation Jesus had with Peter shortly after His resurrection. Jesus prepared a breakfast for His disciples after a night of fishing. Then Jesus invited Peter to go for a walk. Just days before, Peter had denied knowing Jesus. Now, three times Jesus asked Peter if the fisherman-turned-disciple loved Him. By asking this question, Jesus not only let Peter know that he was forgiven for his lapse of faith, but He let Peter know that God still had a purpose and plan for him. He also spoke of how Peter would eventually die for His Gospel.

Peter, maybe a little embarrassed by all the attention he was getting, looked over his shoulder and saw John following them. Peter asked the Lord, "What about him? How will he die?" Peter fell into the comparison trap.

Jesus answered, "What does it matter to you what I have planned for another? Live your life according to My plan. That's all you need to be concerned about."

And that's all Jesus still requires of His followers. God has a unique plan and purpose for each one, equipping them as they keep their eyes on Him and follow Him daily.

*Father, show me Your plan for today and help me
not to compare my path with others'. Amen.*

Day 147

JOY FOR THE JOURNEY

*The LORD is my strength and my shield; my heart trusted in him,
and I am helped: therefore my heart greatly rejoiceth;
and with my song will I praise him.*

PSALM 28:7

There are times when joy seems impossible. When you're going through a rough season, for instance, or when you're face-to-face with a proverbial Goliath. The enemy of your soul would like nothing more than to rob you of your joy. He's skilled at tripping you up, creating havoc.

But guess what? It's possible to praise—to be joyful—even in the middle of the battle. There's a great story in the Old Testament about a man named Jehoshaphat who was facing a mighty opposition—an army, no less! He sent the Levites (the praise and worshippers) to the front lines. In other words, he led the way into the battle with praise on the lips of his warriors. And they prevailed!

The same is true in our lives. We must lead the way with praise. If we will maintain the joy in our hearts, even in the midst of our battles, we will be triumphant in the end. So don't let the enemy steal your joy, even if you're walking through a difficult season. There are plenty of victories ahead if you don't give up.

*Lord, I must confess, I don't always feel like singing a song of praise
when I'm facing a huge battle. In fact, I usually just want to
give up. Thank You for this reminder that I can be joyful,
even when I'm in the middle of a struggle. Amen.*

Day 148

WHAT IF?

The LORD shall preserve thee from all evil:
he shall preserve thy soul.
PSALM 121:7

"Mommy, what if the sun falls down? What if an earthquake swallows our house? What if. . . ?" When the world appears scary to children, they run to their parents with questions. They look to their mothers and fathers for comfort, reassurance, and peace.

Grown-ups are no different. They run to Father God with their what-ifs. "What if I have cancer? What if I lose my job? What if there is a terrorist attack? What if. . . ?"

Psalm 46 provides the answer to all these questions. It says, "God is our refuge and strength, a very present help in trouble. Therefore will not we fear, though the earth be removed, and though the mountains be carried into the midst of the sea; though the waters thereof roar and be troubled, though the mountains shake with the swelling thereof. . . . The LORD of hosts is with us; the God of Jacob is our refuge" (vv. 1–3, 7).

Feeling safe and secure rests not in the world or in other human beings but with God alone. He is a Christian's help and hope in every frightening situation. He promises to provide peace to everyone who puts their faith and trust in Him.

What are you afraid of today? Allow God to encourage you. Trust Him to bring you through it and to give you peace.

Dear Lord, hear my prayers, soothe me with Your words,
and give me peace. Amen.

Day 149

THANKFUL, THANKFUL HEART

I will praise thee, O LORD, with my whole heart;
I will shew forth all thy marvellous works.
PSALM 9:1

———————— *elle* ————————

If you live from the perspective that 10 percent of life is what happens to you and the rest is how you respond, then every situation has a side—positive or negative. Say you're late to work; every stoplight on your way is a red one, and you feel like you just can't make up the time. Instead of complaining, consider the delay was one that God appointed to keep you safe.

When you choose to approach life from the positive side, you can find thankfulness in most of life's circumstances. It completely changes your outlook, your attitude, and your countenance. God wants to bless you. When you are tempted to feel sorry for yourself or to blame others or God for difficulties, push PAUSE. Take a moment and rewind your life. Look back and count the blessings that God has given you. As you remind yourself of all He has done for you and in you, it will bring change to your attitude and give you hope in the situation you're facing. Count your blessings today.

———————— ✦ ————————

Lord, I am thankful for my life and all You have done for me.
When life happens, help me to respond to it in a healthy,
positive way. Remind me to look to You and trust You
to carry me through life's challenges. Amen.

Day 150

GOD IS SOVEREIGN

I will go in the strength of the Lord God: I will make mention of thy righteousness, even of thine only.

PSALM 71:16

God is sovereign. Think about those words for a minute. This means He has the ultimate authority. Supreme power. The highest rank. There is no one else we can run to whose opinion is higher—or holier—than the Lord's. He alone has the answers to what we face, and His sovereignty assures us that we can trust Him, even when everything around us is whirling out of control. Sure, it's not always easy, but it's always the right choice.

Have you acknowledged God's sovereignty in your life? If so, it might be time to take your hands off the situations you're dealing with and trust that He—out of His great love for you—will offer the best solution. No trying to fix things on your end! Relax. Your sovereign Lord has everything under control in His time, and His way.

Dear Lord, I have to admit, I don't always trust Your sovereignty. I trust my own instincts first. Help me to let go and trust You in every situation, trusting You with Your timing and Your answers. Today I choose to let go, releasing my troubles into Your capable hands. Amen.

CLEANING UP

Draw nigh to God, and he will draw nigh to you. Cleanse your hands,
ye sinners; and purify your hearts, ye double minded.
JAMES 4:8

Picture a muddy, unshorn sheep. A shepherd would have a job before him to clean up that animal because the fleece is quite deep. He must dig down with the shears layer by layer, tugging at the wool as he goes. In order to shear the sheep, he has to have hold of it, a firm grasp on a wiggling, uncooperative animal. Whatever it takes, the shepherd cleans the sheep.

Now picture us. Uncooperative, squirming, with insides that need to be cleaned. Our thoughts and actions have not been pure. Maybe we have lost our temper, taken advantage of another, or gossiped. Actions that are not what God wants of us. Actions that are called sin. Sin that blackens the heart. Like the sheep, we must be gathered in and cleaned.

Our most glorious God has promised He will do that for us when we ask. If we draw near to God and ask for His forgiveness, He will cleanse our hearts and make us part of His fold. Hallelujah. What a magnificent and overwhelming plan He has for us!

Dear Lord, is gaining a new life truly as simple as that?
I reach out my hand in surrender and ask You to become the King
of my life. Thank You for all You have done for me. Amen.

Day 152

EYE CARE

*For thus saith the LORD of hosts. . .he that toucheth
you toucheth the apple of his eye.*
ZECHARIAH 2:8

The apple of the eye refers to the pupil—the very center, or heart, of the eye. Consider the lengths we go to in order to protect our eyes. We wear protective glasses in some workplaces. We close our eyes or squint in windstorms or bright light. When dust blows, we turn our heads or put up our hands to keep the dirt from ending up in our eyes.

When we do get something in an eye, the ache and discomfort are instant. Tears form, and we seek to get the particle out as quickly as possible to stop the pain. If we are unable to remove the offending bit, we often become unable to do anything but focus on the discomfort.

To think that we are the apple of God's eye is incredible. Consider the care He must take for us. He will go to great lengths to protect us from harm. When something or someone does attack us, God feels our pain. He is instantly aware of our discomfort, for it is His own. When the storms of life come, we must remember how God feels each twinge of suffering. Despite the adversity, we can praise God because He is sheltering us.

*Thank You, God, that You are so aware of what is happening to me.
Thank You for Your protection. Amen.*

Day 153

GOING ABOVE AND BEYOND

Now unto him that is able to do exceeding abundantly above all
that we ask or think, according to the power that worketh
in us, unto him be glory in the church by Christ Jesus
throughout all ages, world without end.
EPHESIANS 3:20–21

Are you one of those people who goes above and beyond—at work, in your relationships, and at play? Maybe you like to do all you've promised to do, and then some. If this is true of you, then you're more like your heavenly Father than you know. His Word promises that He always goes above and beyond all that we could ask or imagine.

Think about that for a moment. What have you asked for? What have you imagined? It's amazing to think that God, in His infinite power and wisdom, can do immeasurably more than all that! How? According to the power that is at work within us. It's not our power, thankfully. We don't have enough power to scrape the surface of what we'd like to see done in our lives. But His power in us gets the job done. . .and more.

Praise the Lord! Praise Him in the church and throughout all generations! He's an immeasurable God.

Heavenly Father, I feel pretty powerless at times. It's amazing to
realize You have more power in Your little finger than all of mankind
has put together. Today I praise You for being a God who goes
above and beyond all I could ask or imagine. Amen.

Day 154

THROUGH HIS EYES

If ye fulfil the royal law according to the scripture,
Thou shalt love thy neighbour as thyself, ye do well.
JAMES 2:8

Sometimes we wonder if we are doing enough for God. We think about the commandments and the teachings of Jesus and wonder if we are living "Christlike" lives.

A rich young ruler came to Jesus one time and asked Him what he must do to be saved. But the answer Jesus gave reflected the idea that He always taught: there is nothing we can do to earn our way into heaven. It is not a matter of earning our salvation, and certainly God is not impressed by our work. Our walk with Jesus is about a real relationship. It is about loving Him and loving others as ourselves. Isn't it wonderful that we have a God of love?

As we see in James 2:8, we are living as we should if we obey God's law to love one another. We know that this is not always easy to do. It seems that loving the person we like the least is how we love God the most. Sometimes it is quite challenging to look upon others as Jesus does. If we see people through the eyes of Jesus, though, in His words we are "doing" well.

Give me Your eyes, Lord. Allow me to see others as You
see them. Then, with Your help, I can love those
who to me seem unlovable. Amen.

Day 155

WHAT ARE YOU DOING HERE?

The word of the LORD came to him, and he said unto him,
What doest thou here, Elijah?
1 KINGS 19:9

Isn't it surprising when God, who knows everything, asks *us* a question?

At the time God asked Elijah this question, He already knew what had brought Elijah to the point of such despair that he prayed to God to take his life. God knew Elijah had just been victorious over the prophets of Baal. He knew too that Elijah had been threatened by Jezebel and was running in fear for his life. Despite knowing all this, God still asked Elijah why he was hiding out in a cave.

Elijah isn't the first person God has asked a direct question, knowing the answer. God asked Adam and Eve where they were even though He knew they were trying to conceal themselves from Him (Genesis 3:9). In their case as well as Elijah's, fear and despair had driven them to a place of hiding and shame.

Sometimes we live in a manner that causes God to ask us the question He posed to Elijah. Whether we're in a literal place we shouldn't be or our emotions have lead us to a place of captivity, God wants us to stop and consider where we are.

Aren't you thankful He cares enough to ask?

Father, You always see me. To protect me from evil,
sometimes You ask me, "What are You doing here?"
Help me to stop, think, and act according to Your will. Amen.

Day 156

SECOND FIDDLE

He must increase, but I must decrease.
JOHN 3:30

John the Baptist knew exactly who he was and what role he was called to play.

When John's disciples complained that a new preacher, Jesus, was drawing followers from their group, John set his ego aside and said, "Jesus must become greater; I must become less." John understood his call as the forerunner. His job was to prepare the way for the Messiah. He played second fiddle to the first chair.

Every orchestra needs a second fiddle (or trumpet or clarinet. . .) for the music to be complete. The lead in a play needs a supporting actor for the story to come across correctly. John prepared the path for Jesus then stepped out of the limelight.

Maybe we're feeling our call to serve Christ isn't good enough. Not everyone can teach or preach—but perhaps we can make coffee on Sunday or hand out bulletins before the service. Physical limitations may prevent us from even getting to church, but we can pray daily for others. Each role serves a purpose in sharing God's story.

John models the right attitude for serving God: we set our own agendas and egos aside. God's light shines through us more brilliantly when we become less.

Lord, put me where You need me most. Whether it be a lofty place or lowly, I am Your servant, ready and enthusiastic to serve. Amen.

Day 157

GOOD CHEER

For, when we were come into Macedonia,
our flesh had no rest, but we were troubled on every side;
without were fightings, within were fears.
2 CORINTHIANS 7:5

———————— ✑✑✑✑ ————————

When friends are going through prolonged difficult times, it's easy to give them pat answers: "Stay focused on God and continue praising the Lord, no matter what happens; and if you do this, you'll have peace in the midst of life's storms, the storm will soon pass, and all will be well again" (Isaiah 26:3; 1 Thessalonians 5:16–18). That's good advice as far as it goes, but it's not the full picture.

When Paul and his companions were going through extremely hard times in Macedonia—suffering sleep deprivation, surrounded by conflicts, and nearly overwhelmed by problems—Paul frankly confessed that he felt fear. Fear may not have wholly debilitated him, but certainly anxious thoughts constantly tried to fill his mind.

God sent him comfort and peace, and Paul said: "God, that comforteth those that are cast down, comforted us by the coming of Titus." It uplifted Paul to see his good friend, but what caused him to rejoice "the more" was that Titus brought good news (2 Corinthians 7:6–7).

Let's bring comfort and good cheer to the downcast, not just good advice (Proverbs 12:25; Isaiah 61:1–2).

———————— ✆✆✆ ————————

Father, sometimes I don't know what to say to those feeling
downcast. Teach me, please, how I might comfort
them and bring them good cheer. Amen.

Day 158

GREAT NEED MEETS GREATER GOD

Have mercy upon me, O LORD; for I am weak:
O LORD, heal me; for my bones are vexed.
PSALM 6:2

The closer we get to God, the more glaring are our faults. The brighter the light of perfection that we subject ourselves to, the more flaws are revealed. The better we understand the awesome magnificence of God, the more we expose our own imperfection. As the great men and women of the Bible came to realize, the stronger we become in the faith, the more wretched we sometimes feel.

This, however, is no cause for despair. Our Lord wants nothing more than for us to come to depend on Him. We can only truly become dependent as we acknowledge our inadequacies. As the apostle Paul found out, true strength comes from admitting our weakness, and total healing comes by realizing that without God we are sickly and terminally diseased by sin. Cry out for the mercy of God and He will strengthen you; ask for His healing and you will be made whole.

Dear Lord, I try to be perfect and find that I am hopelessly deficient.
Nothing I can do will bring me the perfection You intend for me.
Fill me with Your Spirit and do for me all that
I cannot do for myself. Amen.

Day 159

NOTHING TO FEAR

Precious in the sight of the LORD is the death of his saints.
PSALM 116:15

Benjamin Franklin said, "In this world, nothing is certain except death and taxes."

We can sometimes escape paying a tax, but we cannot escape death. Every one of us will die someday.

In Psalm 116, the psalmist tells of his cries to God for mercy. He cried out to God because he was afraid. "The sorrows of death compassed me, and the pains of hell gat hold upon me" (v. 3). Then he went on to praise God for saving him. We can't know if the psalmist was literally saved from dying or if his words were a metaphor. But we do know from reading Psalm 116 that God saves our souls from dying (v. 8).

The Twenty-third Psalm holds the familiar words "Yea, though I walk through the valley of the shadow of death, I will fear no evil: for thou art with me" (v. 4). Through our belief in Jesus Christ, we know that we are saved; we become God's "saints."

Psalm 116:15 assures us that our transition from this world to heaven is precious in God's sight. God paid the price of our eternal life through the sacrifice of His only Son. In death, we have nothing to fear.

Lord, I must remember that I am not my body. My soul lives within it with You, and after my body dies I will live on in heaven as Your precious child. Amen.

TRUTH, WITH A CAPITAL T

*Pilate saith unto him, What is truth? And when he had said this,
he went out again unto the Jews, and saith unto
them, I find in him no fault at all.*
JOHN 18:38

Most of us are familiar with the trumped-up charges and the kangaroo court that convened to set in motion Jesus' journey to the cross. As Jesus was shuffled from one jurisdiction to another, an interesting conversation begins with Pontius Pilate, the Roman authority figure for the region.

In an attempt to make sense of this latest crisis, which no doubt has interrupted his breakfast, Pilate begins to question Jesus. As Pilate tries to sort out the mayhem the Jewish priests have brought to his door, he finds himself engaging in a philosophical discussion about truth with the prisoner.

Jesus asserts that his purpose is to testify to truth, and for this reason He was born (v. 37). The Way, the Truth, and the Life is testifying in a legal proceeding about who He is.

Pilate asks the right question: "What is truth?" He's on the right track, looking for a semblance of justice in the midst of procedural mockery. But his failing lies in the fact that he doesn't wait for Jesus' answer. Instead, he returns to the bloodthirsty mob who aren't interested in truth—they're only interested in having their position justified.

Jesus approaches all of us with the answer of truth. Will we listen?

*Jesus, You are the way and the truth and the life—the only way
to the Father. Help me always to walk in Your truth
and to listen to Your words. Amen.*

Day 161
TEARS

Jesus wept.
JOHN 11:35

Jesus wept. He cried when He saw the tomb of His good friend Lazarus. Jesus knew He would bring Lazarus back to life, yet His heart still broke with sadness. Jesus experienced sorrow Himself, and He knows the depth of our pain when we lose someone or something important to us.

Grief is an intense emotion. Knowing that Jesus cried helps us to accept our own weeping—especially when our loss is still fresh.

Sometimes we're embarrassed that our tears stream from a seemingly bottomless well. Yet tears are so precious to God that He records and stores each one. The psalm writer said, "Thou tellest my wanderings: put thou my tears into thy bottle: are they not in thy book?" (Psalm 56:8).

Jesus' tears demonstrate God's empathy as we go through the grieving process. God cares deeply about our situation. He desires to gather us in His arms. He understands the sorrow and turmoil we feel when we experience serious heartache.

Crying is a natural response to deep pain and loss. Our tears form wordless prayers connecting us with God. He knows the depth of our sorrow. He comforts us with His love and His tears.

Loving Lord, You know my tears. You value each of my tears so much that You gather them in Your bottle and write them in Your book. Thank You for understanding me. Amen.

Day 162

PRESSING ON

*I follow after, if that I may apprehend that for which
also I am apprehended of Christ Jesus.*

PHILIPPIANS 3:12

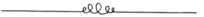

We all need a lot of work when it comes to fulfilling God's perfect plan for our lives. We get sidetracked, we mess up, life distracts us. . .and progress is slow. No matter how sincere our desire to live out God's purpose for us, we fall down again. And again.

But that's okay. God knows us better than anyone, and He knows we're not perfect. He knows we'll make mistakes and have setbacks. All He asks is that each time we fall down, we get back up and keep moving forward.

Think about it. Christ saw potential in us—so much that He died for us. He didn't say, "Oh good grief, look how slow they are! Look at how many times they goof up. Never mind. It's not worth it." Nope. He paid such a high price for us because He knew we were made in His image. And He knew that as long as we trust Him and don't give up and keep pressing forward, our likeness will become closer and closer to His.

That's what He wants for us—for our spirits to mirror His. He wants us to love, for He is love. He wants us to be kind and gentle and compassionate, for He is all of those things. He longs for us to be His representatives in this world. And we will be, as long we keep pressing on.

Dear Father, help me to press on to become more like You. Amen.

Day 163

POWERFUL PRAYER

Rejoice evermore. Pray without ceasing. In every thing give thanks:
for this is the will of God in Christ Jesus concerning you.
1 Thessalonians 5:16–18

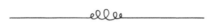

Ever fallen asleep during prayer? Or have you ever told a friend you'd pray for a request and then completely forgot about it until they brought it up again? We've all been there. Squirming inside, you listen to your friend's update, and say, "Oh, yes, I'll keep praying for that." What makes prayer so hard?

We might feel intimidated to talk to a holy God, even though He invites us to tell Him about our lives and ask for what we need. Self-reproach and doubt can get in the way too; sometimes our prayers sound ridiculous to our ears, or we have been praying for the same request for so long that it doesn't seem like God will answer it. Or, we are worn out simply by the thought of the energy, focus, and humility required for prayer.

However, prayer is a discipline where sweetness and hard work flow together. God commands us to pray continually because prayer is an exercise in trust. We ask the Creator of the universe to act on our behalf in faith that He *will* act—it is our faith that makes our prayers effective, not our eloquence.

Whatever your prayer life is or has been, approach God in faith. He is always ready to hear us, and His Spirit will give us the strength to pray (Romans 8:26–27).

Father God, give me strength to pray. I want to be closer to You and to rely fully upon You. Thank You that You always listen. Amen.

Day 164

PLEASING GOD

Let the words of my mouth, and the meditation of my heart,
be acceptable in thy sight, O Lord, my strength, and my redeemer.
Psalm 19:14

The Christian's life should be a walking testimony to Christ's redemption. The way that others around you know that you are a Christian is through your words and your actions. God sees even beyond these to your heart. He knows your thoughts, your motives, and the secret feelings that no one else is able to discern. He hears the words that come from your mouth, but if they do not match what's in your heart, He knows. Both should be pleasing to the Father. As you walk and talk, consider Jesus. The popular slogan "What Would Jesus Do?" has come and gone. At one time it was on bracelets and billboards. Imagine that it still is. Would you desire that every interaction you have with another, each decision you make at work or school, and every thought that crosses your mind be pleasing to the Lord? You can only accomplish this through being in close fellowship with Christ, reading the Word, and allowing the Holy Spirit to enable you where you are weak. Ask God today to help your words and actions be pleasing to Him.

Father, I want to please You with my speech, actions, and thoughts.
Strengthen me through Your Holy Spirit whom You have sent to be
my Helper. Help me to honor You in all I do and say. Amen.

A JOYFUL NOISE

Sing aloud unto God our strength:
make a joyful noise unto the God of Jacob.
PSALM 81:1

Aren't you glad the Bible commands us to "make a joyful noise" to the Lord instead of saying something like "sing like an angel"? Many are born with amazing vocal abilities. They wow us with their choir productions and their amazing solo performances. But some of the rest of us are lucky to croak out a word or two in the right key.

God doesn't care about your vocal abilities. He longs to hear a song of praise rise up out of your heart, even if it's sung in three or four keys. Think about that for a moment. He's listening as millions of believers sing out—in every language, every key, every pitch. And it doesn't bother Him one bit because He's not listening to the technique; He's listening to the heart.

Still not convinced? Read the book of Psalms from start to finish. It will stir up a song in your heart, and before long your toes will be tapping and your heart bursting. Why? Because you were created to praise Him. So don't worry about what others will think. Make a joyful noise!

Lord, my heart wants to sing happy songs today! I'm not going to
worry anymore about my voice, whether I'm singing in church
or in the car or in the shower. I was made to praise You,
Father, so I choose to make a joyful noise! Amen.

Day 166

EVERY GOOD WORK

And God is able to make all grace abound toward you;
that ye, always having all sufficiency in all things,
may abound to every good work.

2 CORINTHIANS 9:8

———————— ✺ ————————

Maybe you cringe every time you hear that God wants to bless you. Perhaps you think that message is overblown by television evangelists or positive thinkers. Here's a biblical truth: We serve a God who owns the cattle on a thousand hills. He has more than enough for every situation. Does that mean He's going to shower down excessive heavenly blessings on you every day? Maybe not, but there will definitely be days—and seasons—when the blessings flow.

Whether you're in a season of plenty or lack, remember that God hasn't forgotten you. Today's scripture is a promise you can take to the bank. He can give you more than you need. When He does, you will have plenty of everything. Specifically, you will have enough to do the work that He has called you to.

So brace yourself! Maybe those TV preachers are onto something. God loves you so much and wants to give you what you need, not so that you can gloat in your possessions, but so that you are equipped to do His work.

———————— ✺ ————————

Lord, I get it. You don't want to bless me just for the sake of spoiling me. You long to give me the things I'm lacking so that I'm well equipped to carry forth Your message to my friends and loved ones. Thank You, Father! Amen.

Day 167

HE WON'T LET YOU DOWN

Now I say that Jesus Christ was a minister of the circumcision for the truth of God, to confirm the promises made unto the fathers.
ROMANS 15:8

Everyone has been hurt at one time or another by a broken promise. When that happens, it is best to forgive and go on. People are just people. They mess up. But there is One who will never break His promises to us—our heavenly Father. We can safely place our hope in Him.

Hebrews chapter 11 lists biblical characters who placed their trust and hope in God and weren't let down. Do you think Noah was excited about building an ark? Surely Sarah and Abraham hadn't planned on parenting at their age. Daniel faced the lion's den knowing his God would care for him. We can find encouragement from their examples, knowing that their faith in the God who'd come through for them time and again wasn't misplaced. They did not grow weary and lose heart. They knew He was always faithful.

Today we choose to place our hope in God's promises. We won't be discouraged by time—God's timing is always perfect. We won't be discouraged by circumstances—God can change everything in a heartbeat. We will keep our hearts in God's hand. For we know He is faithful.

Lord, I choose this day to place my trust in You,
for I know You're the one, true constant. Amen.

Day 168

PERFECT PEACE

Thou wilt keep him in perfect peace, whose mind is stayed on thee: because he trusteth in thee.
ISAIAH 26:3

Peace is an elusive thing. We allow our emotions to control us and then wonder why peace rarely follows. Strangely, peace has nothing to do with emotions. Ponder that for a moment. Your peace—or lack thereof—isn't control by an emotional puppeteer. You can choose peace in the middle of the storms of life.

What's robbing you of your peace today? Take that "thing" (situation, person, etc.) and write it down on a piece of paper, then pray over it and shred it. Release it to God. Keep your mind steadfast on God, not what was written on the paper. It's no longer the driving force in your life. Your trust is in God, and He cares even more about your situation (or that person) than you do, anyway.

Letting go. . .taking your hand off. . .will bring peace. It's never easy to release something that's had a hold on you, but you will be blessed with supernatural peace once you do.

Oh Lord! I've been holding on to things I should have let go of ages ago. Please forgive me, Father! Today I release those things into Your hands. As I let go, flood me with Your peace from on high! Amen.

Day 169

THE SHIELD OF FAITH

*Above all, taking the shield of faith, wherewith ye shall be able
to quench all the fiery darts of the wicked.*
EPHESIANS 6:16

When Paul wrote to the church at Ephesus about the shield of faith, he used the word *thureos*, which means "door." Roman soldiers' shields were large, rectangular, and door-sized. In other words, they covered every single part of the soldier's body. It's the same with our faith. The salvation we've been given in Christ covers us from head to toe. And because He is lavish in love and steadfast in keeping His promises, we'll always have enough for every situation we encounter.

The Roman soldiers' shields had one other distinctive quality: they were made of several hides of leather sewn together. This meant that every morning, a soldier would have to rub oil into the shield in order to keep it pliable and to prevent it from drying out and cracking. This daily renewal was the difference between life and death. . .literally!

In our own faith walk, we must daily allow God's Holy Spirit to refill and re-energize us. The Spirit replenishes our joy, rebuilds our faith, and redirects our thoughts so that we can live boldly and courageously for Jesus. This begs the question: What have we done today to oil our shields? Let's not get complacent and allow distractions to deter us from our duty! In Christ, we have a true shield that won't ever let us down. Praise the Lord!

*Lord, thank You for Your Word and all the riches I find there.
Give me the discipline to come to You regularly for refilling. Amen.*

Day 170

THE NEW ME

Therefore if any man be in Christ, he is a new creature:
old things are passed away; behold, all things are become new.
2 CORINTHIANS 5:17

———————— *ello* ————————

Are you "in Christ"? Is He consistently Lord of your life? Then you are
a new creation.

Regardless of your past, regardless of the circumstances you may
have faced, you're a new creation. All the past guilt is gone—vanished,
obliterated—and everything is new.

It's true that some of us live with the consequences of past choices.
Maybe our children are the result of premarital sex—but they are
nonetheless marvelous miracles of God. Maybe today's health problems
result from years of unwise and harmful choices—but God says the guilt
is all in the past, gone. Everything is new. What's history is done and
over—and Jesus has replaced your old with His new: new peace, new
joy, new love, new strength.

Since God Himself sees us as a new creation, how can we do any
less? We need to choose to see ourselves as a new creation, too. And
we can, through God's grace.

If you are in Christ, you are a new creation. Be glad. Give thanks.
Live each day as the new creation you have become through Jesus.

———————— ∽◦◠◦∾ ————————

Father, I'm so thankful that You are a God of grace—and I thank You
that I am a new creation. Please give me the spiritual eyes
to see myself as a new creation, looking past the
guilt of yesterday's choices. Amen.

Day 171

BUILD FOR TODAY

Build ye houses, and dwell in them; and plant gardens,
and eat the fruit of them.
JEREMIAH 29:5

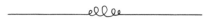

Skeptics sometimes accuse Christians of being so heavenly minded that they are no earthly good. Today few of us would sell all our earthly possessions and camp out on a hilltop, waiting for the Lord's return. However, we still often live in "Tomorrowland."

Tomorrow, we think, we will serve God more fully, after our children are grown and we have more time. Tomorrow we will give more, after we have paid off the car and saved enough for a down payment on a house. Tomorrow we will study the Bible more, after we no longer work full-time.

Jeremiah's audience, Jews deported from their homeland to Babylon, knew all about Tomorrowland. They said, "Soon God will return us to our homes. As soon as that happens, we will serve God." They lived with their suitcases packed, ready to return.

God sent a stern message through His prophet Jeremiah. "You're going to be there a long time. Put down roots where I have sent you."

God sends the same message to us. He wants us to live for today. We can't allow dreams for tomorrow to paralyze our lives today. God's presence enables us to live in the present.

Dear heavenly Father, You have given us the gift of today.
You want us to plant gardens and make homes.
Show us joy and fulfillment in the present. Amen.

Day 172

HE IS

In the beginning God created the heaven and the earth.
GENESIS 1:1

―――――――― ℓℓℓ ――――――――

Sometimes the simplest things are the most profound.

The Bible begins with a clear, direct statement of where our universe came from: God. What the Bible doesn't try to explain is where God Himself comes from. At the very start, scripture simply *assumes* His existence.

But read a few pages into the Bible, and you'll find God's explanation of His own being. . .kind of. Though it's tough for the time-bound human mind to understand, God called Himself "I AM" in response to Moses' question "What is [Your] name?" (Exodus 3:13–14). Those two little words clearly imply existence—and always in the present tense. There was never a time that God wasn't, and there will never be a time when He won't be. God simply *is*.

Scientists and philosophers have debated the origins of the universe and everything in it—including people—for about as long as people have existed in the universe. But the Bible states clearly and simply that everything originated with God.

It takes faith to accept that. But it takes a lot more faith to disbelieve!

―――――――― ༺ ―――――――――

*Father, many things about You are beyond my comprehension.
When I don't understand, please help me just to trust
You, have faith in You, and believe. Amen.*

Day 173

A HEALTHY FEAR

The fear of the LORD is to hate evil: pride, and arrogancy,
and the evil way, and the froward mouth, do I hate.
PROVERBS 8:13

When we think about our fears, our minds and bodies almost always tense. Whether it's a fear of heights, spiders, public speaking, failure, or being alone, everyone has fears. In fact, it's considered perfectly natural to avoid what we fear.

Why does the Bible say we should "fear" God? In reality, to fear God is not the same as fearing the creepy-crawly spider inching up the living room wall. Instead, we fear God when we have a deep respect and reverence for Him.

Imagine that the president of the United States was paying your home a visit. The house would be extra clean, the laundry would be washed and put away, and you would be on your best behavior. Why? Because the visitor deserves respect.

Our lives should reflect a similar reverence for our heavenly Father every day—our souls scrubbed extra clean, sin eliminated, and love for our Creator bursting forth in joy. God wants speech and actions to match. Take time today to stand in awe of the One who deserves our greatest respect and love.

Lord, help my daily actions and speech to reflect
my respect for You. Amen.

Day 174

IT'S ALL THERE

*For God so loved the world, that he gave his only begotten Son,
that whosoever believeth in him should not
perish, but have everlasting life.*

JOHN 3:16

———————— elle ————————

Every once in a while we find a succinct statement that sums up a series of themes in a neat sentence. No, we're not talking about "Lather, rinse, repeat." John 3:16 is fascinating because in one verse we find the fullness of God's message in a nutshell.

We learn that God so loved. God's love was not a pitying love of pure emotion but a practical love. God saw our sinfulness, and He loved. He expressed His love by the greatness of the gift of His Son. When sin would drag us down to perish in the awful pit, Christ died and went there as our substitute.

Sin separated us from God. Jesus' resurrection connects us again to a life-giving God, to an eternal life where we know that God is love. By faith we enter into this relationship. In our sin, deserving of death, we could do no good works to dig ourselves out of our hole. By God's grace, He extends salvation as a gift, obtained by believing in His Son. What a message! What a gift!

———————— ०००० ————————

*God, how can I ever thank You for the gift of salvation through
Your Son, Jesus? Let my life be a testimony to His sacrifice
and Your eternal love. Amen.*

TO THE ENDS OF THE EARTH

And this gospel of the kingdom shall be preached in all the world for a witness unto all nations; and then shall the end come.
MATTHEW 24:14

If you ask many Christians if we're already living in the end times, they'll answer, "Yes, we are, and Jesus can come any day now." However, Jesus tells us that the Gospel must first "be preached in all the world for a witness unto all nations"—and only then the end will come.

We tend to think that in this modern era the Gospel has surely already been preached in all nations—thanks to radios, television, and the internet—even in nations closed to the Gospel. But the Greek word translated as "nations" is *ethnos* and literally means "ethnic groups" or "people groups." Many closed nations are made up of dozens of people groups and tribes in remote mountain valleys and hinterlands who don't have access to modern media—yet they too need to hear the Gospel.

We desire Jesus to return, and when He declares, "Surely I come quickly," we pray, "Amen. Even so, come, Lord Jesus" (Revelation 22:20). But we must do our part to hasten that day: we must help see to it that the Gospel goes to the ends of the earth (Acts 1:8).

Lord, in this age when the whole world seems connected,
there are still some who haven't heard Your name.
Lead us, Your people, to the ones
who need to hear. Amen.

Day 176

PLEDGE OF ALLEGIANCE

*And these words, which I command thee this day, shall be in thine
heart: and thou shalt teach them diligently unto thy children,
and shalt talk of them when thou sittest in thine house,
and when thou walkest by the way, and when
thou liest down, and when thou risest up.*

DEUTERONOMY 6:6–7

God's words in Deuteronomy were originally delivered to the people
of Israel from Moses. These verses (Deuteronomy 6:3–9) later became
known as "the Shema," meaning "hear" in Hebrew.

The Shema is one of the central points of the morning and evening
Judaic prayer services. For Jews and Christians alike, it serves as a spiritual
pledge of allegiance.

In verses 6–7, God gives us the ins and outs of His commandments
in regard to our families. Check out God's desired time commitment:
it's not what you would call hit and miss! These verses in Deuteronomy
remind us that, like breathing, our commitment to God isn't haphazard;
rather, it's a minute-to-minute lifeline!

Today, as we get up and lie down, may we also remember to commit
to this pledge of allegiance as one nation under God.

*Dear God, I promise devotion to You every day of my life,
and I will do my best to honor Your commandments
all day, every day, morning to morning. Amen.*

Day 177

BEYOND BELIEF

Come and see the works of God: he is terrible
in his doing toward the children of men.
Psalm 66:5

———————— elee ————————

In the days of Jesus, a common usage of the word *terrible* meant to be beyond belief. God truly is beyond belief. We cannot begin to understand all He has done and all He continues to do in our world. A walk through the country will expose us to more miracles than we can count. A look at the night sky will fill us with wonder to the core of our being. God has offered us untold questions to explore and contemplate. Come and see the works of the Lord. They are incredible!

———————— ◦ɢ◦◦ ————————

Lord, I do not pretend to understand You, but I do surely love
You. Show me new wonders and teach me new questions,
that I might come to know You better each day. Amen.

I DON'T KNOW!

Else what shall they do which are baptized for the dead,
if the dead rise not at all? why are they then baptized for the dead?
1 CORINTHIANS 15:29

What does this verse mean?

Actually, there are numerous different theological views of what this verse means! We don't really know what Paul meant by this. Those of us who depend for our livelihood on our specialized skills and education hate the three words *I don't know*. But in truth, we don't know.

There is nothing else in all of scripture that even hints at anything related to "baptism for the dead." No great doctrine of the ages has been enunciated by the church about it. In context, Paul refers to it obliquely to illustrate the assuredness of Christ's resurrection. He isn't laying out anything important to salvation.

Many of us take pride in our doctrinal purity. This verse serves as a reminder to all of us that no matter how correct our theology, God is bigger than any of us, and we can never have it all figured out. God cannot be put in a box. Perhaps Paul is just trying to keep us humble!

Shine Your light on the scriptures, Lord. Help me understand them.
And when I can't, remind me that Your ideas are sometimes
too grand for my human mind to comprehend. Amen.

Day 179

JESUS WRISTWATCH

See then that ye walk circumspectly, not as fools, but as wise, redeeming the time, because the days are evil. Wherefore be ye not unwise, but understanding what the will of the Lord is.

EPHESIANS 5:15–17

Time is money, they say. Society preaches the value of making good use of our time—and the expense of wasting it.

In the Bible, Ephesians 5 speaks of using every opportunity wisely. But even though scripture teaches the value of time, Jesus never wore a watch. He didn't view His opportunities within the bounds of earthly time.

Have you ever ended a day with guilt and regret over the growing black hole of work yet to be completed? Or do you feel peace at the end of your day, having walked in the presence of the Lord?

Satan wants to consume you with endless lists of meaningless tasks. Fight back! Concern yourself less with the items you can cross off your to-do list and more with those things the Lord would have you spend your time and energy on. You can strive to be a great multitasker or workhorse—but it's more important and fulfilling to be an efficient laborer for the Lord.

Father, help me to see where You are working and join You there. Let me place my list of tasks aside as I seek Your will for me today. Then give me the ability to show myself grace over the things I do not get done. Amen.

Day 180

(IM)POSSIBLE!

Whom God hath raised up, having loosed the pains of death: because it was not possible that he should be holden of it.
ACTS 2:24

According to science and the natural order, which statement is true?

It is impossible for the dead to return to life.

It is impossible for the dead to stay dead.

Even movies like *The Night of the Living Dead* play on our rock-solid assumption that dead people are meant to remain in the grave.

In his sermon on the day of Pentecost, Peter told his audience that Jesus of Nazareth had indeed died, put to death at their hands only weeks before. For the members of that audience, that should have been the end. If even the great King David's body lay entombed in Jerusalem, how much more this troublesome prophet from Galilee (Acts 2:29)?

But in Jesus, God turned the normal course of nature on its head. He reversed the poles; He turned the impossibility of coming back to life to the impossibility of staying dead. He raised Jesus to life and exalted Him to His right hand (Acts 2:32–33).

May we bow in worship to the One who turned His funeral upside down and opened a new world of (im)possibilities.

Lord, I worship You because You are the only One who brings eternal life to all believers. Thanks to You, I look forward to a new life in heaven someday. Amen.

Day 181

SAY WHAT?

But be ye doers of the word, and not hearers only,
deceiving your own selves.
JAMES 1:22

Have you ever been introduced to someone and immediately forgotten the person's name? Similarly, have you ever tried to talk to someone who is engrossed in a television show? "Yeah, I'm listening," the person replies in a less-than-attentive voice.

James seems to be in a similar situation. He is frustrated by those who pretend to listen and yet do not apply what they have heard. Like a person who sits through a speech and afterward cannot list the main points, so the people to whom James writes have heard the Word of God and cannot—or will not—apply it.

So often we find ourselves tuning out the minister on Sunday morning or thinking about other things as we read our Bibles or sing hymns of praise. We look up at the end of a sermon, a stanza, a chapter, and we don't know what we've heard, sung, or read. We pretend to hear, but we are really letting the Word of God go in one ear and out the other. Our minds must be disciplined to really listen to God's Word. Then we must do the more difficult thing—*act* on what we've finally heard.

Dear Lord, please teach me to be attentive to Your Word.
Help me to act on the things You teach me so that
mine becomes a practical faith. Amen.

Day 182

FILLED WITH THE WORD

This book of the law shall not depart out of thy mouth; but thou shalt meditate therein day and night, that thou mayest observe to do according to all that is written therein: for then thou shalt make thy way prosperous, and then thou shalt have good success.

JOSHUA 1:8

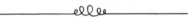

It is so easy for sin to creep into our lives, particularly in this age of technology in which we live. With a single click of the mouse, we can study any subject and instantly have a library of resources on hand. Unfortunately, this technology has a dark side as well. A phrase that has been used often throughout the recent years is "garbage in, garbage out." With another click of the mouse, we can allow images and ideas to enter our minds that we know better than to allow.

Joshua 1:8 speaks clearly to the solution to any temptation we may encounter. Just as the Bible is as relevant today as it was when it was written, we can use its instruction to be successful in our Christian walk. When we fill our minds with God's Word, there will be neither room nor desire to fill our minds with the garbage of this world. As Joshua 1:8 points out, only then will we prosper and succeed in everything we do!

Let us thank the Lord for His holy Word!

"Lead me not into temptation, but deliver me from evil." Lord, plant those words in my heart, and let Your holy Word, the Bible, always be my guide. Amen.

HOLY STANDARD

In those days there was no king in Israel: every man did that which was right in his own eyes.
JUDGES 21:25

———————— eℓℓℓℓ ————————

Reading through the book of Judges conjures up scenes that rival some horror movies produced by Hollywood.

During the era of the judges, the Israelites bounced from one disaster to another while ignoring God's Law, only to be brought back into repentance when oppressed by an enemy. Hearing their cries for help, God would raise up a hero to rescue them.

This hero, or judge, ruled over the people and kept them in line until he died. At that point the Israelites again "did that which was right in [their] own eyes" and the cycle began anew.

This situation is not unlike our own culture. Instead of using God's standard of right and wrong, today's society tells us to determine our own morals. Why? Because it claims there is no lawgiver apart from us, individually.

When each Israelite set his or her own criterion for right and wrong, tragedy and heartache resulted. Ignoring God's standards didn't work for the Israelites, and it won't work for us today. It's wise to periodically examine our personal criterion of right and wrong to keep it in line with God's standards laid out in the Bible. Ask yourself, "Whose standards am I following?"

———————— ⁕⁕⁕⁕ ————————

Separated from You, Lord, the world is spiraling downward. We are so in need of redemption! Send Your people to redeem the lost. Save them from eternal death. Amen.

Day 184

CAN YOU HEAR IT?

Speaking to yourselves in psalms and hymns and spiritual songs,
singing and making melody in your heart to the Lord.
EPHESIANS 5:19

We are surrounded by music. Our alarm clocks awaken us each morning, television musically underscores the dramatic moments in our favorite shows, and commercial writers come up with catchy jingles to sell their latest, greatest whatchamacallit. Our computers reprimand error keystrokes with familiar beeps, and music streaming apps keep us company during our exercise sessions. We live in a symphony (or a cacophony) of sound.

Now, rewind your thoughts to a different era two thousand years ago. Electricity was limited to lightning in the night sky, and amplification depended on the acoustics of the amphitheater. In this relatively quiet environment, Paul suggested that making music together is, in fact, a good way to connect with God.

Picture a solitary soul receiving encouragement from the community of believers worshipping together in song. In a time when music had to be participatory in order to be experienced, imagine the hearts of each worshipper storing up precious phrases of song as treasured memories.

Biblical generations broke the silence of their world by singing praise to God. In the loudness of our modern world, we must create our own times of silence. And in the stillness, our hearts sing their own song of praise. Be still—and listen.

Thank You, Lord, for stillness. Thank You for quieting my heart
so that I can hear Your precious voice. Speak to
me, Father. I'm listening. Amen.

Day 185

JUST AS HE PLEASED

Whatsoever the LORD pleased, that did he in heaven,
and in earth, in the seas, and all deep places.
PSALM 135:6

Imagine the fun the Lord had creating all the animals of this world. With the power to do whatever He pleased, He concocted a menagerie of some wonderful creatures. Consider the giraffe, or the baboon, or the frog. What a host of funny-looking creatures. Think of the splendor of the eagle, the grace of the gazelle, the power of the tiger. God put so much into making His creation a good one. The same is true of His children. God went to great lengths to make sure His children were good. He even imparted in each and every one of them His own image. He offered them free will and all the blessings they could ever hope for. He did these things because they pleased Him.

Our God is a God of love, and nothing pleases Him more than to be able to share that love. Indeed, we may be God's funniest creatures, but that only makes Him love us all the more.

Father, You must have a wonderful sense of humor to put up
with children like me. Forgive me for being less than You
created me to be. Help me to grow and mature
and develop into Your image. Amen.

Day 186

HEARTS OF FLESH

And I will give them one heart, and I will put a new spirit within you;
and I will take the stony heart out of their flesh,
and will give them an heart of flesh.
EZEKIEL 11:19

———————— *elle* ————————

When a person has a heart attack, a portion of the heart muscle dies—making the organ less efficient in pumping life-giving blood throughout the body.

A heart of stone—cold, hard, and immovable—cannot pump life and love within us, either. We are born needing a heart transplant. Our naturally divided hearts chase after the glittering desires of the world, jealous of success of others, harboring deep resentments, bitterness, and anger in their dark chambers. We think the world will satisfy the emptiness we feel inside.

God is willing to give us an undivided heart—a heart that is open and ready to see, hear, and love God. This heart has a single focus: loving God and others with a tenderness that we know comes from Someone beyond us.

The good news is, we have already had successful surgery, and our donor heart is within us. We received our heart transplant when Jesus died for us, creating new spirits within us.

God's heart changes everything and creates us as new people with living hearts.

———————— *elle* ————————

Thank You, Lord, for giving me a new heart, a heart so perfect
in Love that it will last me forever. Amen.

Day 187

FOR YOU AND ME

And the Lord God planted a garden eastward in Eden;
and there he put the man whom he had formed.
GENESIS 2:8

———————— *elle* ————————

Adam wasn't created in the garden of Eden. He was formed from the dust somewhere to the west of the garden. The first thing God did, after giving him life, was to lead the father of mankind to paradise.

Then Adam and Eve blew it and were thrown out. God could have let it go and left mankind scrabbling in the dust, but He didn't. He sacrificed His Son to give us another way to paradise. That's how much He wants us there! Because that's where we were meant to be!

But mankind has been fallible from the start, and as a result, we often don't think we deserve that kind of love. The dust of this world is all many ever aspire to. Heaven is for better people, special people, saints perhaps, not weak, inconsistent, scared people like us. And when we think like that, we break God's heart. He's not waiting for us to prove ourselves worthy. He made the invitation and it's still valid. We just have to accept.

The garden was planted for *you* to walk in. Not some "better" person. You have another chance. Take it. Head eastward or upward. God wants you to come home!

———————— *ૢૢૢ* ————————

I accept Your invitation, Oh mighty God!
I accept that Jesus died for my sins. Amen.

Day 188

WHAT'S THIS THING IN MY EYE?

And why beholdest thou the mote that is in thy brother's eye,
but perceivest not the beam that is in thine own eye?
LUKE 6:41

Whether we admit it or not, we judge others. Maybe it's how they look ("Just how many tattoos does a person need?") or their political leaning ("How can you call yourself a Christian and vote for a president from *that* party?"). Sometimes we pigeonhole others because of an accent ("What an ignorant hillbilly!") or an achievement of some kind ("Mr. Smarty Pants thinks he's better than everyone else because of his PhD.").

Our Father God urges us not to judge others in this way. After all, He doesn't look at our outward appearance. He doesn't pay attention to our political affiliation or anything else in our lives that is open to interpretation. He looks at the heart and judges by whether we have a personal relationship with Him.

In Luke 6:41, Jesus reminds us through His mote/beam analogy that none of us are blameless. It's important to put our own shortcomings into perspective when we face the temptation to judge others. Today, work on removing the beam from your eye and praise God for His gift of grace!

God, please forgive me for the times that I have judged others.
Help me to develop a gentle spirit that can share Your love
and hope in a nonjudgmental way. Amen.

Day 189

CORE STRENGTH

*He giveth power to the faint; and to them that have
no might he increaseth strength.*
ISAIAH 40:29

Regular exercise is essential to keep our bodies functioning the way God designed them to. One of the components of an effective exercise regime is the development of core strength. These muscles—the abdomen, trunk, and back—are responsible for strength, stabilization, and balance. Strong core muscles protect our spines, enable us to stand and move with ease, and prevent the development of chronic pain. Investing time in developing and maintaining core muscles pays enormous dividends.

The same is true for our spiritual core muscles. Our spiritual core consists of foundational elements from which our lives move. It can include core beliefs—about who God is and the role of the Father, Son, and Holy Spirit in our daily lives. It can also be principles on which we build our lives—what is our purpose on earth? What is our motivation for working, living, and interacting with others? Who are we in Christ? We can exercise our spiritual core by reading God's Word every day, praying about everything, and spending time in fellowship with other believers.

A strong spiritual core will help ensure that you remain stable and secure in a changing world, that you are able to keep from falling, and that you are able to move and live with grace. As you exercise your physical body, also make a commitment to regularly exercise your spiritual core as well.

*Father, help me to return again and again to the
core foundations of my spiritual health. Amen.*

WHAT'S TO COME

*Then answered Peter and said unto him, Behold, we have forsaken
all, and followed thee; what shall we have therefore? And Jesus said
unto them, Verily I say unto you, That ye which have followed me,
in the regeneration when the Son of man shall sit in the
throne of his glory, ye also shall sit upon twelve
thrones, judging the twelve tribes of Israel.*

MATTHEW 19:27–28

———————————— ೲೲ ————————————

Peter, always so practical. Here's what he's really saying: "Lord, when
we get to the end, will it have been worth it to follow You?" And Jesus
reassures him with a gigantic yes!

How it must have broken Jesus' heart to know His treasured follower
would be martyred one day. Perhaps Peter had an inkling about this too.
We see that he wanted desperately to know whether life really went on
eternally. The Lord went a step further and related that Peter would not
only be with Christ, the Son of Man, eternally, but he would have work
to do once he arrived in heaven.

None of us will just occupy space in heaven. Our God is always
productive. And this job that Jesus refers to, that of judging the twelve
tribes of Israel, will be given to the disciples.

Have you ever speculated as to what you might do in heaven? Well,
don't worry; it's not going to be anything like what you've done on earth.
Your "boss," after all, will be perfect.

———————————— ೲೲ ————————————

*Lord, I can't even imagine what You have in store for me
in heaven. Please keep me faithful to complete the
duties You've called me to on the earth. Amen.*

AGING WELL

*Therefore remove sorrow from thy heart, and put away evil
from thy flesh: for childhood and youth are vanity.*
ECCLESIASTES 11:10

Our society is youth-obsessed. As soon as movie stars get past a certain age, they're offered fewer roles. Websites post pictures of "past their prime" actors' sagging, wrinkled frames. Even magazines touting the benefits of becoming seasoned often airbrush and edit photos of their subjects.

Why are we reluctant to celebrate aging? It is a natural process, and the alternative isn't good. Perhaps we are uncomfortable with one day being less useful, dependent on our loved ones, or feeble in body and mind. Maybe we're afraid of death. Heaven seems far away at times.

However, God takes a different view of getting older. In Leviticus 19:32, the scriptures say, "Thou shalt rise up before the hoary head, and honour the face of the old man, and fear thy God." Job 12:12 says, "With the ancient is wisdom; and in length of days understanding."

Look for godly men and women in your church or community who have aged well. Ask them how they feel about getting older. You'll probably discover they love the age they are and wouldn't trade their hard-won wisdom for anything in the world.

*Lord, show me Your perspective on getting older. As I age, help me
to become more in tune with You and less in tune with the world.
Thank You for healthy role models. May I become one for
younger believers as I sail into my later years. Amen.*

SAVORING THE WORD

But he answered and said, It is written, Man shall not live by bread alone, but by every word that proceedeth out of the mouth of God.
MATTHEW 4:4

Potlucks are meals of chance, roulette for the taste buds. The strategic guest fills their plate with a small bite of everything. There are surprises— what everyone thought was lemon meringue turned out to be a gelatinous banana pudding, while an untouched sauce swelled with savory, meaty flavors.

Studying the Bible's sixty-six books can feel like a potluck, and our reading habits might be picky too. Psalms and Proverbs might be sweet and easy to read, but the book of Numbers might have the attraction of week-old dry bread. The "good stuff" gets scooped up and the other books are overlooked.

As unsavory as they might seem, don't be so quick to pass on challenging sections of the Bible. Jesus said that men and women live by *every* word that proceeds from the mouth of God, not just some of them. Unlike a hit-or-miss potluck dish, all of scripture is meant for the Christian's nourishment (Romans 15:4). Seek the Father as you chew on the book of Judges or contemplate the life of the prophet Ezekiel. All of His Word is sweet when you can see Him in it.

Father God, thank You for Your entire Word. Please open my eyes to see You and Your goodness in the difficult passages as I spend time with You daily. Amen.

FREE AT LAST

Now the Lord is that Spirit:
and where the Spirit of the Lord is, there is liberty.
2 CORINTHIANS 3:17

———————— *elle* ————————

Rules exist to keep order in our lives and to establish boundaries. Parents have rules for their children; the police have rules for drivers. All are necessary for men to get along with each other, to cooperate. And when people operate completely outside the rules, chaos can ensue. So when we begin life as a Christian, we learn that Jesus did not come to bring chaos—He came to bring each of us a new life.

In scripture, Paul was speaking to the church in Corinth, but he certainly wasn't telling them to throw caution to the wind and live completely outside the box. What he was saying was once the Spirit of the living God lives inside you, there is freedom, an emancipation from bondage, a release from sin. What a cause for rejoicing! Free indeed.

But we cannot live this way in our own power. When we form this covenant with God, and are saved, then with Jesus and the Holy Spirit we can defeat the enemy who is trying to steal and destroy. Put on this armor to face the world. Be ready for the fight. Look to the Word to provide you with the needed tools to walk through each day.

———————— ᵒᵧᵧᵒ° ————————

Father God, thank You for the Holy Spirit, which You have placed
inside my heart. Quicken me to hear Your voice. Amen.

Day 194

WRITTEN ON HIM

Can a woman forget her sucking child, that she should not have compassion on the son of her womb? yea, they may forget, yet will I not forget thee. Behold, I have graven thee upon the palms of my hands; thy walls are continually before me.

Isaiah 49:15–16

God's people, during the life of the prophet Isaiah, were under threat of captivity, and they saw impending doom. They knew their dark and rebellious hearts brought this about, and they feared that Jehovah would forget or forsake them. God responded by likening Himself to a mother—the ultimate symbol of love and devotion. Mothers care for their children to guide and protect them. However, in this fallen world there are also women who abandon their children. God says that unlike weak and broken earthly parents, He will remain steadfast. He can do no less when He says that He engraved His children on the palms of His hands. Carved into His hands! This image comes to life when Jesus took nails through His hands to save sinners and make them children of God. What a powerful promise: He will never leave us nor forsake us.

Holy God, thank You that we can call You Abba, or Daddy. Thank You that Jesus suffered, died, and rose again so that people of all tribes and nations could know You as Father. Thank You that You never forget Your children. Help us to never doubt Your compassion, provision, and love. Amen.

Day 195

BRINGING US TO COMPLETION

Being confident of this very thing, that he which hath begun a good work in you will perform it until the day of Jesus Christ.

PHILIPPIANS 1:6

Remember the old saying "If at first you don't succeed, try, try again"? That's an encouraging statement. But it doesn't tell us how many times we should try. It doesn't tell us when we should throw in the towel and give up.

While there may be an appropriate time to give up on a certain skill or project, we should never give up on people. We should continue to hope, continue to pray, continue to love them. After all, that's what God does for us.

No matter how many times we fail, no matter how many times we mess up, we know God hasn't written us off. He's still working on us. He still loves us. He knows our potential, because He created us, and He won't stop moving us forward until His plan is completed.

Those of us who have been adopted into God's family through believing in His Son, Jesus Christ, can be confident that God won't give up on us. No matter how messed up our lives may seem, He will continue working in us until His plan is fulfilled and we stand before Him, perfect and complete.

Dear Father, thank You for not giving up on me.
Help me to cooperate with Your process
of fulfilling Your purpose in me. Amen.

Day 196

KEEP PRAYING

Pray without ceasing.
1 Thessalonians 5:17

⁓

"Talking to men for God is a great thing, but talking to God for men is greater still" (E. M. Bounds). Did you realize that we can witness all day to someone and never reach that person for Christ until prayer energizes our words?

Perhaps you have a wayward friend or an unsaved family member. You're heartbroken, and you've tried to share the message of salvation repeatedly to no avail. You've prayed, but nothing changes. Hoping to open their eyes, you continue to "preach," but soon your preaching becomes nagging and they resist your words all the more. So what should you do? Stop sharing the truth that you know will set them free? Keep silent and hope for the best?

Jesus said, "No man can come to me, except the Father which hath sent me draw him" (John 6:44). Prayer is a prerequisite to salvation. Consistent and passionate prayer for others moves God to draw them through the power of the Holy Spirit. Our prayers soften hardened hearts and prepare the heart's soil to receive God's Word.

It's our job to pray specifically for the needs of a person, and it's God's job to change that person's heart to receive the Gospel message.

So don't despair. Just keep praying.

⁓

*Lord, when I get frustrated and fail to see the results
of my prayers, encourage me to keep praying. Amen.*

Day 197

I SURRENDER

Yet I will rejoice in the LORD, I will joy in the God of my salvation. The LORD God is my strength, and he will make my feet like hinds' feet, and he will make me to walk upon mine high places.

HABAKKUK 3:18–19

Sometimes life seems like an uphill battle and we certainly don't feel like celebrating. We find ourselves frustrated by the demands of the day and worried about the future. It's just too difficult to stay the course—keep on keeping on. We're tempted to throw up our hands in frustration and quit. That's when we must realize we're in the perfect position: hands raised in surrender.

Learn that God's promises are true. He *will* be with us in all our difficulties, so we can relax in His care and focus on Him, instead of the problem. After all, He didn't promise a life with no problems. He did promise to carry us through, to be a source of strength we can lean on come what may.

So, are we leaning on and surrendering to the Lord? Do we trust Him with our future and the future of those in our care?

Surrender and *trust.* Two words that lead to life and joy. Choose to surrender and trust this day. He'll then bring you safely over the mountains.

Dear Lord, surrendering and trusting doesn't come naturally. Gently guide me so I might learn of You and become confident in Your care. Enable me to live life to the fullest. Amen.

Day 198

LAZINESS VS. REST

*Come unto me, all ye that labour
and are heavy laden, and I will give you rest.*
MATTHEW 11:28

In our society, we are so very *busy*. Many people work seven days a week. Even children's schedules are packed with lessons and tutoring, special classes, and clubs. They play instruments and sports. They go, go, go. . . just like the adults in their lives. Why are we all so busy? Are we running from the quiet? Are we afraid to rest? We complain about the busyness but continue to pack our calendars and to-do lists. Do we think we might appear lazy or strange if we simply choose to stay home, to have quality time with God and with our families?

Certainly, the Bible warns against laziness with such verses as Ecclesiastes 10:18, which says: "By much slothfulness the building decayeth; and through idleness of the hands the house droppeth through." But Jesus Himself rested. He often went away from the crowds to rest and to pray, to rejuvenate. We are commanded to remember the Sabbath and keep it holy. This involves rest. We are encouraged to be still and know that He is God.

Don't confuse laziness with rest. Just because you are not busy one day or one evening does not mean you should experience unnecessary guilt. Find a balance between work and play, busyness and rest. You will be better off for it in the long run.

*God, help me to avoid laziness and instead seek out
rest when it is needed in my life. Amen.*

GREAT EXPECTATIONS

*And, behold, there was a man in Jerusalem, whose name was
Simeon; and the same man was just and devout, waiting for the
consolation of Israel: and the Holy Ghost was upon him. And it was
revealed unto him by the Holy Ghost, that he should not
see death, before he had seen the Lord's Christ.*
LUKE 2:25–26

Simeon was an old man. He was righteous and devout. But surely there
were other old men hanging around the temple who were righteous
and devout. Of all the Pharisees and Sadducees nearby, of all the truly
devoted, religious people of that day, why Simeon? Why did God choose
this man to welcome His Son into the temple and proclaim His coming
to all who would listen?

One key phrase offers a clue: "[he] was. . .waiting for the consolation
of Israel." In other words, Simeon knew God's promises, and he was
looking for good things to happen.

What a lesson we can learn from this old saint! God has promised
many good things to His people. But often we mope around, stressed
and anxious, worried that things won't go well for us. Why do we do
that? Like Simeon, we should wake up each morning looking for God
to do great things. We should greet each new day expecting God to
work, to fulfill His promises.

*Dear Father, thank You for Your promises. I know You have good
things in store. Help me to watch and wait, expecting You
to do great things each and every day. Amen.*

FEARFULLY AND WONDERFULLY MADE

*For thou hast possessed my reins: thou hast covered me in my
mother's womb. I will praise thee; for I am fearfully and wonderfully
made: marvellous are thy works; and that my soul knoweth right well.
My substance was not hid from thee, when I was made in secret,
and curiously wrought in the lowest parts of the earth. Thine eyes
did see my substance, yet being unperfect; and in thy book
all my members were written, which in continuance were
fashioned, when as yet there was none of them.*

PSALM 139:13–16

———————— ☙ℓℓ℮ ————————

Are you one of those people who picks up a new book and reads the
last page first? Well, if your life could be compared to a book, only God
knows the "ending" as well as the beginning. Despite the "pages" in
the middle that might prove disappointing at times, God has a definite
purpose for your life. And if you are in His will, the last page will have
a very happy ending!

As we survey the "sea of humanity," we can feel as insignificant as
a grain of sand. And yet one granule piled on top of another makes for
a gorgeous beach.

Each of us has not only an inborn sense that there is a God, but
also an understanding that we possess a designed intent. Your parents
aren't responsible for your creation—God is. Had He not willed your
very existence, you would not have happened. God wants to use your
life to further His kingdom.

———————— ☙☙℮ ————————

*Lord, please renew my understanding that You created me in Your
own image and likeness with a body, mind, and spirit. Amen.*

Day 201

CAN GOD INTERRUPT YOU?

A man's heart deviseth his way: but the LORD directeth his steps.
PROVERBS 16:9

Before rushing out of the house each morning, our day is efficiently planned. We are eager to check off our to-do list. But wait! The phone suddenly rings. There is an unexpected knock at the door. The car tire is flat.

How do we react when our plans are interrupted? Do frustration, resentment, and anger quickly surface? We have places to go and people to meet. We do not have time for interruptions!

Have you ever considered that perhaps God has ordained our interruptions? A friend could be calling in need of encouragement. God knew you'd be just the right person to lift their spirits. Maybe the knock on the door is a lost child seeking help. Perhaps, just perhaps, God may be trying to get your attention.

There is nothing wrong with planning our day. However, we have such limited vision. God sees the big picture. Be open. Be flexible. Allow God to change your plans in order to accomplish His divine purposes. Instead of becoming frustrated, look for ways the Lord might be working. Be willing to join Him. When you do, interruptions become blessings.

Dear Lord, forgive me when I am so rigidly locked into my own agenda that I miss Yours. Give me Your eternal perspective so that I may be open to divine interruptions. Amen.

Day 202

HONOR YOUR PARENTS

*Honour thy father and thy mother: that thy days may
be long upon the land which the LORD thy God giveth thee.*
EXODUS 20:12

Honoring your parents is a lifelong duty. It looks different at four, fourteen, and forty, but it is a commandment important enough that almighty God chose to include it in a list of just ten.

This commandment may be difficult for adults to know how to obey. You know you should honor your mother and father, and yet it is not always simple. What exactly does honor entail? You are an adult, and yet they are still your parents. What if your parents are unbelievers?

These are not easy questions to answer, but the commandment is fairly cut-and-dried. Honor them, respect them, treat them well, listen to them, and never speak ill of them to others. You may not follow all of your parents' advice. Now that you are an adult, you are not required to do so. It is still admirable to seek it at times. They know you well, and they have lived longer than you have. They may have helpful input.

If your parents are not believers, honor them in every way possible so long as it does not cause you to stumble in your walk with the Lord. We are always called to put the Lord first.

*God, help me to honor my parents as
You have instructed me to do. Amen.*

Day 203
INSIDE OUT

And he saith unto them, Are ye so without understanding also?
Do ye not perceive, that whatsoever thing from without entereth
into the man, it cannot defile him. . . . That which cometh
out of the man, that defileth the man.
MARK 7:18, 20

People have generally focused on keeping the outside clean. The Jews of Jesus' day made sure they washed the same hand first each time. In keeping with the law, they refused to eat certain foods, declaring them "unclean."

We act in much the same way today. Some foods turn our stomach and become "unclean" to us. Americans consider daily baths the norm.

If only we exercised the same care in keeping our *minds* clean. Jesus listed some of the unclean things that flow from our minds: lust, pride, envy, and slander, among others. Unfortunately, once we have allowed images or thoughts into our minds, we can't "scrub" them away the way soap washes away dirt.

Safeguarding our thought life starts with what we allow into our minds. As much as possible, we should "see no evil" and "hear no evil." Music, television, movies, books, and even our friendships must be filtered.

We can't erase bad thoughts from our minds, but we can crowd them out—by filling our minds with noble, lovely, and true thoughts. "Wherewithal shall a young man cleanse his way? by taking heed thereto according to thy word" (Psalm 119:9).

The blood of Christ cleanses us, and the Bible helps to keep us clean.

Lord, search my thoughts, and show me my impurities.
Fill me with Your Word. Amen.

Day 204

STAND IN THE GAP

*And I sought for a man among them, that should make up the hedge,
and stand in the gap before me for the land, that I should
not destroy it: but I found none.*
EZEKIEL 22:30

———— ✺ ————

Each prayer request you offer up to God is important to you, and when
you ask others to pray, you're counting on them to help carry you through
the tough times.

Do you give the same consideration to those who ask you for prayer?
It's easy in the busyness of life to overlook a request someone else has
made. Maybe you don't know the person very well or you don't really
have an understanding of what they're going through. Perhaps the
request came in an email that you quickly glanced at and then deleted.
Yet even with emailed prayer requests, others trust you to stand in the
gap for them during difficult times in their lives.

Don't delay. Take time right when you receive a request to talk to
the Lord on the requester's behalf. Be the bridge that carries that person
through the valley of darkness back to the mountaintop of joy.

———— ✺ ————

*Heavenly Father, help me to have a heart of compassion for those
I know and even for those I don't know who need Your comfort
and love. Help me never to be too busy to pray for them. Amen.*

Day 205

MODEL CHILDREN

And said, Verily I say unto you, Except ye be converted,
and become as little children, ye shall not enter
into the kingdom of heaven.
MATTHEW 18:3

On the road to Capernaum, Christ's disciples were arguing among themselves about which of them was the greatest. When Jesus asked what they had been arguing about, they kept quiet (Mark 9:33–34). Maybe they were embarrassed to say.

Matthew 18 provides more insight into this story. It says that the disciples asked Jesus, "Who is the greatest in the kingdom of heaven?" (Matthew 18:1). In other words, "What do we have to do to attain greatness when we get there?"

In Matthew 18:3, Jesus answers their question by using little children as examples. He tells His disciples that they need to change their attitudes and think with the righteous heart of a child.

Very young children approach the world with innocence. They are free from selfish ambition, are humble and dependent on their parents. This simple, meek spirit is what God requires of us. Instead of worrying about being great here on earth or when we get to heaven, Matthew 18:3 indicates we should be concerned about whether we will enter His kingdom at all.

Oh Lord, make me like a little child, innocent and humble in Your
company. Take away my selfish ambitions, and point
my sight in the direction of heaven. Amen.

Day 206

LET IT GET YOU DOWN

And ye now therefore have sorrow: but I will see you again,
and your heart shall rejoice, and your joy no man taketh from you.
JOHN 16:22

Knowing that Jesus is your Savior, do you ever get sad? With the promise of heaven ahead of you, do you ever get down and depressed?

Of course you do—and nonbelievers will use that as a weapon against you. "If you really believed you were saved," they say, "you would be singing and dancing all the time!" Churchgoers, while avoiding addressing their own failings, will tell you that joy comes—if only you believe harder!

One of the devil's most effective weapons is to make you believe your lack of joy is due to your own shortcomings. But we are sad because we are broken. The fall separated us from Love, and ever since then, in many and various ways, that sadness has been seeping through.

Here Jesus makes the beautiful promise, "I will see you again, and your heart shall rejoice." Our hearts will rejoice because Jesus is the Physician who will heal our wounds. He is the Counselor who will restore us to Love.

Until then, if you feel a bit down, don't beat yourself up. Remember, there's a good reason for it—and it's all going to get much better soon.

It is part of being human, Lord, when sadness seeps into my heart.
But You are my joyful promise. I smile when I remember
that I will see You again. Amen.

Day 207

SEEING JESUS

And he turned him unto his disciples, and said privately,
Blessed are the eyes which see the things that ye see.
LUKE 10:23

What would you give to have been down by the Sea of Galilee when Jesus was calling His disciples? "The Twelve" were blessed, blessed men to have been in the right place at the right time. It wasn't that they were particularly special—not until Jesus chose them—but no man or woman before them or since them has been as blessed.

The disciples were lucky enough to see Jesus in the flesh, to live, eat, and walk with Him as a human being, something none of us will get to do. And they paid dearly for the privilege.

But Jesus' mission wasn't finished once the flesh was left behind. He would appear to the disciples and guide them as they spread the good news in foreign lands, and He had also taught them to look for Him in "the least of these."

We didn't get to be part of the Twelve, but that doesn't mean we don't get to see Jesus. We just have to look in different places. Until we join Him in His eternal kingdom, we will see the Lord in the humble, the hungry, the lonely, the destitute—and our eyes will be blessed too!

Jesus, allow me to see Your divine self through the world's humanity.
Open my eyes to Your gentle compassion, the truths of Your
teaching, Your profound forgiveness, and Your deepest love. Amen.

BEANS OR STEAK?

*Every man shall give as he is able, according to the blessing
of the Lord thy God which he hath given thee.*
DEUTERONOMY 16:17

———————— ₰₰₰₰ ————————

At the harvest celebration, every Jew was to thank God with a sacrifice according to the blessings he'd been given. God's Word assumes that every believer would receive a blessing of some sort. At the very least, His people were alive because He provided food for them. Those who didn't have much more than that would bring a small but heartfelt offering. Others, blessed with physical abundance, brought a generous offering of much greater value.

Our blessings may not be the kind we'd like. We may look for extra money to pay off bills whereas God sends us spiritual strength. But just as God provided for His Old Testament people even in the years of lean harvests, He provides for us.

We may be eating more beans and rice than steak and lobster, but isn't the former better for us in the long run? While we're looking for the good life, God's looking at what's good for us. Sometimes that means physical blessing—but other times it's a spiritual challenge.

No matter what our circumstances, God is blessing us—if we're following Him with steadfastness. Let's bless Him in return with our thanksgiving.

———————— ₰₰₰₰ ————————

*Lord, I thank You for the many blessings You give. In exchange,
I offer You the gift of my heart and life. Amen.*

Day 209

OVERWHELMED BY LIFE

*When the waves of death compassed me, the floods of ungodly men
made me afraid. . . . In my distress I called upon the LORD,
and cried to my God: and he did hear my voice out of
his temple, and my cry did enter into his ears.*
2 SAMUEL 22:5, 7

———————— ✍ ————————

Some days the "dailyness" of life seems like a never-ending grind. We get up, eat, work, rest—and do it again the next day. Then when tragedy strikes, we're swept up in grief. What once seemed doable now seems a huge challenge. Depression sinks its claws deep into our spirit. Fatigue sets in, and we are overwhelmed. Life is hard. We may be tempted to question, "Is this all there is?"

Here's the good news: There's more. God never meant for us to simply exist. He created us for a specific purpose. He longs for us to make a difference and show others His love and grace. What's more, He never asked us to do life alone. When the waves of death swirl around us, and the pounding rain of destruction threatens to overwhelm us, we can cry out to our heavenly Father, knowing that He will not let us drown. He will hear our voice, and He will send help.

So, next time you feel that you can't put one foot in front of the other, ask God to send you His strength and energy. He will help you to live out your purpose in this chaotic world.

———————— ✐ ————————

*Lord, thank You for strengthening me when the "dailyness" of life,
and its various trials, threatens to overwhelm me. Amen.*

Day 210

NEW THINGS

Behold, I will do a new thing; now it shall spring forth;
shall ye not know it? I will even make a way in
the wilderness, and rivers in the desert.
ISAIAH 43:19

Sometimes it seems like we're standing in the middle of a thick forest. Lost. No way out. No path, no help to be found. Trees block the sunlight; we have no cell phone reception, no idea which way to go. At least, that's what it feels like, right?

God says when we're in a wilderness with no clear path, He'll make a path. He'll clear a way for us. If we turn around and try to live in the past, we'll lose our way. If we follow Him, He'll show us a better way. At times it might feel like we don't have the provisions we need to do this. We struggle to pay bills, or we long for friendship or lost love. We feel physically, financially, or spiritually destitute. But even then, God will provide. When we find ourselves in a desert, God will bring a river! In order to find that river, we can't return to our former way of life. We must keep moving forward, keep following Him, keep trusting His love for us. He is good, and all His plans for us are good. In faith, we can leave the past behind and step forward into a future filled with His bountiful provision.

Dear Father, I trust You with my future. I can't wait to see
what You have in store. Amen.

Day 211

REFLECTING (ON) CHRIST'S GLORY

*But we all, with open face beholding as in a glass the glory of the
Lord, are changed into the same image from glory to glory,
even as by the Spirit of the Lord.*

2 CORINTHIANS 3:18

What are you thinking about? Careful. The act of contemplation is powerful. Why else would teachers chide students when their attention is anywhere but on the lesson? Their daydreams about recess won't fuel their brains for mathematics. Contemplation is a moral and transformative action too. Contemplating the difficulties of a relationship could sway a person's commitment; contemplating wealth (or the lack thereof) can create heart-sinking envy. We pay attention to what we care about; what we care about shapes and changes us.

Christians are called to "[look] unto Jesus" (Hebrews 12:2). Here in 2 Corinthians, Paul writes about contemplating Jesus' glory—the Greek word translated into English as "beholding" means both "to meditate upon" and "to reflect." Dwelling on Christ's life *transforms us* into being more like Him.

Thinking on Jesus means to meditate on the truth we believe about Him. The Word shows us a Savior who gave up His holy, perfect life to restore the undeserving to Himself, who rose again victorious over death! The Holy Spirit enables us to reflect Jesus' loving, sacrificial character more and more as we know and love Him better.

*Father God, when my mind wanders, teach me to turn my
attention again to Christ and His glory. Let me know Him
better so I can show Him better to others. Amen.*

LIVING TEMPLES

*Know ye not that ye are the temple of God,
and that the Spirit of God dwelleth in you?*
1 CORINTHIANS 3:16

The Samaritan woman asked Jesus where people ought to worship God—on Mount Gerizim (where a Samaritan temple once stood) or at the Jewish temple in Jerusalem. Jesus surprised her by saying that the time was soon coming when men would not worship God at *either* spot, but "the true worshippers shall worship the Father in spirit and in truth" (John 4:23). Indeed, as Stephen later said, "The most High dwelleth not in temples made with hands" (Acts 7:48).

If God doesn't dwell in temples built by men, where does He dwell? Jesus promised His disciples that although, up to that time, the Holy Spirit dwelled *with* them, He would soon dwell *in* them (John 14:17).

Paul stated it clearly when he asked Christians, "Know ye not that ye are the temple of God, and that the Spirit of God dwelleth in you?" He further stated, "Your body is the temple of the Holy Ghost which is in you," and emphasized that fact as the reason why we ought to live holy lives (1 Corinthians 6:19; 2 Corinthians 6:16–17).

What an awesome privilege—to be a temple of the Spirit of God!

Heavenly Father, how wonderful it is that You have chosen my body as a dwelling place for Your Holy Spirit. Keep me always aware of Your presence. Amen.

Day 213

A PROMISED HEALING

*Behold, I will bring it health and cure, and I will cure them,
and will reveal unto them the abundance of peace and truth.*
JEREMIAH 33:6

Are you longing to be healed of an affliction? Mary Magdalene suffered with seven demons before Jesus touched her and restored her to life. Scripture doesn't tell us much about how, when, or where Jesus healed Mary. It does tell us that Mary, along with several other women, provided for and supported Jesus so that He could do what God had called Him to do. After Jesus healed her, she became one of His most ardent followers.

This woman, who had been tormented by Satan himself, became a walking testimony of the power of the Light to dispel darkness: "The light shineth in darkness; and the darkness comprehended it not" (John 1:5).

Whether or not God chooses to cure you here on earth, one day He *will* restore you to total health. In heaven, our bodies will be perfect and no diseases will be allowed to touch us. We will live in peace and prosperity.

Such a promise should make us rejoice. Jesus will strengthen us for this life, whatever it may hold, and will one day turn on the light that will make the darkness scatter for all time. Hallelujah!

*Heavenly Father, thank You for Your promise of healing.
Strengthen me as I walk this earth, and give me
hope as I look toward heaven. Amen.*

Day 214

LEAD BY EXAMPLE

*But ye shall not be so: but he that is greatest among you,
let him be as the younger; and he that is chief,
as he that doth serve.*

LUKE 22:26

Sometimes when we're wrong, we're *really* wrong. We look at the map and turn right, thinking we are headed west. After driving for miles, we find we're going in the opposite direction. It is the same thing when it comes to being great. We think being great involves commanding hundreds of people, holding a place of authority.

Surprise! If we wish to be great in the kingdom of God, we may have to do a U-turn. Greatness is found in being a servant. The leader is not one who tells others what to do; the leader leads and teaches by example. He doesn't point the way to go; he simply does what must be done.

Jesus did not simply tell His disciples how to live. He humbled Himself to serve, and He never rose above that station. Because He left us an example of humble service, shall we exalt ourselves? We have the promise that as Christ served even to death, and God therefore highly exalted Him, we who serve Him faithfully will reign with Him.

*Jesus, help me to be a servant not only to You but also to the world.
Teach me to be humble like You were humble. Amen.*

Day 215

UNIQUELY THREE-IN-ONE

*I am Alpha and Omega, the beginning
and the end, the first and the last.*
REVELATION 22:13

Over and over we find that the titles God gave to Himself in the Old Testament are being applied to Jesus Christ as well. In the Old Testament, the Lord God called Himself a shepherd, the Alpha and Omega, the Beginning and the End, and the Almighty. He is called the First and the Last. In the New Testament, we find the same titles given to Jesus.

This makes our God unique among the religions of the world. No other religion has a God whose Son is equal to the Father. The Jews and Muslims reject the idea of God having a Son. Only Christianity has a triune God—three persons in one God.

The Bible is unique because in it God fully reveals who He is. Since Jesus is fully God, let it renew our hope and faith in our Savior. He who created all things out of nothing will recreate this world into a paradise without sin.

*Jesus, I trust in You as my God—Father, Son,
and Holy Spirit—three persons, one God, one perfect You! Amen.*

Day 216

PERFECT IN FAILURE

For that which I do I allow not: for what I would,
that do I not; but what I hate, that do I.
ROMANS 7:15

Who is this weak-willed, indecisive wimp? Has he no faith, no moral fiber?

Actually, he was the worldwide leader of the early church, and this verse comes from his letter to Christians in Rome. So what kind of impression was he giving them?

He was laying out the harsh reality that faith does not make us perfect. Paul lived, suffered, and died for his adoration of the Lord, but in day-to-day life he frequently and consistently failed to live up to his own ideal. That's because his ideal life was Christ's, and no one could live up to *that* example.

Still he tried, because, while his body belonged to sin, his soul belonged to the Lord—and his mind was the general directing the battle between the two.

It can be disheartening to fail. Some people fall away from faith because of it. But here is the remedy to that situation. In your struggle you are no better or worse than Saint Paul. Thankfully, your ultimate success won't be measured by the number of times you fall; it will depend entirely on the number of times you reach for Jesus to help you back up.

I struggle with perfection, Lord. I try my best and still I fail.
But my best is good enough for You! Teach me
not to be so hard on myself. Amen.

Day 217

I LOVE YOU MORE!

*If any man come to me, and hate not his father, and mother,
and wife, and children, and brethren, and sisters, yea,
and his own life also, he cannot be my disciple.*

LUKE 14:26

———————— *eelee* ————————

Jesus must have seriously wanted to discourage people from following Him. He told the listening crowds, "If you don't hate your family, you can't be My disciple."

Ouch.

But Jesus was using hyperbole to make a point: "Love Me so deeply that your love for your family will seem like hatred by comparison." When He gave the twelve disciples instructions before sending them out, He repeated the point in less strident terms: "He that loveth father or mother more than me is not worthy of me: and he that loveth son or daughter more than me is not worthy of me" (Matthew 10:37).

To love Christ is our ultimate aim. But from that love springs more love, the kind of others-centered love He lavishes on us. Love for Christ and love for others flows in a circle. The more we love Christ, the more we love others. . .and the more we love others, the more we show our love for Christ.

———————— *ele* ————————

*Jesus, I love You with all my heart; please help me to love
You more. Fill me up with love for You. Then let Your
love shine through me to others. Amen.*

Day 218

REACH OUT

But the natural man receiveth not the things of the Spirit of God:
for they are foolishness unto him: neither can he know
them, because they are spiritually discerned.

1 CORINTHIANS 2:14

Imagine yourself visiting another country but you're unable to speak the language. Everywhere people are conversing in a tongue that you cannot decipher. Although you're lost, asking for directions seems useless. You drive around aimlessly, confused by street signs that don't make sense. People honk as you enter the exits and yell as you navigate the roundabouts. Even though you're trying your hardest, onlookers judge you as an idiot.

In the same way, unbelievers may feel confused trying to navigate the unfamiliar territory of spiritual truth. They don't have the ability to understand it because they don't have the Holy Spirit as a teacher to guide them. The Bible may not make sense to them, but don't be quick to judge. Hope isn't lost!

God likely has placed unbelievers in your life that He wants you to reach out to. Share your faith with them in words and actions they can understand. Pray the Lord opens their hearts to receive Jesus as Lord and Savior. Then the Holy Spirit will dwell with them, giving them the ability to comprehend spiritual truth. Pray that these lost "tourists" will find Jesus soon!

Dear Lord, help me not to judge those that don't know You.
Instead, may I pray that You intercede to show them the way. Amen.

Day 219

FULL OF GRACE

Let your speech be always with grace, seasoned with salt,
that ye may know how ye ought to answer every man.
Colossians 4:6

Inflection. Tone of voice. Attitude. Maybe you remember your mom saying, "It's not what you say, but how you say it." Words not only convey a message; they also reveal the attitude of our hearts. When our conversation is full of grace, even difficult truths can be communicated effectively. But how do we season our words with grace?

Grace is undeserved favor that extends unconditional love to another. Whether you're communicating with friends, family, or coworkers, it's important to show that you value them. Put their needs above your own. Communicate truth within the context of love. Show compassion and forgiveness. Demonstrate understanding and an openness to receive their input. Respect their opinion. Rather than striving to drive home your point, try to understand theirs. Seek to build them up. Convey encouragement and hope. Be positive.

When our conversations are full of grace, people will enjoy communicating with us. They will walk away blessed by the love we have shown. Today, in your conversations, extend God's grace to those hungry to experience His love.

Dear Lord, may I view each conversation as an opportunity
to extend Your grace to others. May my words be a blessing. Amen.

Day 220

ASKING FOR IT

Confess your faults one to another,
and pray one for another, that ye may be healed.
JAMES 5:16

Forgiveness is hard enough to grant, let alone to request. Taking responsibility for your mistakes and asking for mercy from the person you've offended are not easy things to do.

Most people would rather make excuses for their behavior than own up to it. However, asking for forgiveness is one of the most powerful testimonies of your faith that you can demonstrate. When we ask for forgiveness, we acknowledge we have trampled the dignity of another human being. We admit that we have hurt God as well by sinning against a person He deeply loves. In asking for forgiveness, we humble ourselves and throw ourselves on mercy—the mercy of the person we've hurt and our Father's mercy.

It is a gift to be forgiven. Sometimes forgiveness is withheld—a "reasonable" human reaction to sin, but painful nonetheless. Even if the person in question refuses to forgive you, you must do all you can to make peace, and then leave it in the Father's hands—He can bring peace where peace seems impossible. Take heart: if you have confessed your sin to the Father, He has forgiven you and will never hold that sin against you.

Father, help me to be humble and ask for forgiveness from those
I sin against. Thank You for Your forgiveness that frees me
to admit my weakness and foolishness to others. Amen.

Day 221

WAITING

*Wait on the LORD: be of good courage, and he shall
strengthen thine heart: wait, I say, on the LORD.*
PSALM 27:14

—————— ✺ ——————

In our society, we wait in line to buy groceries, to make bank deposits, and to pick up our kids from school. We wait in classrooms, exam rooms, and even in rooms called "waiting rooms." Waiting is part of life. Because we dislike it, we seek to make things faster. With the invention of drive-through windows, we don't have to get out of the car. The meal is handed to us from a window as we drive by and pay. Microwaves have shortened cook times. We can even sign in online at an after-hours medical clinic to avoid waiting with all the other sick people. We can wait at home instead, where we are able to multitask!

Some things are worth waiting for. Would you agree? The right spouse is definitely worth the wait. Some people drive around for a few minutes waiting for that front-row parking spot to open up. Sometimes we wait for just the perfect moment to share some news, whether good or bad, with family members or friends.

Waiting for God to answer our prayers is easier said than done. God does not hurry. Nor is He ever late. He is always right on time to bless us, and He has our best interests at heart. Seek God's answers for your questions, and be patient. Waiting on the Lord will always pay off.

—————— ✺ ——————

*Help me, Lord, to be more patient. I know that when You ask me to
wait, You have a reason. Thank You, Lord, for Your provision. Amen.*

Day 222

INTERCEDING FOR US

For he that is mighty hath done to me great things;
and holy is his name.
LUKE 1:49

Troubling issues in our nation are complex and too numerous to count. Sometimes it is difficult to know what to pray for, how to pray, or even where to begin. There are many Christians who have given up on praying for our country altogether. It can feel hopeless at times, and actually it is. Without God it is hopeless.

Thank God that He does hear, for we have an intercessor in Christ—by the power of the Holy Spirit—who is always there interceding on our behalf. He is our hope. Hope for a nation grounded in His principles but fallen like the rest of the earthly world.

Let us pray and thank Him for what He is already doing, then look expectantly for what God will do through a people who love Him and seek to shine for Him in truth and love.

Lord God, thank You for seeing our every need and for the ability
to come to You anytime, all the time, in prayer. Amen.

Day 223

HOW GREAT IS OUR GOD!

*And said, I beseech thee, O LORD God of heaven, the great and
terrible God, that keepeth covenant and mercy for them
that love him and observe his commandments.*
NEHEMIAH 1:5

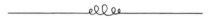

When Dorothy finally met the wizard she had been searching for in *The Wonderful Wizard of Oz*, she was disappointed. The "Great and Terrible" magician, who had promoted himself as an all-powerful man with a short temper, turned out to be a normal person behind a curtain—albeit one who was good at special effects.

Rest assured, when we finally meet God, we won't have the same kind of letdown. The Bible notes God's inestimable qualities—unconditional love, unending mercy, unimaginable strength—with reverence. The New Testament authors also repeatedly wrote about God's mercy and compassion, lest we despair of ever coming near Him.

Of course, we need to fear the holy Creator and Maker of all things and strive to do His will, but as the One who formed us, God knows that we will fail (and loves us anyway). His love is why He sent Jesus to die on the cross.

Today, think about God's love, mercy, and strength as you go about your day. When you face problems, ask Him to solve them, instead of trying to fix them yourself. Repeatedly and reverently surrender to Him—because He is great, but He's certainly not terrible.

*Creator, Maker, Redeemer God—You are wonderful.
Thank You for Your wisdom, strength, and love. Amen.*

TEMPTED BY SATAN

*And the devil said unto him, If thou be the Son of God,
command this stone that it be made bread. And Jesus
answered him, saying, It is written, That man shall
not live by bread alone, but by every word of God.*

LUKE 4:3–4

Have you ever found yourself so tempted to sin that you ached all the
way to your soul? Christ understands that pull toward evil. Satan wasn't
just present in the wilderness to "bug" the Lord Jesus Christ. This was
a full-on, frontal attack.

In this first temptation, Satan intimated that there must be something
wrong with the Father's love for the Son since He allowed Him to go
hungry. Satan's fiery darts of doubt were aimed directly at the triune God.

With the second temptation, Satan led Christ upward for a better
view of "all the kingdoms of the world" (v. 5). Satan attempted to get
Christ to bypass the cross and seize the power.

The third temptation involved a literal leap of faith. Satan dared
Jesus to prove Himself to be the Son of God and stand on the pinnacle
of the temple and throw Himself down. This time the evil one meant to
question the Father's faithfulness toward the Son. After all, the scriptures
did say that God would give His angels charge concerning Him.

The stakes were high in the wilderness. If Christ had succumbed
to Satan's snare, He would have been ineligible to make that perfect
sacrifice on the cross as the Lamb of God without blemish. But He didn't!

Lord, I thank You for Your Son's perfect victory over Satan. Amen.

PEOPLE PLEASER VS. GOD PLEASER

*But as we were allowed of God to be put in trust with
the gospel, even so we speak; not as pleasing
men, but God, which trieth our hearts.*

1 THESSALONIANS 2:4

Much of what we say and do stems from our desire to be accepted by others. We strive to make a certain impression, to shed the best light possible on ourselves. Wanting to be viewed as successful, we may decide to exaggerate, embellish, or even lie. It's difficult to be true to ourselves when we care so much about the acceptance and opinions of others. Impression management is hard work, so it's good to know God has a better plan!

Rather than being driven by the opinions of others, strive to live your life for God alone and to please Him above all else. God knows our hearts. He perceives things as they truly are. We cannot fool Him. When we allow ourselves to be real before Him, it doesn't matter what others think. If the God of the universe has accepted us, then who cares about someone else's opinion?

It is impossible to please both God and man. We must make a choice. Man looks at the outward appearance, but God looks at the heart. Align your heart with His. Let go of impression management that focuses on outward appearance. Receive God's unconditional love and enjoy the freedom to be yourself before Him!

*Dear Lord, may I live for You alone. Help me transition
from a people pleaser to a God pleaser. Amen.*

Day 226

TREASURE VAULT

For where your treasure is, there will your heart be also.
LUKE 12:34

─────────── ℓℓℓℓ ───────────

Where is your greatest treasure? Do you own something so valuable it sits in a safe-deposit box in your bank? Maybe you take it out once in a while then return it for safekeeping.

If that's really your life's greatest treasure, you're in trouble, for according to this verse, your heart is locked up in a narrow, dark, safe-deposit box, where it's awfully difficult to love others and enjoy the world God has given you.

Maybe you don't own that kind of valuable, but you're inordinately proud of the vehicle you drive. Would you really want your heart to sit out in all weather, where it could eventually rust away? Even the best care will never make a car last forever. Hide it in a garage, but it still has a limited life.

But when your best treasure is your relationship with Christ and His eternal reward, you don't have to worry about where your heart is. It's safe with Jesus, free to love others, and valuable to both you and the people with whom you share Christ.

Are you gathering earthly treasures or eternal ones? Those on earth won't last. Sending treasures before you to heaven is the wisest thing you can do. Worldly goods fade, but not those in Jesus' treasure vaults.

─────────── ⁘⁘⁘ ───────────

Lord, help me send treasures ahead of me into eternity instead of grabbing all the earthly items I can get. Amen.

Day 227

ARE YOU WILLING?

And he put forth his hand, and touched him, saying, I will:
be thou clean. And immediately the leprosy departed from him.
Luke 5:13

This touching verse sums up Jesus' mission. The leper asked for healing—if Jesus was willing. Of course, Jesus was willing. He willingly took human form; He willingly suffered ridicule. Willingly He cured many—and willingly He died.

He didn't have to do any of it, but He did.

In return, God asks the same from us. He can do great works through us—if we are willing. But that's difficult, isn't it? After all, who are we? We can't perform miracles. And there lies the stumbling block—for God to work in the world, we have to get past thinking of ourselves as His *partners*. The apostles didn't cure anyone. God used them to perform many cures, but none of the power came from them. They simply allowed themselves to be instruments in His hands.

Great things are yet to be done in this world—and we can be a part of them when we stop worrying about our capabilities and put more faith in *His*.

In the quest to be more like Christ, the simplest and most effective thing we can do is be willing. Then hand that willingness over to God and see what He does with it.

God, I am willing. Use me. Work through me to accomplish
whatever You desire. Whether it is something great
or something small, I am ready. Amen.

Day 228

WHY DO YOU ASK?

*The blind receive their sight, and the lame walk, the lepers are
cleansed, and the deaf hear, the dead are raised up,
and the poor have the gospel preached to them.*

MATTHEW 11:5

What did Jesus say when the Pharisees and Pilate asked Him if He was the Son of God? Well, let's just say He didn't give them any answers they understood. Those powerful questioners were left deeply frustrated.

But when John the Baptist sent messengers to ask, "Are you the one who was to come?" Jesus specifically told them about the work He was doing. Why the difference?

Well, the Pharisees and Pilate were asking for reasons of earthly power. They didn't really want to know the Lord, whereas John, helplessly chained in a cell, wanted nothing more than that. Within days of death and with doubts gnawing at his soul, John asked for words of comfort. Jesus' reply must have made John's beleaguered soul sing. This was what he devoted his life to! His Lord was walking on the earth!

Those ruled by earthly passions will never understand when Jesus speaks. But servants of God, no matter how desperately flawed they are or how foolish their questions might seem, can call on Him and receive an answer. It might be comforting; it might be challenging. You just have to be prepared to listen.

*My heart listens for You, almighty God. I question You, and I trust that
You will answer me. Prepare my heart to receive Your words. Amen.*

NOT THE BAD GUY

*And it repented the LORD that he had made man
on the earth, and it grieved him at his heart.*

GENESIS 6:6

—————— ✣ ——————

Because of the flood, God has often been painted as the bad guy. "I can't trust a God who got angry and wiped everyone out!" people say. Yet this verse tells us God was *sorry*, not angry.

God did everything possible to avoid the flood. He gave humanity several generations to turn from its wickedness. His long-suffering was so great that He waited until there was only one righteous man left—Noah. And God didn't send the flood without warning. Noah and Enoch were preachers of righteousness. Though they warned the world for a hundred years (the time it took to build the ark), no one believed them. By the time the rains began, the world reeked of sin. Genesis 4:23–24 indicates there was murder without guilt. A world of killers received the death penalty.

Considering the details of an event, we see a whole new story—and the righteousness of God. Don't be quick to put God down, but carefully research those questions you find disturbing. The Bible has given us every reason to put our whole life into His hands, today and forever.

—————— ✣ ——————

*You knew that humans would continue to sin, and so You
sent Jesus to save us. Your love for us is greater than
any other love, Oh just and forgiving God! Amen.*

Day 230

USE-FULL!

As every man hath received the gift, even so minister the same one
to another, as good stewards of the manifold grace of God.
1 PETER 4:10

———————— *elle* ————————

You might think people incapacitated by illness are taken out of the game by God—but they have a role in bringing out the best in others. People who are swamped by the evil around them might feel unable to do any real good—but their courage is a great example.

There are lives taken out of service, however. God doesn't do that, and His enemy isn't responsible, either. Those lives are put "on the bench" by the people living them.

This message is for the ones who through fear of failure or worry about their inadequacy deliberately sideline themselves. There are no useless lives. There is a point to your being on this earth. If the least you can offer is a smile, if you can only sit and listen, then smile and listen. The most seemingly insignificant act on your part might be what makes the difference to another struggling soul.

Think you have nothing to offer? You're wrong. Get back in the game and make your play, however feeble it might seem to you. God will take it and do great things with it. He just needs you to be in the game.

———————— *oooo* ————————

Lord, when I am physically or emotionally unable to give my all,
remind me of my gifts, especially those I'm unaware of,
and teach me to share them with others. Amen.

Day 231

REMEMBER AGAIN

Take, eat: this is my body, which is broken for you:
this do in remembrance of me.
1 CORINTHIANS 11:24

———— *elle* ————

For the most part, when people remember heroes, they celebrate their accomplishments. But with the Lord's Supper, Jesus commands us to remember His death.

Why not let a cup of wine remind us of the time He turned the water into wine? Or have the bread remind us of when He multiplied the loaves to feed five thousand? Instead, He calls us to the circumstances of His death.

At the Passover, a lamb was sacrificed. But Jesus was the Lamb of God who came to take away the sins of the world. That is why we remember His death. Only by His dying on the cross then rising again could we be saved from our punishment of hell and the slavery of sin.

Some things lose their fascination with familiarity. It's normal for a familiar passage of scripture to lose its force over time. Chances are, if we have taken Christ's death for granted, we have accommodated sin too. Let us stir up our hearts over the death, burial, and resurrection of Christ, for it is the bedrock of our faith and will lead us to triumph over all sin.

———— *ఠ౷ ఠ* ————

Jesus, fill my mind and heart with thoughts of Your death,
burial, and resurrection. I am so grateful for Your sacrifice.
I don't ever want to take it for granted. Amen.

Day 232

GOD'S SANCTUARY

Praise ye the LORD. Praise God in his sanctuary:
praise him in the firmament of his power.
PSALM 150:1

———————— elle ————————

Before there were churches, before there were preachers, before Christ came to this earth, God had created His sanctuaries. On the mountaintops, God was worshipped. In the valleys, God was worshipped. In the forests, by lakesides, in caves wherever God's handiwork was found—there He was worshipped.

We can praise God anywhere. Church isn't a place; it is an entity made up of living parts. Wherever we gather in the name of God, there is His sanctuary. Lift your voice to the Lord. Praise Him wherever you may be. He is with you where you are.

———————— ooooo ————————

I will praise and worship You with all my heart and mind
and soul. Hear my words, Lord, and be pleased
by the love I have for You. Amen.

Day 233

UP ALL NIGHT

He will not suffer thy foot to be moved:
he that keepeth thee will not slumber.
PSALM 121:3

⁓⁓

Ever stayed up all night studying for a major test, waiting for a loved one to come home, or rocking a sick child? The next day or two your mushy brain barely functions, and your body, drained of all energy, finds it difficult to accomplish even the most simple tasks.

You'll regain your balance and energy only after several nights of refreshing sleep. The human body requires regular periods of rest in order to thrive. Unlike humans, the psalms tell us that God does *not* sleep. He watches over us, never once averting His eyes even for a few quick moments of rest.

God guards our every moment. He stays up all night, looking after us as we sleep. He patiently keeps His eyes on us even when we roam. He constantly comforts when fear or illness makes us toss and turn. Like a caring parent who tiptoes into a sleeping child's room, God surrounds us even when we don't realize it.

We can sleep because God never slumbers.

⁓⁓

Oh God, how grateful I am that You never sleep.
When weariness overtakes me, You guard me like a mother
who watches over her child. I love You, Father! Amen.

Day 234

COMPLETE CONTROL

*And the LORD said unto Satan, Behold, all that he hath is in thy power;
only upon himself put not forth thine hand. So Satan went
forth from the presence of the LORD.*

JOB 1:12

———————— ℓℓℓℓ ————————

Many people picture God and Satan as opposing forces locked in eternal combat. When the good times roll, then God must have the upper hand. When things go south, Satan is winning.

This fascinating verse opens a window to the inner workings of God's day-to-day administration. In Job 1, Satan first gave an account to God of his travels through the earth. Then God informed Satan of Job's uprightness. Satan replied that Job was on God's side because the Lord had blessed him so much: "Just take away his goods and watch what happens then." At that point, God allowed Satan to test Job but issued a strict charge not to touch his person.

Clearly, Satan is under God's complete authority. The devil can't work without God's permission. No matter how bad things may get, they are never out of control. And a day is coming when God will rid the universe of Satan, casting him into eternal fire.

One final thought: Job was blessed more at the end of his life than the beginning (Job 42:12).

———————— ∽∽∽∽ ————————

*Job—I feel like him sometimes. I ask, "Why do bad things happen
to good people?" Father, remind me that You are always
in control and You love me. Amen.*

Day 235
SO, TALK!

No man can come to me, except the Father
which hath sent me draw him.

JOHN 6:44

───────── *ellee* ─────────

In some of the psalms, the writers seem to shake their fists at God, shouting, "Where are You, Lord? Why are You so slow? Are You sleeping? Wake up and help me!"

Interestingly, the psalmists never doubted God's existence, only His methods. They loved Him, they believed He would triumph over enemies, and they knew He was the one true God. But they had some strong opinions about the way He went about His business. And they had no qualms about telling Him!

Fortunately for us human beings, God isn't easily offended. He is deeply committed to holding up His end of our relationship, and He doesn't want us to hide anything from Him. He already knows every thought we have, anyway. Why not talk to Him about those thoughts? Every concern we have, every little thing that's good, bad, or ugly.

Our Father always wants to talk. In fact, the very impulse to pray originates in God. In his book *The Pursuit of God*, author A. W. Tozer wrote, "We pursue God because, and only because, He has first put an urge within us that spurs us to the pursuit."

So, talk!

───────── ༄༅ ─────────

Lord God, it boggles my mind that You want to hear from me!
And often! Your Word says that I can call out Your name with
confidence. That You will answer me! Today, Lord, I give You praise,
honor, and glory—and my heart's deepest longings. Amen.

Day 236

STAYING ON TRACK

I have fought a good fight, I have finished my course,
I have kept the faith.
2 TIMOTHY 4:7

In our hustle-bustle world, it's easy to get so busy we forget our priorities. Hopefully, as believers, we've established our priority list with God at the top. Staying in touch with Him and walking in His will should be our number one goal.

Paul knew this when he exhorted the churches to stick closely to the teachings of Jesus. He knew the fickle heart and how easy it would be for them to stray. In his letters to Timothy, he reminded the young man of the importance of drawing close to God, hearing His heartbeat. Despite the pain and afflictions Paul suffered in his life, he kept his eyes on Jesus, using praise to commune with God.

Likewise, we can keep in constant communion with the Father. We are so blessed to have been given the Holy Spirit within to keep us in tune with His will. Through His guidance—that still, small voice—we can rest assured our priorities will stay focused on Jesus.

Lord, throughout my life, I want to echo the words of
scripture, "I have stayed on track. I have kept the faith."
Be with me today as I refocus on You. Amen.

HE ENJOYS YOU

The LORD thy God in the midst of thee is mighty; he will save,
he will rejoice over thee with joy; he will rest in his love,
he will joy over thee with singing.
ZEPHANIAH 3:17

―――――― ◦◦◦◦ ――――――

Memory is a powerful part of each one of us. Perhaps you can see your father cheering you on in a sports event or you remember your mother stroking your feverish forehead while you lay sick in bed. With those mental pictures comes a recollection of emotion—how good it felt to be cheered and encouraged, how comforting it was to be loved and attended.

Zephaniah's words remind us that God is our loving parent. Our mighty Savior offers us a personal relationship, loving and rejoicing over us, His children, glad that we live and move in Him. He is the Lord of the universe, and yet He will quiet our restless hearts and minds with His tender love. He delights in our lives and celebrates our union with Him. We can rest in His affirmation and love, no matter what circumstances surround us.

―――――― ◦◦◦◦ ――――――

Lord, help me remember that You are always with me and that You delight in me. Remind me that I am Your child and that You enjoy our relationship. Amen.

Day 238

TIMES OF TROUBLE

*Thou hast turned for me my mourning into dancing: thou hast put off
my sackcloth, and girded me with gladness; to the end that my
glory may sing praise to thee, and not be silent. O LORD
my God, I will give thanks unto thee for ever.*
PSALM 30:11–12

_____ ℓℓℓℓ _____

David knew times of trouble, and he also knew what it meant to be
relieved of trouble. He experienced want and he experienced abundance.
He hid in fear of losing his life to a king that he knew hated him. . .and
later, he danced with joy, praising God, amazed at God's provision and
protection. Can you relate? You probably have never been chased by
a king and his armies. But every life is full of ups and downs. There will
be times when all you can hope to do is survive in the shelter of the
Lord's wing. You know He is there, but you cannot sense His presence.
You trust Him, but you don't know how in the world He will turn things
around. Just keep trusting. Just keep believing. Just keep praying. David
cried out to the Lord for mercy. Not just this psalm but many others are
filled with David's pleas to the Lord. God is faithful to hear our prayers.
Just as He turned David's sorrow into joy, He can do the same for you.

_____ ༼༼༽ _____

*Father, I ask You to turn my weeping into laughter.
Teach me to praise You no matter my circumstances. Amen.*

MAPQUEST

Shew me thy ways, O LORD; teach me thy paths. Lead me in
thy truth, and teach me: for thou art the God of
my salvation; on thee do I wait all the day.
PSALM 25:4–5

Stopping to ask directions is almost a thing of the past. Today we have GPS systems and Mapquest: plug in the info we need and we're off—choosing our own paths. But are they always the right ones? Scripture calls for the Lord to *teach* us. To *guide* us. When we use the Bible as our manual, we can trust that the Lord will direct us on the right roadway.

The words of the psalm assure us that God is faithful and that the paths in which we are led are the correct paths, ultimately leading us home. But to have God show us our way, to guide us, means we must have teachable spirits. We must be willing to listen and follow. We must plug into His power and grace, *before* we begin our journeys.

Father God, help me hear Your voice.
Let me know Your heart and guide me always. Amen.

Day 240

WHITER THAN SNOW

*Purge me with hyssop, and I shall be clean:
wash me, and I shall be whiter than snow.*
PSALM 51:7

—————— ✺ ——————

If you've ever looked out over a pristine, white field covered in glistening mounds of white snow, you know what purity looks like. Everything underneath those mounds of snow has disappeared from view, to be seen no more. The white snow covers it all, making it irrelevant.

That's how forgiveness works. When we come to God and confess our sins, He is faithful and just to forgive us. His forgiveness washes over us in exactly the same way that the snow covers the ground below. All traces of yesterday—the awful things we've done, the pain we've caused, the heartache we've gone through—are gone. In place of the bad memories is glistening white forgiveness, sparkling with the hope of better days to come.

If you haven't yet asked Jesus to be the Lord of your life, if you haven't accepted His forgiveness for the sins you've committed, this is the perfect day—the perfect season—to do so. He can wash your sins away and leave you whiter than snow.

—————— ✺ ——————

*Father, I love the image of snow that I find in this scripture.
It's a reminder that my past really can be in the past. I want to
live for today, Lord, so that I can have the courage to step
into tomorrow without worrying about what happened
yesterday. Cleanse me, Lord! Amen.*

Day 241

HE CHOSE

The Lord did not set his love upon you, nor choose you, because ye
were more in number than any people; for ye were the fewest
of all people: but because the Lord loved you.
DEUTERONOMY 7:7–8

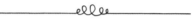

In the book of Deuteronomy God tells the people of Israel that they are unique. Who else has "[heard] the voice of God speaking out of the midst of the fire" and lived (Deuteronomy 4:33)? What other nation could claim that Jehovah was on their side as they saw all the miracles God did for them? However, God says that this special treatment, this unique relationship with the one true God, is not a result of anything done by the Israelites. They did nothing to deserve this love; it was freely given to them. They were actually a terribly rebellious and ungrateful people. Yet God still reached down to them and constantly assured them of His love and presence.

People today seek to do things to gain acceptance or affection. They judge their worth by their accomplishments, looks, possessions. But God says He loves His people and it is nothing they do that makes them right with God. It is only God's grace, evidenced most powerfully through the death and resurrection of Jesus, that produces the Maker's love. He chose to love and to save. What's more, He chose to love the least.

Father, humble us when we think we can reach You by
our own strength. When we are discouraged and weary,
let us remember that You love us still. Amen.

Day 242

LOOK UP!

Thy mercy, O LORD, is in the heavens;
and thy faithfulness reacheth unto the clouds.
PSALM 36:5

In Bible times, people often studied the sky. Looking up at the heavens reminded them of God and His mighty wonders. A rainbow was God's sign to Noah that a flood would never again destroy the earth. God used a myriad of stars to foretell Abraham's abundant family, and a single star heralded Christ's birth.

The theme of the heavens traverses the scriptures from beginning to end. The Bible's first words say: "In the beginning God created the heaven[s]." The psalmist David shows God's greatness in comparison to them: "The heavens declare the glory of God" (Psalm 19:1). And in the New Testament, Jesus describes the end times, saying, "There shall be signs in the sun, and in the moon, and in the stars. . . . Then shall [people] see the Son of man coming in a cloud with power and great glory" (Luke 21:25, 27).

Some of God's greatest works have happened in the sky.

This immense space that we call "sky" is a reflection of God's infinite love and faithfulness. It reaches far beyond what one can see or imagine, all the way to heaven. Too often jobs, maintaining households, parenting, and other tasks keep us from looking up. So take time today. Look up at the heavens, and thank God for His endless love.

Heavenly Father, remind me to stop and appreciate Your wonderful creation. And as I look upward, fill me with Your infinite love. Amen.

Day 243

A TRUE HEART

He answered and said unto them, Well hath Esaias prophesied of you hypocrites, as it is written, This people honoureth me with their lips, but their heart is far from me. Howbeit in vain do they worship me, teaching for doctrines the commandments of men.

MARK 7:6–7

Jesus considered the Pharisees hypocrites because they were pretending to honor the Lord so that others would think they were holy and hold them in high regard. But their hearts weren't in it.

God wants our hearts *and* our words. The Bible says in Luke 6:45 that "a good man out of the good treasure of his heart bringeth forth that which is good." What you think and feel inside is eventually what will come out. If your heart isn't really set on the Lord, people will see that your actions don't match up with what you're saying.

When you pray, always be honest with God and with yourself. When asked to pray in public, there is no need to use large, flowery words to impress others. God is the only One who matters.

A man was asked to pray a blessing before a big holiday dinner. He complied but spoke so softly that not many could hear him at all. When he said "amen," the family looked up to see if he was really finished.

"We couldn't hear you!" the family said.

"Well, I wasn't praying to you!" replied the man.

Dear Jesus, let my heart, my words,
and my actions always be true to You. Amen.

Day 244

SEEK GOD

*I love them that love me; and those
that seek me early shall find me.*
PROVERBS 8:17

Did you ever play hide-and-seek as a child? Sometimes it was easy to find your sibling or friend. A foot sticking out from behind the couch or chair was a dead giveaway! Other times, a playmate may have selected a better hiding place. He was harder to find. You searched high and low. You looked behind doors and beneath beds. You lifted quilts and moved aside piles of pillows. But you didn't give up. Not until you found him!

Scripture tells us that God loves those who love Him and that if we search for Him, we will surely find Him.

Seek God in all things and in all ways. Search for Him in each moment of every day you are blessed to walk on this earth. He is found easily in His creation and in His Word. He is with you. Just look for Him. He wants to be found!

*Father in heaven, thank You for Your unfailing love for me.
Help me to search for You diligently. I know that
when I seek, I will find You. Amen.*

Day 245

MELTING POINT

*Now if any man build upon this foundation gold, silver,
precious stones, wood, hay, stubble; every man's work
shall be made manifest. . .because it shall be revealed by fire.*
1 CORINTHIANS 3:12–13

———————— ~ellee~ ————————

Wood, hay, and straw—they all burn. We use them as kindling and fuel.
Apply a flame to each and they leap to life—providing light and heat
until they're totally consumed.

Gold and silver, though, are different. They don't burn; they *melt*.
As they turn from solid to liquid, the impurities of their natural state
burn away.

In a similar way, tribulation reveals the quality of our inner lives. Trials
consume the worthless parts of our character, activities, and spending
habits. What isn't consumed melts, turning our stability on its head. Then
we're prepared for a reformation of what remains.

When we consider what we say, do, purchase, or pursue, we can
use today's verse as our standard. Is our pursuit *ignitable*—temporary
and unimportant—or is it *malleable*—something that can be reshaped
and used as God directs?

What happens when the fires of tribulation blow through our lives?
Do we reach an ignition point or a melting point?

———————— ~oo6oo~ ————————

*Oh Lord God, You test me to transform me into the image
of Your Son. Teach me to invest in what will last
and not that which passes away. Amen.*

Day 246

GO WITH THE FLOW?

And so Pilate, willing to content the people, released Barabbas
unto them, and delivered Jesus, when he had
scourged him, to be crucified.
MARK 15:15

———————— *elle* ————————

Pilate didn't want anything to do with this Jesus fellow. Even his wife had warned him not to get involved. So he stalled. Then he released a murderer and killed an innocent man.

Why? Because Pilate was a bad man? No. To please the crowd.

The people in the crowd, whipped into a self-serving frenzy, chose what they knew—a sinner like them—instead of reaching for something better. That's what crowds do.

We deal with crowds like that all the time, even though they might not be howling in the street. The "crowd" might be school friends who want to ostracize someone, the party crowd who want you to get as drunk as them, even fellow church members who focus on earthly traditions above heavenly love.

As sociable beings, we often enjoy being in groups. Usually they're fun and harmless, and because of that, it's often tempting just to go with the flow. But when the crowd laughingly suggests something that makes your soul hesitate, ask yourself: Are you choosing Barabbas or Jesus?

———————— *ଦ୍ରୋ* ————————

I choose You, Jesus! When the crowd presses in around
me desiring to drive me away from You and Your
teaching—Jesus, I choose You! Amen.

Day 247

GOD, INC.

Bring forth therefore fruits worthy of repentance, and begin
not to say within yourselves, We have Abraham to our father:
for I say unto you, That God is able of these stones
to raise up children unto Abraham.

LUKE 3:8

Being one of the faithful isn't an inherited position, much as some people might like to think so. We aren't automatically saved because our parents were.

Thinking of themselves as the chosen race had made some of the people of Jesus' day lazy about their faith. John pointed out that the *choice* was God's—and they shouldn't give Him cause to regret it.

Imagine God as an employer. He's hiring, but He doesn't want people who think they're owed a job. He doesn't "do" nepotism—you won't get the job because your old man worked for the company way back. God has no place for "seat warmers" in His business. He seeks people who want to be there, people who will "produce fruit" from the raw materials He provides.

God, Inc., is a thriving business that's really going somewhere. There are always vacancies for those willing to work. It's a lifelong, recession-proof position with a wonderful retirement package.

It's too good an opportunity to risk losing through complacency. You can bet those stones would jump at the chance—if stones could jump!

Jesus, put me to work. What can I do to spread Your Word?
How can I recruit others into Your business of salvation?
I am ready, willing, and able, Lord. Amen.

Day 248

THE HAND OF GOD

For I the LORD thy God will hold thy right hand,
saying unto thee, Fear not; I will help thee.
ISAIAH 41:13

If there is a scripture you need to have handy in times of trouble, this is it! Post it on your fridge; write it on a sticky note and put it in your car; commit it to memory so that the Spirit of God can bring it to mind when you need to hear it most.

While you're at it, look for the many other encouraging verses found in scripture. Like Psalm 139, which tells us that God created us and knows everything about us. He knows when we sit and when we get up. Psalm 139:7–10 tells us that no matter where we go, His hand will guide us and hold us.

God's Word is exactly what we need when facing hard times. Heading to the emergency room? Repeat Isaiah 41:13 and remember that God is holding your hand. Afraid of the future? Stop worrying and trust the God who loves you and has great plans for you. Facing a problem that you cannot possibly bear? Take hold of God's mighty hand and believe that He will help you.

Father God, help me not to fear. Take hold of my hand
and guide me. I put my faith and trust in You alone. Amen.

Day 249

GOODBYE AND HELLO

For which cause we faint not; but though our outward man perish,
yet the inward man is renewed day by day. For our light affliction,
which is but for a moment, worketh for us a far more exceeding and
eternal weight of glory; while we look not at the things which are
seen, but at the things which are not seen: for the things which are
seen are temporal; but the things which are not seen are eternal.
2 Corinthians 4:16–18

One of the most difficult things in life is watching a loved one nearing the end of their life. Maybe you know someone who is caring for such a person right now. Those last miles in the earthly journey can be long and hard.

The American author and clergyman Henry van Dyke offers encouragement in his poem "Parable of Immortality." He compares a person to a beautiful and strong ship spreading its sails in the morning breeze and slowly sailing for the horizon. In time, she fades into where the ocean meets the sky, and someone says, "There she goes." But at that exact moment, those on the other side see her appear on the horizon just as strong and powerful as when she began her journey, and they shout joyfully, "Here she comes!"

Isn't it magnificent that God promises Christians eternal life? The journey may be hard, but the destination is magnificent.

Dear God, thank You for the assurance of eternal,
joyful life for all who believe in Jesus. Amen.

Day 250

THUNDER ROARS

Whosoever shall call on the name of the LORD shall be delivered.
JOEL 2:32

—————————— ~~~~~ ——————————

Do you ever tremble with fear? Whether it be from dangers without or emotional distress within, fear can paralyze people. It is as though a hand grips us by the throat and we are pinned in place with nowhere to go. Yet the Lord our God has said do not be afraid, He will save us.

The book of Psalms reveals a man who quivers and hides in caves to escape his enemies. Time and again David calls out to the Lord, because he has been taught that God will calm his fears. The circumstances do not always change, the thunder may still roar, but just like David we can know our lives are secure in the hand of the almighty Creator of the universe. He *will* save us. It's a promise.

Today, make a list of those things that cause you to quake in your boots. Read the list out loud to the Lord and ask Him to provide the necessary bravery to overcome each one. Ask Him to see you through the deep waters and to hold you tightly over the mountaintops. For when you call on His name, He hears and answers. Listen closely and remember He saves.

——————————  ——————————

Father, I'm scared. Please hold me close and calm my anxious heart. Tune my ears to hear Your Word and know what to do. Amen.

Day 251

THE ULTIMATE ACT OF LOVE

Rejoice the soul of thy servant: for unto thee, O Lord, do I lift up my soul. For thou, Lord, art good, and ready to forgive; and plenteous in mercy unto all them that call upon thee.
PSALM 86:4–5

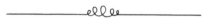

The modern theologian Lewis Smedes once said, "You will know that forgiveness has begun when you recall those who hurt you and feel the power to wish them well." It seems the most unnatural thing in the world for us to forgive someone who has hurt us deeply, let alone hoping good things will happen for them. However, that is really the only loving thing to do.

Forgiveness doesn't require that the person who did the hurting apologize or acknowledge what they've done. It's not about making the score even. It doesn't even require forgetting about the incident. But it is about admitting that the one who hurt us is human, just like we are. We surrender our right for revenge and, like God, let go and give the wrongdoer mercy, therefore blessing them.

Gracious and loving Father, thank You that You love me and have forgiven me my sins. May I be more like You in forgiving others. Although I may not be able to forgive as easily as You do, please encourage me to take those small steps. In forgiving others, Father, I am that much closer to being like You. Amen.

Day 252

JUNGLE OF LIFE

For the word of God is quick, and powerful, and sharper than any twoedged sword, piercing even to the dividing asunder of soul and spirit, and of the joints and marrow, and is a discerner of the thoughts and intents of the heart.

HEBREWS 4:12

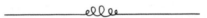

Since the time Adam and Eve disobeyed God, the consequences of sin have often stood between us and God's best for our lives. Choosing a life of faith can feel like we are lost in a jungle, tangled in the underbrush. But God has given us a powerful tool that will cut through the debris of life in a fallen world.

When you take the Bible and live according to God's plans, obeying Him, God's Word cuts like a machete through the entanglements of life. When you choose to use the Sword of Truth, it clears a path and can free you from the weights of the world that try to entrap and ensnare you.

No matter what the challenges of life are saying to you today, take His Word and speak His plans into your life. Choose His words of encouragement and peace instead of the negative things the circumstances are telling you.

God, I want to live in Your Truth. I want to believe what You say about me in the Bible. Help me to speak Your words today instead of letting the problem speak to me. Help me believe. Amen.

Day 253

A WAY OUT

There hath no temptation taken you but such as is common to man: but God is faithful, who will not suffer you to be tempted above that ye are able; but will with the temptation also make a way to escape, that ye may be able to bear it.
1 CORINTHIANS 10:13

———————— ✑✐✐✐ ————————

Is there a hang-up in your life that is hard to get over or get rid of? Temptation comes in all shapes and sizes, so what might be tempting to you isn't a problem for someone else. The opposite is also true. But no matter what hinders you today, everyone has been sidetracked by temptation. We all make mistakes, and whatever is tempting you, you can bet that it has also tripped up many others, too.

Here's the encouraging thing: Whenever you face temptation, God promises to provide a way out. Look for it! In every moment that you are tempted, look for it! Pay attention to the interruptions that occur during temptation and grasp hold of them. They may just be "divine appointments" there to lead the way out!

———————— ✴✴✴✴ ————————

Dear Jesus, I cry out for grace and mercy and praise You that Your love has covered my sin completely. Help me find the way out in every temptation. Amen.

A HEALTHY BODY

*Beloved, I wish above all things that thou mayest
prosper and be in health, even as thy soul prospereth.*
3 JOHN 1:2

————— ✦ —————

If you've ever faced a health crisis or watched a loved one go through a catastrophic illness, you realize the value of good health. There's nothing like almost losing it to realize what you've had all along! In spite of modern technology, great doctors, and the advance of research, health issues persist.

We face seasons when our bodies refuse to cooperate with us. During those times we have to remember who our healer really is. Doctors are great, but ultimately, God is our healer. He longs for us to turn to Him—to trust Him—during our seasons of physical and emotional weakness. He also longs for us to take care of the body He's given us. How can we do this? By watching what we put in it and by getting the proper amount of rest and exercise. Our vessels are precious gifts, and we can't afford to wreck them.

If you're in a rough place health-wise, pour out your heart to the Lord. Ask Him to show you how to best care for yourself. Visit your doctor and get his or her input as well. Working as a team, focus on turning your health issues around.

————— ✦ —————

*Father, I don't want to abuse this precious vessel You've entrusted
to me. I need to take better care of my body. Show me Your
plan for my health, Lord, then guide me as I take
steps toward better health. Amen.*

Day 255

KEEP AN EYE OUT

Therefore we ought to give the more earnest heed to the things
which we have heard, lest at any time we should let them slip.
HEBREWS 2:1

The fishing industry flourished in the Sea of Galilee, since no other freshwater lake existed nearby. This body of water lay nearly seven hundred feet below the level of the Mediterranean Sea, which was about thirty miles to the west.

The nearby hills reached as high as fifteen hundred feet. To the east, mountains with peaks of more than thirty-three hundred feet surrounded the sea, whose name means "circle." The geography created a beautiful but dangerous setting, subject to sudden and violent storms.

The fishing boats commonly used held four men, and a boat's typical small size at that time made it quite vulnerable to vicious weather. If fishermen were careless as to what was happening around them—where they were and if the clouds showed signs of changing—they could find themselves in trouble quickly. Their boat would be carried off by the wind and waves.

A similar slipping away can easily happen to us as we navigate the sea of life. Keeping an open eye for the early warning signs of danger helps us stay on the course God has given us. We need to pay careful attention to all we learned in order to arrive safely at the end of our journey.

Heavenly Father, I know that Satan can find countless ways
to send me off course. Help me to keep my eyes
open and my destination set on You. Amen.

OLDER AND WISER

Likewise, ye younger, submit yourselves unto the elder.
Yea, all of you be subject one to another, and be
clothed with humility: for God resisteth the proud,
and giveth grace to the humble.

1 PETER 5:5

———————— *elle* ————————

Do you suppose teenagers enjoy hearing this verse? If it was only for teens, they might have a right to feel put upon. But it isn't. We can *all* find someone older and wiser, if we have the eyes to look.

So the question is this: Do we have the humility to learn from those older people? If we do, our submission becomes a positive thing. Through it we move onward and upward. If we don't, we set ourselves up as the authority, as people who know it all. That's exactly the kind of person the next generation likes to rebel against and try to topple. So the generations are separated because of pride.

It's tougher to rebel against humility. If our children see the benefits of positive submission—the peace and wisdom it brings—they might follow the example and learn from us. In turn, they become the teachers. It's a process that never ends. We will always be younger than someone, so we'll always have more to learn. And even when we're "old as the hills," we won't be as old as God.

———————— *white* ————————

Father, open my heart to wisdom offered by those older than I am.
Set their wise words inside my heart so I might learn from them
and pass them on to younger generations. Amen.

Day 257

NEVER FAR

How long wilt thou forget me, O LORD? for ever?
how long wilt thou hide thy face from me?
PSALM 13:1

———————— ✑✑✐ ————————

There is no worse feeling than feeling a distance from God. When we cry out in prayer, we need to feel His presence with us. When that feeling is absent, hopelessness and despair set in. We need to know, however, that the Lord has not really gone far from us, but we have pushed Him from ourselves. The Lord is always as close as a prayer, and we need only to open our hearts to Him, and His presence will be felt once again. The Lord never hides His face from us, though often He will wait, stepping back like the loving Father that He is, to see whether or not we can struggle through a problem on our own. God wants to see us grow, and He often has to let us struggle a bit in order to allow that growth to occur. Even in those times of trial, however, the Lord is never far away, and He will not allow us to be tried beyond our endurance.

———————— ✑✐✐ ————————

Help me to know that You are with me in every situation at every
moment of the day. I need Your comforting presence in
my life, Oh Lord. Without it, I cannot go on. Amen.

Day 258

STOP PRETENDING

Let love be without dissimulation.
ROMANS 12:9

Many times in our lives we are hurt deeply by those closest to us. And because they are family members or people that we must maintain a relationship with, we pretend to love them by sweeping issues under the rug. We go through the motions of relating to them in peace while nursing bitterness in our hearts. Mother Teresa said, "If we really want to love we must learn how to forgive."

God wants our relationships to be real. He wants us to be real with Him and real with others. Pretending is being dishonest. He says in Matthew 15:7–8 that the religious leaders honored Him with their lips but their hearts were far from Him. He calls them hypocrites.

Are you hypocritical in your close relationships? Are you pretending to love when you feel nothing even close?

Tell the Lord how you feel. Ask for His help to overcome your fear of sharing your heart and being real with Him and others. Learn how to forgive, and watch as the Lord transforms your relationships into something that honors Him.

Heavenly Father, help me overcome my fear of sharing my true feelings. Forgive me for pretending to love when my heart is not in it. I want to live in authentic relationship with You and with those I love. Amen.

Day 259

IN THE DEPTHS AND SHALLOWS

Out of the depths have I cried unto thee, O LORD.
PSALM 130:1

Funny how some people never ask for help until everything comes crashing down on them. They wait until the last minute, then send out the distress signal. Many people work their relationship with God that way. They call on Him infrequently while things are going well, but when trouble rears its ugly head, they are pounding on His door for help. It is a wise person who learns to include God in everything he does. When God is a full part of your life, you never feel panic when things go wrong. Still, it is good to know that God will hear us when we cry out of the depths and that He will always come to the aid of His children.

Make me remember You in all times, Lord, not just times of trial. Help me to share my whole life with You and to glory in Your presence. Thank You for staying beside me always. Amen.

Day 260

FEARLESS

God is love; and he that dwelleth in love dwelleth in God, and God in him. . . . There is no fear in love; but perfect love casteth out fear: because fear hath torment. He that feareth is not made perfect in love.
1 John 4:16, 18

First John 5:3 says that if we love God, we will do what He commands. It sounds simple enough, but fear can creep in when we consider what it means to show Him complete devotion. Putting Him first in our lives might cost us more than we expect—in our relationships, in our jobs, in how we spend our money or time. We might worry about what others might think of us or fear that we can't accomplish what God calls us to do.

God's unconditional love frees us from fear—the fear of punishment, failure, or harsh judgment from other people—because His opinion of us matters most. Through everything, He has promised to be with us and strengthen us. We may feel ashamed of our fear, but God is not angry. Instead, He gives us exactly what we need to strengthen our faith, whether it's the sign of a damp sheepskin (Gideon, Judges 6) or inviting us to touch His wounds (Jesus to Thomas, John 20:24–29).

Do not fear. Christ shows us the vastness of His love to drive out our worries and anxieties. When we rely on Him, we can accomplish *anything* He asks of us.

Father God, I want to step out in faith and do what You command. Banish my fears by showing me how perfectly You love me. Amen.

Day 261
WISH LIST

They cried the more, saying, Have mercy on us, O Lord,
thou son of David. And Jesus stood still, and called them,
and said, What will ye that I shall do unto you?
MATTHEW 20:31–32

The two blind men heard that Jesus was passing by. They called out a generic plea: "Have mercy on us!"

The man they addressed as Lord and son of David stopped in His tracks. He responded with a simple question: "What do you want?"

Wasn't it obvious? Jesus knew their thoughts and what their hearts desired. But that wasn't enough. They had to verbalize their request: "We want our *sight*"—the one thing they could not receive without divine intervention. Jesus answered their prayer by opening their eyes—and they responded by following Him.

God wants us to bring specific needs to Him. Do you need a job? Tell Him what salary you desire, what kind of work you like to do, and where you want to commute. Do you need a new home? Tell Him exactly what you'd like.

God doesn't *need* us to tell Him our desires. He already knows them. But He delights in going above and beyond what we can ask for. He loves to demonstrate His lavish love. Even if He doesn't give us what we want, it's because He has something better in store.

God wants us to bring the wishes of our hearts to Him in prayer.

Heavenly Father, I thank You that You care about the smallest
details of my life. Teach me the joy of specific prayer. Amen.

Day 262

BREAKDOWN

*And the Lord turned, and looked upon Peter. And Peter
remembered the word of the Lord, how he had said unto him,
Before the cock crow, thou shalt deny me thrice.*

Luke 22:61

What do you think Peter saw when he looked into the eyes of the Lord
he had just abandoned?

In His time of greatest need this King turned to His man and heard
him lie, heard him put his own safety before his previously declared
loyalty. The expression on His face made Peter run away. Not to hide or
go into voluntary exile but to weep bitterly, because, undoubtedly, he
would have seen only love and understanding on Jesus' face.

In a way, it is necessary that we fail, necessary that we are broken
down. How else do we come to realize that the things of this world will
not sustain us? How else do we come to the place where God can build
us back up?

Like others who betrayed their king, Peter died. Those bitter tears
signaled the death of the man he thought he was. But the love of Jesus
allowed him to be reborn as the Peter his Lord knew he really was.

---

*Mighty God, I leave my old self behind. I shed my sinful past
and give my life to You. Shape it into something grand,
something that will bring You glory. Amen.*

Day 263

HEAVENLY VISION

And God shall wipe away all tears from their eyes; and there shall be no more death, neither sorrow, nor crying, neither shall there be any more pain: for the former things are passed away. And he that sat upon the throne said, Behold, I make all things new.
REVELATION 21:4–5

Longing for heaven is a learned longing. How could it be natural when so much beauty exists on this earth for us to see, taste, and touch? As wonderful as this short life can be, it will not compare to what awaits us—seeing the loveliness of the Savior with our own eyes and hearing His voice with our ears, knowing that we will never part from Him.

In His presence, all imperfection, pain, and sadness will vanish, and the earth will be remade. We will be reunited with our loved ones in Christ who were separated from us on Earth by death or distance. The expectation of that day helps us persevere through the hurt and brokenness of the present. Knowing that complete peace and joy lie ahead gives us courage.

Even now, Christ's work isn't on hold—He is making us new by renewing our hearts and strength; He is teaching us how to love as He loves in order to draw more people to Himself. Hold this world loosely, for it will fade in the light of the Savior's face. He who calls us Beloved is coming again soon!

Dear heavenly Father, thank You that You gave us the hope of heaven when You sent Jesus. Give me a heart that longs for heaven and longs for Your presence even more. Amen.

THE DIFFERENCE BARNABAS MADE

*But Barnabas took him, and brought him to the apostles,
and declared unto them how he had seen the Lord in the way,
and that he had spoken to him, and how he had preached
boldly at Damascus in the name of Jesus. And he was
with them coming in and going out at Jerusalem.*
ACTS 9:27–28

Did you know that the man we know as Barnabas was not given that name at birth? His name was Joseph. The apostles later gave him the name Barnabas, which means "one who encourages." Isn't it apparent why he was given this name? Barnabas was an encourager.

When Saul literally "saw the light" on the road to Damascus and instantaneously was converted, there were many who did not believe it. Saul had been a Jew among Jews, a Pharisee, a murderer of Christ followers. The apostles did not want to accept him. They were skeptical. But Barnabas stood up for Saul. He testified to the change of heart he had witnessed in the man. Barnabas not only encouraged Saul, but he encouraged the apostles to accept him as a brother in the Lord. Did this encouragement make a difference? Indeed it did. It caused the apostles to accept Saul into the fold. He went throughout Jerusalem with them, preaching Christ as Savior. You never know when a bold word of encouragement may make all the difference in the world.

*God, use me as an encourager in this world. Allow my bold words
of encouragement to make a difference in the lives of others. Amen.*

Day 265

PREPARE THE WAY!

The voice of him that crieth in the wilderness, Prepare ye the way of the LORD, make straight in the desert a highway for our God.

ISAIAH 40:3

An ancient custom in the Near East required that a representative be sent ahead of a dignitary to prepare the road. He removed obstacles like rocks and boulders and filled in the potholes. Travel was easier when the crooked road became straight and even.

People wanted to get through the hot, parched desert quickly. Travelers were prone to injury while walking on the rocky ruts in the road. If they found the straightest route, they arrived quicker at their destination, often an oasis. Here they found cool refreshing water and much-needed rest to regain their strength to complete their journey.

Our journey in life often veers into the valleys of spiritual dryness. We crave God's living water to quench our thirst, yet feel we are alone on a long, winding highway. We want to do what is right, but stumble over the uneven terrain.

God prepares our way for us and, through Jesus' death and resurrection, removes the obstacles and makes straight our paths. We may still have dry times, but we journey onward, relying on God's strength.

Dear God, like the pillar of fire in Moses' time, You go before me and light my way. You make for me a straight and even path. Thank You, Father God! Amen.

GOD'S WORK

Except the Lord build the house, they labour in vain that build it: except the Lord keep the city, the watchman waketh but in vain.
PSALM 127:1

———— ﾟℓℓℓℓﾟ ————

A great cathedral was constructed to God's glory, while hungry and sick people sat outside its walls. The cathedral was called "The Greatest Achievement in the Name of God." Millions flocked from all over to enter its doors. Thousands went away disturbed that the ministry of the church was contained completely within its walls. As the years passed, the church lost its luster, and it became just another church. The poor were still there, but nothing had been done yet to help them. God must have looked down on the cathedral and said, "This is the poorest excuse for a church I have seen."

When men and women try to take the church out of God's hands, it ceases to be the church. Only churches built on the spiritual rock of salvation can claim to be God's churches. Our achievements in the name of God must bear His signature, not our own, otherwise they have been done in vain. God is the author of all that is good; we are merely His helpers. Whatever God builds will last forever, while humankind's creations crumble to the dust.

———— ﾟ℃℃ﾟ ————

Use my talents to do Your will, Lord, not my own. Remind me that I am doing Your work with You, not my own work for You. Bless all my endeavors in Your name. Amen.

Day 267

ENTERING HIS REST

There remaineth therefore a rest to the people of God.
For he that is entered into his rest, he also hath ceased
from his own works, as God did from his.
HEBREWS 4:9–10

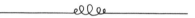

What is the ideal way to practice the Sabbath? Christians have given as many answers to that question as there are ways to spend the day. The Bible teaches that the Sabbath is for resting from the work and cares of the week just like the Father modeled for us when He created the world (Genesis 2:2–3).

In Hebrews, however, Sabbath rest takes on another meaning. The writer of Hebrews exhorts readers to enter God's rest. In the letter's context, this rest is a peace that goes *heart deep*. Instead of fretting that we are not right with God, we point to Christ's perfect life and work, trusting in Him alone to be accepted in God's sight.

Just as God declared that His creation was perfect and complete ("very good") on the seventh day, Christ pronounced His saving work to be perfect and complete ("It is finished") on the cross. We can approach our Creator boldly and without fear of rejection, resting in the knowledge that we are fully pleasing in His sight because of His Son. We do not have to work to be worthy. We can rest in Him.

Dear heavenly Father, help me rest in the work Your Son did to save me. Deepen my faith so that Your peace and Your truth will answer my worrying heart when I fear I am unworthy to be Your child. Amen.

Day 268

A MATTER OF LIFE OR DEATH

For if ye live after the flesh, ye shall die: but if ye through the
Spirit do mortify the deeds of the body, ye shall live.

ROMANS 8:13

A diabetic is dependent upon insulin. A cancer diagnosis demands medical treatment. For the blind, a cane or a seeing-eye dog is essential. These are matters of life and death.

The Bible teaches of another such matter. It is an ongoing war within the believer that simply must be won by the right side! It is spiritual life versus spiritual death.

The Holy Spirit indwells believers in Christ. Jesus Himself taught His followers about this third part of the Trinity before He ascended into heaven. He promised that a Helper would come. This Helper, the Holy Spirit, came when Jesus went away. The Spirit convicts us of sin. The Spirit, sometimes referred to as our Counselor, also guides us in truth.

If you are a Christian, the Holy Spirit is your personal power source. The strength to do what is right is within you if you choose to live by the Spirit and not by the flesh. You will be tempted to follow voices that tell you to do as you please or that "it's okay if it feels right." You will experience anger and other emotions that can lead you astray in life. But if you pay attention, your Helper, the Holy Spirit, will reveal the Father's ways. It is a matter of life *or* death. Which will you choose?

Father, today I choose life. May Your
Holy Spirit lead me in truth. Amen.

Day 269

RENEW YOUR STRENGTH

*But they that wait upon the LORD shall renew their strength;
they shall mount up with wings as eagles; they shall run,
and not be weary; and they shall walk, and not faint.*
ISAIAH 40:31

———————— ✍ ————————

Andrew Murray was a South African writer, teacher, and Christian pastor in the late 1900s who captured the heart of prayer with these words about Jesus: "While others still slept, He went away to pray and to renew His strength in communion with His Father. He had need of this, otherwise He would not have been ready for the new day. The holy work of delivering souls demands constant renewal through fellowship with God."

Each day you give a part of yourself to that day—spiritually, emotionally, physically, financially, and socially. Within each of those areas of life, you need to refuel. Spiritually, the only way to recharge is a renewal that comes from God. Waiting for a fresh outpouring of His life-giving Spirit brings a newness and a fresh perspective on all the other areas of your life. Give your best each day by drawing on the strength of your heavenly Father and spending time with Him.

———————— ✍ ————————

*Heavenly Father, Your Word and prayer are strength to my soul.
Renew me and pour Your life into me. Fill me with Your
power and give me courage for a new day. Amen.*

Day 270

MISSION IMPOSSIBLE

*And he said, The things which are impossible
with men are possible with God.*
LUKE 18:27

As capable as we may be, some things will always remain impossible for us. No matter how much education we get, how determined we are, or how much money we have, some things are out of our control.

Yet just because something is impossible for us doesn't mean we don't have any hope. Where we can't, God can. The God who created the universe, who set the moon and stars in the sky, who put the sun in place, and who brought Lazarus back to life after four days in the grave is a God who knows no limits.

Whatever we face, we can face with confidence. God, who loves us more than anything, will move heaven and earth to fulfill His purpose. And He is a God who likes to show off, who likes to take things to the limit before acting, just so He can get the glory. He is an amazing, all-powerful God, and He cares deeply about each and every one of His children.

It may seem like we are facing the impossible. And left up to us, it may be impossible. But we must never, ever forget. Nothing is impossible with God.

*Dear Father, thank You for being a God of miracles.
Help me to trust in Your ability to accomplish Your purpose,
even when it seems impossible to me. Amen.*

WHISPERS IN THE WIND

Jesus saith unto him, Thomas, because thou hast seen me, thou hast believed: blessed are they that have not seen, and yet have believed.
JOHN 20:29

―――――――――

The wind blew hard, as a good old-fashioned Midwestern rainstorm descended on the town. Trees bent over, their limbs thrashing about. Leaves scattered across yards, and the wind chime clanged a raucous song instead of the gentle, soothing one normally heard.

The wind is invisible. We can feel it as it crosses our skin. We can sometimes smell it as it transports a scent. We can't see *it*, but we can see the effect it has with the blowing leaves. It is powerful. The wind is very much like our faith in God.

We can't see Him. We can't take Him by the hand or even converse with Him face-to-face like we do a friend. But we still know He is present in our lives because we can experience the effects.

God moves among His people, and we can see it. God speaks to His people, and we can hear the still, small voice. And, just like we can feel the wind across our cheeks, we can feel God's presence. We don't need to physically see God to know that He exists and that He's working.

―――――――――

You are like the wind, Lord. Powerful and fast moving, soft and gentle. We may not see You, but we can sense You. Help us to believe, even when we can't see. Amen.

Day 272

I.C.E.

*I will bless the LORD, who hath given me counsel: my reins
also instruct me in the night seasons. I have set the LORD always
before me: because he is at my right hand, I shall not be moved.*
PSALM 16:7–8

Think about the people in your life that you have on speed dial. Whom do you call first when crisis hits? Many phones actually have an I.C.E. programmed at the top of the contact list so that EMTs can have a phone number to call "in case of emergency."

And while having an emergency contact is important and necessary, sometimes we can come to depend on these people more so than God. Especially if our first response to any kind of crisis is to call a best friend, a mentor, or a professional counselor instead of going straight to the Lord. We think that just because our friends have skin on, they'll be able to help us in more tangible ways.

The truth is that God is able to do way more than we could ever ask or imagine (Ephesians 3:20), and He wants us to come to Him with everything first. He will counsel us and set our feet in the right direction.

There is nothing wrong with calling a friend or spiritual mentor and getting godly advice! Oftentimes God uses those very people to help you. The problem arises when we put those people before God.

*Heavenly Father, forgive me for the times that I haven't trusted You
enough with my problems. Help me to come to You first. Amen.*

Day 273

HAND HOLDERS

And it came to pass, when Moses held up his hand, that Israel prevailed: and when he let down his hand, Amalek prevailed. But Moses hands were heavy; and they took a stone, and put it under him, and he sat thereon; and Aaron and Hur stayed up his hands, the one on the one side, and the other on the other side; and his hands were steady until the going down of the sun. And Joshua discomfited Amalek and his people with the edge of the sword.
Exodus 17:11–13

―――――――― ✑ ――――――――

How do you view your pastor? Do you see him as the cheerleader of your congregation, trying to motivate them to be better Christ followers? Perhaps the teacher? Maybe even the ultimate decision maker? The truth is, some pastors feel that they are expected to be all things to all people and to do it with perfection.

Our verse today shows that Moses was an ordinary (but called) person trying to do a huge job by himself. No one could be expected to hold his hands up for the duration of a battle. He needed help. One way we can help our pastors in the work they have been given is by the power of consistent prayer for them personally, for their families, and for their ministry.

―――――――― ✑ ――――――――

Father, our pastors are precious to us. Yet we know they have been given big assignments with sometimes unrealistic expectations. Remind us to keep our pastors, their families, and their ministry in prayer. It is one way we can hold their hands high to You. Amen.

Day 274

ASK IN FAITH

But let him ask in faith, nothing wavering. For he that wavereth is like a wave of the sea driven with the wind and tossed.

JAMES 1:6

———— ✑✑✑ ————

What does it mean to ask God for something *in faith*? Does it mean we believe that He *can* grant our requests? That He *will* grant our requests? Exactly what is required to prove our faith?

These are difficult questions. Many who have prayed for healed bodies and healed relationships have received exactly that, this side of heaven. Others who have prayed for the same things, believing only God could bring healing, haven't received the answers they wanted.

There is no secret ingredient that makes all our longings come to fruition. Yet we still pray in faith that God is who He says He is. That God is good and will use our circumstances to bring about His purpose and high calling in our lives and in the world.

When we don't get the answers we want from God, it's okay to feel disappointed. He understands. But we must never doubt His goodness or His motives. We must stand firm in our belief that God's love for us will never change.

———— ✑✑✑ ————

Dear Father, I know that You are good and that You love me. I know Your love for me will never change, even when my circumstances are hard. Help me cling to Your love, even when You don't give the answers I want. Amen.

Day 275

CASTING CARES

Casting all your care upon him; for he careth for you.
1 PETER 5:7

———— ◦ℓℓℓℓ◦ ————

Do you have tiresome work that beckons, follows, and awaits you? No matter how demanding it is, the way you handle that work can reflect God.

Do you have relationship challenges with a spouse, parent, sibling, friend, or child? The way you handle those challenges can be a bright spot for everyone involved.

Are you fearful about the future, either for yourself or your family? The way you handle that fear can be a blessing into eternity.

Are there health issues that you or a loved one face? What you do with those can speak to the lives of many.

Do your friends, neighbors, or coworkers have things they are deeply struggling with that they have asked you to talk about with them or pray for? Listening and praying can make a world of difference for them in so many ways.

Does it seem that there are too many burdens, people, problems, and things to pray for? Give them all to God. He wants to take care of every one.

———— ◦◦◦◦◦ ————

*Lord God, thank You for being the sovereign
Almighty who can handle all of the cares we have. Amen.*

Day 276

THANK YOU, LORD

I will bless the LORD at all times:
his praise shall continually be in my mouth.
PSALM 34:1

―――――― ‿‿‿ ――――――

While imprisoned, the apostle Paul gave thanks to God, even singing His praises, and it resulted in the salvation of the jailer. What a great lesson for every Christian—when you feel least like giving thanks, that's precisely when you should!

What is your response when you find yourself trapped in traffic, late for a meeting, frustrated in your plans, sick in bed, hurting emotionally, overwhelmed with work, lonely, tired, or confused? Our human nature teaches us we should gripe and fret. Yet scripture says we should give thanks. Only when we surrender our lives to Him and His control is this possible.

Learn to thank Him. Thank Him for being your help in times of trouble. Thank Him for His great wisdom and power. And thank Him for causing every situation in your life to work together for your good.

Giving thanks may not change your circumstances significantly, but it will change you. You'll feel yourself focusing on God—His goodness, kindness, and grace—rather than your own anger, pride, sickness, or inconvenience. Maybe that's why it's such fertile soil for miracles. The biblical commentator Matthew Henry stated it well: "Thanksgiving is good, but thanks-living is better."

―――――― ‿‿‿ ――――――

Lord, I choose to give You thanks today for whatever comes my way.
I love You, Lord, and I am grateful for Your goodness. Amen.

PRAYER TOUCHES GOD

A devout man, and one that feared God with all his house,
which gave much alms to the people, and prayed to God alway.
ACTS 10:2

In the book of Acts, a centurion named Cornelius received a vision from God. Though a Gentile, this man loved God, praying and fasting regularly. While he prayed, an angel of the Lord told Cornelius that God heard and honored his prayers. Accordingly, God instructed the centurion to go talk to Peter, God's servant.

Peter, having received a vision that God would cleanse and accept anyone whom the Jews deemed "unclean," agreed to meet this Gentile despite Jewish law. Cornelius invited his Gentile neighbors, friends, and family members when he met Peter in Caesarea. Realizing God orchestrated the meeting, Peter preached the Gospel to Cornelius and all who joined him, and the entire group of Gentiles received the Holy Spirit (Acts 10:44–48).

Jesus takes note of a praying, giving heart like Cornelius had. Denominations mean little, while a contrite, teachable spirit touches God. Cornelius was a good, God-fearing man who needed to hear about salvation through Christ. So God honored his prayers and led him to the preacher—while teaching the preacher a thing or two at the same time.

Have you hesitated to share your faith with someone you think unseemly or beyond your realm of comfort? Begin now. Look what happened when Peter did.

Father, forgive me for my self-righteousness. Open the way for me to witness to whomever You have prepared to hear the Gospel. Amen.

START YOUR DAY WITH GOD

My voice shalt thou hear in the morning, O Lord; in the morning
will I direct my prayer unto thee, and will look up.

PSALM 5:3

Mornings are hard for a lot of people—especially night owls who get more done in the evening. And verses like this one can make night owls feel like they aren't as spiritual as those who get up early to be with God.

The reality is that God wants to be the very center of your life. He doesn't want to be at the top of your priority list—just another box to check off each day. He wants your heart and attention morning, noon, and night. You won't get more points with God if you read ten Bible verses before your morning cup of coffee.

So how can you start your day with God even if you haven't gotten up hours earlier for devotions? As you wake up in the morning, thank the Lord for a new day. Ask Him to control your thoughts and attitude as you make the bed. Thank Him for providing for you as you toast your bagel. Ask that your self-image be based on your relationship with Christ as you get dressed and brush your teeth. Continue to pray as you drive to work or school. Spend time in His Word throughout the day. End your day by thanking Him for His love and faithfulness.

God wants a constant relationship with you, and He is available and waiting to do life with you twenty-four hours a day.

Dear Lord, thank You for the gift of a new day. Help me be
aware of Your constant presence in my life. Amen.

Day 279

WALK A MILE IN THE MASTER'S SHOES

*And beside this, giving all diligence, add to your
faith virtue; and to virtue knowledge.*
2 Peter 1:5

———————

Remember when you bought a new pair of shoes and had to break them in? They tended to pinch the toes a bit. But after a few weeks, they conformed to your foot and became more comfortable. So it is with the Christian life. When we start out on our walk of faith, it's not always a comfortable journey; we try to emulate Christ and His ways, to walk in His shoes, and we need to learn it takes time to get the correct fit.

God, in His infinite grace and mercy, knows we'll stumble. We can place our hope in Him with confidence that He'll understand. He's not there with a "giant thumb" to squash us as we toddle along, new in our spiritual walk. He doesn't look for opportunities to say, "Aha, you messed up!" Quite the contrary: He encourages us with His Word.

For example, we read that the patriarchs in the Bible weren't perfect. Filled with flaws, David was still called "a man after [God's] own heart" (Acts 13:22). In the same way, as we grow and learn with the aid of the Spirit, our lives will also reflect more of Him. And as we grow ever more sure-footed, we'll reach our destination—to be like our Father.

———————

Gracious Lord, thank You for Your ever-present guidance. Amen.

Day 280

JUST IN TIME

Let us therefore come boldly unto the throne of grace, that we may obtain mercy, and find grace to help in time of need.

HEBREWS 4:16

As believers, our lives become exciting when we wait on God to direct our paths, because He knows what is best for us at any given moment. His plans and agenda are never wrong. We just need to practice living on His schedule and spending time in prayer. But that's easier said than done! Often we are chomping at the bit, and it's hard to wait.

Once we fully realize He knows best and turn our lives over to the Spirit for direction, we can allow God to be in charge of our calendar; His timing is what is paramount.

When chomping at the bit for something we yearn for, His timing might seem slow. "Hurry up, God!" we groan. But when we learn to patiently wait on His promises, we will see the plans He has for us are more than we dared hope—or dream. God promises to answer us; and it never fails to be just in time.

Lord, I want Your perfect will in my life.
Help me learn to wait upon You. Amen.

Day 281

BUILDING FRIENDSHIPS

A friend loveth at all times, and a brother is born for adversity.
PROVERBS 17:17

Today's world isn't designed for friendship. It's too fast paced, with too many demands and too much stress. Oh, we're connected to everyone all the time through text messaging and cell phones and social media. But as fun as technology may seem, it robs us of face-to-face time. We're so distracted with everything at once, we find it hard to focus on one thing, one person at a time.

But friendship demands one-on-one, face-to-face time. And although most of us don't feel we have a lot of time to give, we must! We simply must make friendship, and building real flesh-and-blood relationships, a priority.

God created us for relationships. And although a well-timed email or text message may lift us up at times, there's simply no replacement for a real, live hug. There's no substitute for a friend sitting beside you in the hospital, holding your hand. And we won't have those things unless we're willing to put aside our high-tech gadgets and invest time in the people around us.

Today, let's make it a point to turn off our cell phones. Let's step away from our computers for a while and have a real conversation with someone. That person may just turn out to be a true friend.

Dear Father, teach me to be a true friend. Help me to make friendship a priority and invest in the people around me. Amen.

Day 282

ARE THERE ANY QUESTIONS?

He hath made every thing beautiful in his time: also he hath set the world in their heart, so that no man can find out the work that God maketh from the beginning to the end.

ECCLESIASTES 3:11

Our souls know there is a God. The souls of unbelievers know it too. By setting "the world in their heart," God gave us a longing for Him. That deep desire is fulfilled in those who accept Jesus, but those who deny Him have to find something else to scratch the itch. That unfulfilled longing is the best explanation for abuses of alcohol, drugs, and power.

Of course, earthly desires are traps, but sometimes they are even used by believers to bolster faith weakened by a lack of understanding. Our human nature needs to understand. It's a problem that holds many a believer and unbeliever back. No one can completely "find out the work that God maketh." That's what makes Him God. And yet, still we try.

Thankfully, our hearts don't need to understand; neither do they need earthly "fixes." They just need to be set free, to find God and revel in the beauty of His never-ending Creation. Believers, stop letting unanswerable questions prevent you from loving Him more completely. And unbelievers, ask yourself, if you had every material thing you could want, wouldn't your heart still be reaching out for eternity?

I have questions, God, so many unanswered questions about life and about You. Increase my trust in You. Help me to set aside my uncertainty and delight in Your never-ending love. Amen.

Day 283

FIX YOUR THOUGHTS

*Finally, brethren, whatsoever things are true, whatsoever things
are honest, whatsoever things are just, whatsoever things are
pure. . .if there be any virtue, and if there be any
praise, think on these things.*

PHILIPPIANS 4:8

In a world loaded with mixed messages and immorality of every kind, it becomes increasingly difficult to have pure thoughts and clear minds. What can believers do to keep their minds set on Christ? Replace the negative message with a positive message from God's Word.

Think about the negative messages that you struggle with the most. Maybe you struggle with some of these: You're not attractive. You're not spiritual enough. You've made a lot of mistakes, etc.

Dig through the scriptures and find truth from God's Word to combat the false message that you're struggling with. Write the passages down and memorize them. Here are a few to get you started:

- God looks at my heart, not my outward appearance. (1 Samuel 16:7)
- I am free in Christ. (1 Corinthians 1:30)
- I am a new creation. My old self is gone! (2 Corinthians 5:17)

The next time you feel negativity and false messages slip into your thinking, fix your thoughts on what you know to be true. Pray for the Lord to replace the doubts and negativity with His words of truth.

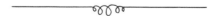

*Lord God, please control my thoughts and help me
set my mind and heart on You alone. Amen.*

Day 284

BREATH OF LIFE

He healeth the broken in heart, and bindeth up their wounds.
PSALM 147:3

As a result of sin, every person on the earth is born into a fallen world. The sinful condition brings hurt and heartache to all men—those who serve the Lord and those who don't. The good news is, as a child of God, you have a hope and eternal future in Christ. Jesus said, "These things I have spoken unto you, that in me ye might have peace. In the world ye shall have tribulation: but be of good cheer; I have overcome the world" (John 16:33).

When your life brings disappointment, hurt, and pain that are almost unbearable, remember that you serve the One who heals hearts. He knows you best and loves you most. When the wind is knocked out of you and you feel like there is no oxygen left in the room, let God provide you with the air you need to breathe. Breathe out a prayer to Him and breathe in His peace and comfort today.

Lord, be my breath of life, today and always. Amen.

BEHAVE YOURSELF!

I will behave myself wisely in a perfect way. O when wilt thou come unto me? I will walk within my house with a perfect heart.

PSALM 101:2

_____

Home is where the heart is.

Home is a refuge, a place of rest.

Home is the smell of fresh-baked bread, the sound of laughter, the squeeze of a hug.

Because home is a place of comfort and relaxation, it is also the place where we are most likely to misbehave. We would never think of yelling at family members in public, for example, but if they push our buttons *just once* at home, we will instantly level them with a verbal machine gun.

David himself knew the danger of walking unwisely at home. He was home—not in battle—when he saw Bathsheba on the rooftop. His psalm reminds us that we must behave wisely all the time, but especially at home.

Because more is caught than taught, our family must see mature behavior from us. We must model integrity—we must keep our promises and act the way we want those around us to act. Hypocrisy—"Do as I say, not as I do"—has no place in the home of a mature Christian who has been made complete in Christ.

May God grow us up into maturity, and may we walk accordingly, especially at home.

_____

Father God, how often I fail at home. Make me sensitive to the Spirit so that I will recognize when I am straying from the path of maturity. I'm an adult; help me to act like one. Amen.

Day 286

YOUR HEART'S DESIRE

*Trust in the LORD, and do good; so shalt thou dwell in the land,
and verily thou shalt be fed. Delight thyself also in the LORD: and he
shall give thee the desires of thine heart. Commit thy way unto the
LORD; trust also in him; and he shall bring it to pass.*
PSALM 37:3–5

It's easy to look at this verse and think, "Hey, if I just delight in the Lord,
He'll give me everything I want!" But when we really start to delight in
the Lord, God changes our hearts so completely that all we ever want
is what *He* wants. When you commit everything you do to the Lord, you
will begin to see how your desires line up with God's desires.

What does this look like in everyday life? Start your morning with
thankfulness. Ask God to bless your day and to provide opportunities
to be a blessing to those you encounter. Interact with God about each
issue and problem you face. Thank Him for big and little blessings
that come your way. Seek His will and guidance when you make plans.
Pray for loved ones that don't know Christ. Intercede for friends and
neighbors who need divine help. Be on the lookout for new ways to
delight yourself in the Lord.

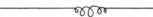

*Lord, I commit my whole heart to You—and all of my plans and ideas.
I want Your will in my life. Thank You for Your blessings and Your great
love for me. Show me how to delight in You, Lord. I love You. Amen.*

STAY TEACHABLE

And when he was disposed to pass into Achaia,
the brethren wrote, exhorting the disciples to receive him.
ACTS 18:27

Apollos was a powerhouse for the Lord. The scriptures describe him as "an eloquent man, and mighty in the scriptures. . . . He spake and taught diligently the things of the Lord" (Acts 18:24–25).

So it's interesting that even with those credentials, Priscilla and Aquila, having heard him, invited him to their house for additional teaching. Afterward, Apollos desired to preach in Achaia, and the couple encouraged him to do so. They immediately contacted the disciples there to welcome him. The result? Apollos refuted the Jews in public debate, proving that Jesus was the Messiah while helping the apostles at the same time (Acts 18:27–28).

We all have room for spiritual growth and godly knowledge no matter how long we have known the Lord. The Bible encourages us to encourage one another. What would happen to advance the kingdom if every believer, despite their position or spiritual seniority, exercised the humility of Apollos? Though scholarly, he accepted more instruction from other believers, who, in turn, encouraged his ministry. Jealousy, pride, or one-upmanship didn't exist.

We are to encourage one another, just as God encourages us.

Lord, keep me teachable so that I can become more effective
for You to encourage others in their ministries. Amen.

Day 288

WORKING HARD

And whatsoever ye do, do it heartily,
as to the Lord, and not unto men.
COLOSSIANS 3:23

Paul told his readers to work hard, with all their heart. Many of the new converts were enslaved to non-Christian masters. The tension between Christians and non-Christians increased when the non-Christian had the authority to lord it over the Christian.

But the wisdom in this verse applies to us today. We should always work hard, always give our best, even if we don't like our bosses. Ultimately, the quality of work we do reflects on our Father. If we're lazy or if our work is below standard, it has a negative impact on the body of Christ. But when we meet our deadlines and our work exceeds expectations, we give others a positive impression of what it means to be a Christian.

If we want to get ahead in our jobs and we want to help build the kingdom of God, we must have impeccable reputations. One way to build a positive reputation is to be a hard worker. When we do our absolute best at any task, people notice. When we consistently deliver quality products and services, people notice. We honor God and we honor ourselves when we work hard at the tasks we've been given.

Dear Father, I want to honor You with the work I do.
Help me to work hard, with all my heart. Amen.

Day 289

PRAYING FOR PEACE

Pray for the peace of Jerusalem: they shall prosper that love thee.
PSALM 122:6

With the news of yet another outbreak of unrest in the Middle East, this phrase comes to mind: "Pray for the peace of Jerusalem." One might think that King David had prophetically understood how war-torn this area of the world would be over the centuries. And, while it is good for us to pray for peace from war in Jerusalem and other places in the world, we should also be praying for peace with God.

As the Prince of Peace, Jesus overcame the world—its wars, pain, and evil. Jesus is the way to peace, both our inner peace and the peace of the world. But it all begins with us as we seek God's will for our lives, get closer to Him, quiet our minds, and listen to that still, small voice. There can be no lasting peace anywhere without us being renewed day by day, praying for inner peace, growth of grace, and the love of ourselves and others.

Dear Father, thank You for sending the Prince of Peace to be our peace. Let me be a peacemaker by praying for peace for Jerusalem and elsewhere. I pray that I can be an instrument of Your peace and show love so that others will seek to love You with all their heart. You are the God of peace; bless me with Your peace forever. Amen.

Day 290

THY ROD AND STAFF

Yea, though I walk through the valley of the shadow of death,
I will fear no evil: for thou art with me; thy rod
and thy staff they comfort me.

PSALM 23:4

———— ❧ℓℓℓ ————

Do a rod and a staff sound comforting to you? These well-known verses in Psalm 23 bring hope to many people, yet little is mentioned about the shepherd's tools—the rod and staff.

Sheep traveled into valleys for food and water, but the valley also contained danger. The high ridges created perfect places for lions and coyotes to wait to snatch an innocent lamb. Anticipating new grass, sheep often wandered away where they slipped into swamps or fell down steep cliffs. Tiny flies bit their ears.

But the shepherd was prepared. He constantly watched over his flock for any signs of danger. With his tall staff with crooked end, he could snare a sheep from a swamp or guide it in fast-moving waters. His rod, a short stick with leather strips on the end, kept the flies and mosquitoes away and could be used in cleaning and grooming.

As stubborn, somewhat dumb creatures, we (like sheep) get into dangerous situations in the valleys of life. But the Lord stays with us, protecting us from the nuisances, cleaning us of our sins, and redeeming us when we fall.

———— ⦾⦿⦿⦾ ————

Lord, You are my shepherd. You direct me where I should
go, steer me from danger, and rescue me when I stray.
You never leave me, and I am so grateful. Amen.

Day 291

WHAT NEXT?

*If any of you lack wisdom, let him ask of God, that giveth to all men
liberally, and upbraideth not; and it shall be given him.*

JAMES 1:5

Ever been lost in an unfamiliar place? Trees block street signs, and other streets aren't marked at all; construction causes confusing, squiggly detours. Embarrassment or even panic grows as the minutes pass.

In life, we hit unexpected detours that make us unsure where to turn next. They might be difficult decisions involving family, healthcare, jobs, or relationships at church. Maybe the weight is migrating from the tension in your shoulders to settle in your heart.

The good news is that our heavenly Father knows the way out of our confusion and will help us when we are at our most frantic. James tells us that God promises to give wisdom to those who ask for it in faith; He gives wisdom "liberally," and He "upbraideth not." Sometimes it's intimidating to ask for advice from others, but God doesn't look down on us for admitting our weakness. He chooses to lavish His love and His gifts on error-prone people because they are a part of His family in Christ. We can entrust ourselves and our lives to our heavenly Father, knowing that through Christ we have access to "all the treasures of wisdom and knowledge" that our Savior possesses (Colossians 2:3).

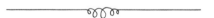

*Dear heavenly Father, thank You that You have my days planned
out for me and I am safe in Your hands. Please grant me
wisdom when I am at a loss and help my spirit be
sensitive to Your Spirit's leading. Amen.*

SINS OF THE FATHERS

*What mean ye, that ye use this proverb concerning the land
of Israel, saying, The fathers have eaten sour grapes,
and the children's teeth are set on edge?*
EZEKIEL 18:2

───────── ℓℓℓℓ ─────────

The Jews of Ezekiel's day were basically saying, "Our fathers sinned, and we're suffering for their sins." They had it wrong. It wasn't just their *fathers* that God was punishing for their idol worship and sins and disobedience. It was *them*! They were suffering for their *own* sins because they were just like their fathers (see also Matthew 23:29–32).

The people of Judah were lamenting that they were innocent but suffering for their ancestors' sins of hating God in fulfillment of Exodus 20:5. They failed to see that by not loving and obeying God, they too were part of the "hate God" generation and were being punished for it.

God told them to stop using that proverb and declared that every person would be punished for their disobedience or blessed for their obedience. It didn't matter how bad a man's father had been: if that man broke the bad habits he'd been taught, loved God, and did what was right, he'd be blessed (Ezekiel 18:3–18).

We are the products of our upbringing, too, but we can break free of the negative heritage and love and serve God. We can make the right decisions.

───────── ∞∫∫∫∞ ─────────

*Father God, You whisper in my heart what is right and what
is wrong. Help me always to make right decisions
that align with Your will. Amen.*

JUST THE PITS

*But as for you, ye thought evil against me;
but God meant it unto good.*
GENESIS 50:20

We can speak of ourselves as "being in the pits," which is symbolic of deep difficult experiences in life. Many times we are in the pits because of our mistakes and wrongdoings. But sometimes there's no explanation. And while in that pit, we can become comfortable. The pit makes us bitter, or we can let it make us better.

In Genesis, Joseph's brothers threw him into a pit to end his life. Instead, he was sold into slavery and had many life experiences that transformed him into a godly man. He experienced extremes in life—literally from rags to riches. Yet his character shone through because whether in the pits or the palace, his faithfulness to God never wavered. He defined his success as doing God's will. Then he was able to see the evil turned into good.

It might take some time to get to a mountaintop when we're in the valley, but we can struggle out of the murky depths with God's help. The Holy Spirit within can enable us to turn things around so we are at least on level ground.

*Dear Lord, help me. I'm so down I don't know which way is up.
Please, Father, take me by the hand and pull me from this pit. Amen.*

FAN THE FLAME

*Wherefore I put thee in remembrance that
thou stir up the gift of God, which is in thee.*
2 TIMOTHY 1:6

In his letter to Timothy, Paul exhorted his spiritual son to "stir up the gift of God" within. Literally, this directive meant to blow the coals into a flame as one would stir embers under a fire. A similar metaphor in Latin, *excitare igniculos ingenii*, means to "stir up the sparks of genius."

This passage is a reminder to every believer. It demonstrates that our God-given gifts remain strong only through active use and fostering. Gifts left unattended or unused become stagnant and, like an unattended fire, die. But if, like the parable of the talents, we continue to exercise the gifts God gives us, they will increase, strengthen, and even multiply.

Just as wood or coal fuels a fire, faith, prayer, and obedience are the fresh fuels of God's grace that keep our fires burning. But this takes action on our part. Are you using the gifts God has given you? Can He entrust you with more? Perhaps today is the day to gather the spiritual tinder necessary to stoke the fire of God within.

God, You have given me special talents and inspiring gifts. I pray, open my eyes to sharing those gifts. Through faith and obedience I will use them to serve You. Amen.

Day 295

HANG IN THERE

But let patience have her perfect work,
that ye may be perfect and entire, wanting nothing.
JAMES 1:4

Perseverance can't be rushed. The only way to develop perseverance is to endure pressure, over a long period of time. A weight lifter must gradually add more weight if he wants to build up his muscles. A runner must run farther and farther, pushing past what is comfortable. If these athletes want to grow and improve, they must persevere through pressure, over time.

The same is true for our faith. If we want to grow as Christians, we have to endure pressure. God allows difficult things into our lives to help build our strength and endurance. Just as the athlete who gives up at the first sign of hardship will never improve, the Christian who abandons faith during times of distress will never reach maturity.

No one ever said the Christian life was an easy one. In fact, Christ told us we'd endure hardships of many kinds. But He also said not to get discouraged. When we stick it out and follow Him no matter what, we will become mature and complete, perfectly fulfilling God's plan for our lives.

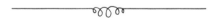

Dear Father, help me to persevere when life gets hard. Help me cling
to You and do things Your way, even when it feels like I can't go on.
I trust that You won't give me more than I can handle and
You're working to make me mature. Amen.

Day 296

CHOOSE HAPPY

A merry heart doeth good like a medicine:
but a broken spirit drieth the bones.
PROVERBS 17:22

Feeling gloomy, blue, out of sorts? Do you have an Eeyore personality, always "down in the dumps"? Scripture exhorts us to choose joy, to choose happy. And it's not always an easy task.

When a person is ill, a gloomy spirit can make it difficult for God's healing power to work. William J. Parker, a theologian, stated, "Let the patient experience an inward awareness of [God's] healing force and let him overcome his heaviness of heart and he will find his new outlook to be like medicine." Despite the sickness, we look to our heavenly Father for encouragement and strength, a heavenly tonic. A glad heart heals us from within and also helps those who come into the circle of its influence.

At times it might seem impossible to cultivate a cheerful outlook on life, but in our Christian walk it should become an intentional act as much as learning to control our temper or to be kind. This new spirit within grows from a faith that all things can work together for good when we walk in God's light and look to Him for everything.

Dear Lord, today my spirit is heavy, my heart downtrodden. Help me
lift my eyes to You and choose to believe You are at work in my life.
Create in me a happy, clean heart, Oh Lord. Amen.

Day 297

SEEK PEACE

Depart from evil, and do good; seek peace, and pursue it.
The eyes of the Lord are upon the righteous,
and his ears are open unto their cry.
PSALM 34:14–15

If something is worth searching for, it is often very valuable. Pirates search for treasure. We search for lost keys. A woman may search for just the right dress for a party. Children playing hide-and-seek search for the participant who is hiding—in order to win the game!

God's Word, in the Psalms, tells us to search for peace. Peace is more valuable than all of the wealth on earth. To lay your head on your pillow at night and know that you are at peace with God and with those around you is a tremendous blessing. True peace is known only by the Christian. The world offers counterfeit versions, but only God can give true and lasting peace that passes all understanding. Seek peace. Search for it. Protect its presence in your life at all costs. If you are on a path that does not bring you peace, you are on the wrong path. Ask God to give you the strength to say no to the things that curtail peace in your life. Peace is essential.

Father, help me to find peace. Reveal to me any area of my life
that is not pleasing to You, so that I might rid myself of it. I want to
be at peace with You and with those around me. Amen.

MAKES SENSE!

*Beware lest any man spoil you through philosophy and
vain deceit, after the tradition of men, after the
rudiments of the world, and not after Christ.*

COLOSSIANS 2:8

"There is no such thing as absolute truth." Ever heard an argument like this? It sounds good on the surface—until you take a step back and start to ponder its meaning. The trouble with this statement is that it declares an absolute truth while maintaining that there is no such thing.

Adam and Eve were deceived in the garden, as the serpent manipulated truth and logic into something that seemingly justified evading God's established guidelines. This legacy of deception continues in our modern world. Positions and viewpoints that appear intellectually solid at first glance break down upon further examination of their components and consequences.

Human logic falls apart in the face of divine wisdom. Worldly philosophy captures and enslaves; the all-knowing, omniscient presence of God radiates both truth and grace. What arguments have you heard lately that have their origins in the roots of this world, rather than the fullness of Christ?

---

*Oh mighty God, keep me focused on the truth of Your Word.
Remind me to dig deep to the roots of human logic
to determine if You planted its seed. Amen.*

Day 299

ARE YOU SURE?

He staggered not at the promise of God through unbelief;
but was strong in faith, giving glory to God.
ROMANS 4:20

———— *elle* ————

Doubt and uncertainty can upend us if we let them. When we are unsure of something, our steps falter, our words stutter, and our hearts rattle in our chests. Fear can set in. We must guard against this anxious spirit and trust the word God has spoken. To protect against an onslaught of concern, we must learn to lean on Him and allow the Holy Spirit to flow within us.

Paul wrote about doubting God's promises and said that feeling can only be combated by rejoicing. He—who was chained, in prison, shipwrecked, and often in danger—speaks of singing praises and being full of joy! But how, in our world, are we able to overcome our moods and rejoice? It is difficult, most certainly, and has to be a conscious choice. Steeping your heart in the Word of God, knowing verses that will comfort you, is a great beginning.

A doubting spirit is not of God, for He is not the author of confusion. Theologian Matthew Henry stated, "God honours faith; and great faith honours God." To truly give Him the glory, we must trust. Of this we are sure.

————  ————

Lord, help us in our unbelief. Our very human nature causes us
to look to the right and to the left. Help us to keep our
focus on You and to trust implicitly. Amen.

Day 300

GOD'S LOVE SONG

The LORD thy God in the midst of thee is mighty; he will save,
he will rejoice over thee with joy; he will rest in his love,
he will joy over thee with singing.

ZEPHANIAH 3:17

God's passion for His people shows itself in many ways.

His mighty power saves us. He delights in us. His love brings peace and quietness to our hearts. And His pleasure is revealed as He rejoices over us with singing.

Angels sang the night Jesus was born (Luke 2:13–14). The psalms are full of lyrics people have used to praise God over the centuries. And Revelation 5:11–12 paints a glorious picture of heaven, complete with continual songs of praise.

But there is a song that's been written just for you. It has your name as its title. And the composer, God Himself, sings your song over you as you go about life here on earth.

Close your eyes. Listen carefully. Do you hear God's melodious voice? He's singing your song. Raise your voice and join Him in the heavenly music!

Oh Lord, what a powerful image—Your voice singing to
me—my song: a melodic poem, an encouraging refrain,
a gentle lullaby. Open my ears to Your voice! Amen.

Day 301

UNCHAINED!

For ye have not received the spirit of bondage again to fear; but ye have received the Spirit of adoption, whereby we cry, Abba, Father.
ROMANS 8:15

Imagine how difficult life would be inside prison walls. No sunlight. No freedom to go where you wanted when you wanted. Just a dreary, dark existence, locked away in a place you did not choose, with no way of escape.

Most of us can't even imagine such restrictions. As Christians we have complete freedom through Jesus Christ, our Lord and Savior. No limitations. No chains.

Ironically, many of us build our own walls and choose our own chains. When we give ourselves over to fear, we're deliberately entering a prison the Lord never intended for us. We don't always do it willfully. In fact, we often find ourselves behind bars after the fact, then wonder how we got there.

Do you struggle with fear? Do you feel it binding you with its invisible chains? If so, then there's good news. Through Jesus, you have received the Spirit of adoption. A child of the most high God has nothing to fear. Knowing you've been set free is enough to make you cry, "Abba, Father!" in praise. Today, acknowledge your fears to the Lord. He will loose your chains and set you free.

Lord, thank You that You are the great chain breaker! I don't have to live in fear. I am Your child, and You are my Daddy-God! Amen.

Day 302

HURT HAPPENS—LOVE ANYWAY

As the Father hath loved me,
so have I loved you: continue ye in my love.
JOHN 15:9

Do you ever feel like Jesus overcame life's challenges more easily than you because He was God? It's important to realize that Jesus lived His life as a man—empowered just as you are today as a believer. He relied on His relationship with God and the Holy Spirit working in Him to do all that He did. He too was human. He suffered pain, hurt, and disappointment just as you do.

Imagine His feelings when brothers, sisters, aunts, uncles, and cousins refused to believe He was the Messiah or discounted His words of truth because He was family. How painful it must have been to have those closest to Him reject Him. Jesus knew that Judas would betray Him and that Peter would deny Him. Jesus must have felt that hurt deeply—and yet He loved them anyway. In the face of the cross, He asked God to forgive those who put Him there.

When faced with pain or disappointment, it's easier to become angry, defend yourself, or even sever the relationship. The same Spirit that empowered Jesus to live His faith can empower you. When hurt happens—choose to love anyway!

Lord, You have shown me how to respond in love.
Give me strength by Your Holy Spirit to love others in the
face of pain, disappointment, and hurt. Comfort me and
provide ways for me to show love to others. Amen.

PLEASE GOD

For do I now persuade men, or God? or do I seek to please men?
for if I yet pleased men, I should not be the servant of Christ.
GALATIANS 1:10

———————— ℓℓℓℓℓ ————————

"Why does she stay with him?" Or, "Oh, he could do so much better than her." Who hasn't seen someone stay in a one-sided relationship, trying desperately to please a self-centered partner? It's often a tragic waste of love. And to what end? To win the affections of a flawed individual?

Everyone who puts their faith in this world ends up trying to please a flawed individual or system. It might be a partner, relative, or boss. We give them credit for being somehow better than us, but they are, after all, only human. Even our best attempts to fulfill their noblest desires could never be better than imperfect.

There is someone out there who can take our love and make it all it should be. Through Him the romantic ideal of "happy ever after" becomes a reality. He has already died for us, and what greater sacrifice could a lover make?

No earthly partner or authority figure could give more or do more with what we have to offer. So why focus on humans when we could do so much better?

———————— 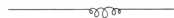 ————————

Jesus, You must really love me to have suffered and given Your
life for me. You loved me before any human did, and Your
love for me lasts forever. I love You too. Amen.

MADE BY GOD

I will praise thee; for I am fearfully and wonderfully made:
marvellous are thy works; and that my soul knoweth right well.
PSALM 139:14

The potter sat at his wheel, turning the clay into beautiful pots. It was hypnotizing to watch. After a time, the pot looked as though it was emerging directly from the potter's hand. With love and care, the potter put his style and mark on every piece he created. Each piece was different, but each bore the striking mark of its maker.

We too are fearfully and wonderfully made. We are individual, yet we bear the stamp of our maker. God's image dwells within us all. With love and care we are fashioned, emerging from the Father's hand, and one day we will return to Him, where we will be afforded a place of honor and love. God's works are marvelous, and His Spirit fills them all.

By Your hand I came into being. Make me useful, Lord, to do what
I was created for. Then, when the time comes, I may stand before
You, fulfilled and confident that I have served You well. Amen.

Day 305

I AM

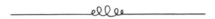

And God said unto Moses, I Am That I Am: and he said, Thus shalt thou say unto the children of Israel, I Am hath sent me unto you.
EXODUS 3:14

The words *I Am* ring out in the present tense. These words are used some seven hundred times in the Bible to describe God and Jesus. When Moses was on the mount and asked God who He was, a voice thundered, "I Am." In the New Testament, Jesus said of Himself, "I am the bread of life; I am the light of the world; I am the Good Shepherd; I am the way; I am the resurrection." Present tense. Words of hope and life. I Am.

Who is God to you today? Is He in the present tense? Living, loving, presiding over your life? Is the Lord of Lords "I Was" or "I've Never Been" to you? Have you experienced the hope that comes from an everlasting "I Am" Father? One who walks by you daily and will never let go? "I am with you always" (Matthew 28:20).

We are surprised when we struggle in the world, yet hesitate to turn to our very Creator. He has the answers, and He will fill you with hope. Reach for Him today. Don't be uncertain. Know Him. For He is, after all, I Am.

Father, we surrender our lives to You this day. We choose to turn from our sins, reach for Your hand, and ask for Your guidance. Thank You for Your loving-kindness. Amen.

Day 306

GOD'S PROVISION

*But my God shall supply all your need according
to his riches in glory by Christ Jesus.*
PHILIPPIANS 4:19

Sometimes the littlest words in our language pack a lot of meaning into them. *All* is one of those words. Three letters encompass the total extent of the whole. Everything is in the word *all*.

In the letter to the Philippians, Paul is wrapping up a discussion of how God had used the church to provide for Paul's need while he was in prison, even though many of them didn't have much to give. Paul spoke out of experience when he told them God would supply all their financial needs because they gave sacrificially to help another person with a greater need.

But God meeting their financial need isn't all that is encompassed in the meaning Paul intended to convey when he chose this particular word. When Jesus taught this principle to His disciples, Luke recorded it in his Gospel: "Give, and it shall be given unto you; good measure, pressed down, and shaken together, and running over, shall men give into your bosom. For with the same measure that ye mete withal it shall be measured to you again" (Luke 6:38). Jesus indicated that whatever a person has to give, when they give it, they will receive as they have given. Emotional, spiritual, physical, material—whatever the need, God will supply it abundantly, pressed down, shaken together, and running over.

*Father, thank You for this promise that You will abundantly supply
every need I have through the riches of heaven in Christ Jesus. Amen.*

Day 307

OPEN THE BOOK

*For whatsoever things were written aforetime were
written for our learning, that we through patience
and comfort of the scriptures might have hope.*

ROMANS 15:4

"Out with the old and in with the new!" is unfortunately some Christians'
philosophy about the Bible. Yet the Old Testament scriptures are vital to
every believer. We cannot understand the power of the New Testament
until we embrace the teachings, wisdom, and moral laws of God revealed
in the Old Testament. After all, the Old Testament points directly to the
coming of the Messiah, Jesus, and our salvation.

The apostle Paul reminds us that everything in the Bible was written
with purpose—to teach us that through our trials and the encouragement
of God's Word we might have hope. Life is tough, after all. We get
discouraged and, at times, disheartened to the point of such despair
that it's hard to recover. Yet the Word of God ignites the power of a
positive, godly fire within.

Reading *all* of God's Word is paramount. It is the source of hope,
peace, encouragement, salvation, and so much more. It moves people
to take action while diminishing depression and discouragement. As the
writer of Hebrews put it, "For the word of God is quick, and powerful,
and sharper than any twoedged sword" (Hebrews 4:12).

Need some encouragement? Open the Book.

*Lord, help me read Your Word consistently to empower me
with the hope and encouragement I need. Amen.*

Day 308

LEAD US, LORD

O Lᴏʀᴅ, I know that the way of man is not in himself:
it is not in man that walketh to direct his steps.
Jᴇʀᴇᴍɪᴀʜ 10:23

So many changes would happen in our lives if we lived Jeremiah's words. If we really believed God was in control. We would be able to release our worries and problems in a prayer of thanksgiving and then wait. And that's the difficulty that trips us up. In our frenzied world, we feel we need immediate answers, and we rush to solve situations our own way. Sometimes that works; however, often we become enmeshed in less than desirable circumstances.

The last line of today's scripture entreats God to correct us, and that's certainly not a desirous thought. Not many hope to be straightened out. But when we yield our lives to Him and trust Him implicitly, understanding full well that our creator God wants the best for us, then our prayers of thanksgiving and trust fall more easily from our mouths. Adoration and praise should fall from our lips before our requests.

A prayer of total surrender gives glory to God the Father and pleases Him. It allows Him to work in our lives in ways we often don't understand.

Lord, I bless You and give You my heartfelt praise.
Thank You for all You do to work on my behalf. Amen.

Day 309

PROPHETIC!

*Thus saith the LORD to his anointed, to Cyrus, whose right
hand I have holden, to subdue nations before him.*

ISAIAH 45:1

—————— ✀ ——————

Who will be president in 2028? What will be the name of a child who will
be born to one of your neighbors in ten years? Why don't you know?

What's so fascinating about this verse is that God tells us in advance
the name of the person who will liberate Israel from Babylonian
oppression—150 years before his birth! Much of Bible prophecy is
literal, where God gives names (such as Cyrus the Great), times (such
as seventy years before Israel is released from captivity), and places
(such as Bethlehem, where the Christ child was to be born).

So when we read Matthew chapter 24 and other places where end-
times prophecies are recorded, we can be sure of their literal fulfillment.
For instance, we do not look for a Christ to come out of a nation but out
of the sky when the sun has turned dark (Revelation 6:12–14). Prophecy
confirms the presence of God and keeps us from being deceived.

—————— ✀ ——————

*Dear God, I am wary of false prophets; there are so many these days,
but I know that I can always rely on the truthfulness
of the prophecies in Your Word. Amen.*

WHAT RESPONSE DOES GOD REQUIRE?

Wherewith shall I come before the LORD, and bow myself before
the high God? . . . He hath shewed thee, O man, what is good;
and what doth the LORD require of thee, but to do justly,
and to love mercy, and to walk humbly with thy God?
MICAH 6:6, 8

———————————

They drag themselves across the uneven pavement until their knees are bloodied and their exhausted bodies finally fall against the splintered wooden doors to the church. In this way, many in Mexico seek to do their yearly public penance for sin.

Christ has already paid the price that needed to be exacted for our sins. He took the whips, the lashes, the nailing to the cross, the verbal rebukes, and also the physical agony on our behalf. The God of this universe looked upon our futility and became a man, and then He sacrificed His life so that we who did not and could not ever deserve His mercy might obtain it. Jesus Christ did all this because He is both just and kind.

Isaiah prophesied the promise of Christ's cross. "Surely he hath borne our griefs, and carried our sorrows. . . . But he was wounded for our transgressions, he was bruised for our iniquities: the chastisement of our peace was upon him; and with his stripes we are healed" (Isaiah 53:4–5).

———————————

Though I expend every effort, Lord, I can never rid myself of sin.
You've already provided the only way that I can be cleansed. Amen.

Day 311

MEEK IS BEAUTIFUL

For the LORD taketh pleasure in his people:
he will beautify the meek with salvation.
PSALM 149:4

───────── ~ℓℓℓℓ~ ─────────

Jesus looked around at the people of Nazareth. There were people of all kinds there. He knew that He had been sent to them all, but He also knew that there were some who would reject Him. He knew there would also be those who would accept Him readily: His people. His people were the poor and oppressed. They were the slaves and the widows and the orphans. They were the outcasts: prostitutes and tax collectors and lepers. In a world where so much value was placed on beauty, His people were the dregs. But he had something to offer them that would make them beautiful. Through His grace, His people would be elevated to the level of angels, and even higher. In God's wisdom, the last—His people—would be first, and the first would be last. Jesus set out, looking to find His people.

Are we His people? Do we accept Him and fashion our lives to His will, or do we reject Him, continuing to live by our own rules? Christ will beautify the meek with salvation. It is in our meekness that we realize our need for God. Let God beautify you, and you will find His pleasure.

───────── ~෴~ ─────────

Make me meek, Lord. Break my spirit of willfulness
and recreate me with Your beauty. Amen.

Day 312
CLEAR VISION

So shall the knowledge of wisdom be unto thy soul:
when thou hast found it, then there shall be a reward,
and thy expectation shall not be cut off.
PROVERBS 24:14

If you've ever worn glasses, you know what it's like to try to go without them. Talk about a fuzzy world! You take tentative steps, cautiously moving forward, knowing that, at any minute, you might trip over something or knock something down.

Clarity of vision is a wonderful gift. Once you put those glasses on, you can clearly see the road ahead and take bold, big steps. Confidence rises up inside of you as you focus on the path set before you.

In this same way, God can bring clarity/vision to your path when you ask for His wisdom. Picture yourself in a rough situation. You don't know which way to go. You ask for the Lord's wisdom. He offers it, and the road ahead of you is suddenly clear. It's as if you've put on spiritual glasses! That's what His wisdom does—it gives definition, boldness, and confidence. It makes clear the path.

What are you waiting for? No need for a fuzzy road ahead. Put on those glasses then take a bold step forward!

Father, I'm so excited that I don't have to walk around confused and blinded. No fuzzy roads for me, Lord! Today I pause to ask for Your wisdom so that the road ahead will be clear. Thank You for great vision and the confidence to move forward. Amen.

Day 313

WITHOUT BLEMISH

The LORD shall judge the people: judge me, O LORD, according to my
righteousness, and according to mine integrity that is in me.
PSALM 7:8

If we are honest with ourselves, we have to admit that it's a very scary thought that God might actually judge us according to our measure of righteousness and integrity. Under the careful scrutiny of the Lord, all our blemishes surface and we are exposed for what we really are: sinners in need of a good cleaning! Praise God that the cleaning is available to us through the blood of the Lamb, Jesus Christ. By the forgiveness of sin offered through the death and resurrection of Christ, we are made clean and pure and able to pass the scrutinous eye of God. Christ's righteousness becomes the righteousness of all who believe in Him and turn their hearts over to Him. Jesus paid the penalty that would have come to us. We now have no fear of condemnation from the Lord. All we have is the promise of love and forgiveness to those who repent of their sins and follow in the ways of the Lord.

Make me like You, Oh Lord. In the ways I am lacking,
remake me in the image of Christ. Create in me a new and
clean heart, and bless the paths I am to walk. Amen.

Day 314

OPEN UP

Confess your faults one to another, and pray one for another,
that ye may be healed. The effectual fervent prayer
of a righteous man availeth much.

JAMES 5:16

James encourages us to admit our faults to other trusted Christians. Why? So that we can support and pray for each other that we might be healed. The healing mentioned in this verse isn't limited to physical healing. More often, it means healing the heart of its sinfulness. James adds that the earnest prayers offered by Christians bring results. The results might not be what we expect, but we can be assured that they are God's results—His will for our lives.

Are you carrying the burden of your faults all by yourself? Why not have a heart-to-heart talk with a Christian friend?

Heavenly Father, there are things that I am keeping to myself
that weigh heavy on my heart. Help me to share my burden
with the right Christian friend. Lead me, Lord. Amen.

Day 315

EMPTINESS

Thou hast made known to me the ways of life;
thou shalt make me full of joy with thy countenance.
ACTS 2:28

Imagine you're looking at a full-to-the-brim rain barrel. You've been in a season of abundant rain. It never occurs to you that a dry season might be around the corner.

Now picture yourself, weeks later, staring down into the barrel, noticing that it's bone dry. Drought has taken its toll. Now you have a picture of what it's like when you go through a season of spiritual wholeness and spiritual drought. Your rain barrel—your heart—is only as full as what's poured into it.

Did you realize that God can refill your heart with just one word? When He sees that your well is running dry it breaks His heart. The only solution is to run to His arms and ask for a fresh outpouring of His holy water, the kind that will replenish your soul and give you the nourishment you need to move forward in Him.

It's up to you. God is waiting to meet with you. His everlasting water is prepped and ready to be poured out on you. All you need to do. . . is run to Him.

Father, I've been blaming my dry spell on so many different things:
Exhaustion. Frustration. You name it, I've pointed the finger
at it. Lord, I need the kind of water that You provide—
the kind that will never run dry. Today, Lord, I run
into Your arms, ready to be refreshed! Amen.

Day 316

DON'T WORRY!

*Be careful for nothing; but in every thing by prayer and supplication
with thanksgiving let your requests be made known unto God.
And the peace of God, which passeth all understanding,
shall keep your hearts and minds through Christ Jesus.*

PHILIPPIANS 4:6–7

The Bible tells us plainly not to worry. But that can be difficult when the economy is poor, bills need to be paid, health issues arise, and families face crisis after crisis. Jesus helps us make sense of this in Luke 12:25: "And which of you with taking thought can add to his stature one cubit?" The answer is obvious. It can't be done. So why waste precious time and energy worrying when it will change nothing?

When you start to worry, pray instead. Tell God how you feel and what you need. Tell Him that you're struggling with worry and ask Him to take your fears away. He replies to your heartfelt plea gently in Luke 12:32: "Fear not, little flock; for it is your Father's good pleasure to give you the kingdom."

How comforting, those words from the mouth of Jesus! Don't be afraid! Don't worry! You've got the kingdom of God to look forward to for all eternity. No need to worry about the rest.

*Dear Jesus, thank You for Your promise of eternal life! Give me
peace that exceeds my understanding when I start to worry. Amen.*

PRAYER IS

O my God, I cry in the day time, but thou hearest not;
and in the night season, and am not silent.

PSALM 22:2

Prayer is a tricky thing. It was never meant as just a "gimme" list by which we can automatically get things from God. It is not a gripe time to vent frustrations and woes. It is not a time to show off our piety. Rather, it is a time to draw close to God in order to be open to His will and guidance. So often we feel that God is not listening because we don't get what we ask for. We want results immediately, and we decide beforehand what we will accept as an answer and what we will not. Who says that we get to make the rules?

The Lord hears us, and He is true to answer us, but He always measures His responses according to His divine wisdom. He knows what is best for us, even when it doesn't agree with what we want. It is natural and human to doubt the Lord sometimes. He understands that. Just don't give up. The Lord breaks through our desert spots, to comfort us when we cry.

Lift me, Lord, into Your loving arms. Grace me with the sweet
memory of Your care, that I might never doubt You. Amen.

Day 318

GRACE ACCEPTED

*But God, who is rich in mercy, for his great love wherewith
he loved us, even when we were dead in sins,
hath quickened us together with Christ,
(by grace ye are saved).*
EPHESIANS 2:4–5

———————— ⁊⁊⁊ ————————

Have you ever been wrongly accused of something or completely misunderstood? Have the words of your accusers struck your heart, making you feel like you have to make it right somehow, but no amount of reasoning with them seems to help?

If anyone understands this situation, it's Christ Himself. Wrongly accused and misunderstood, yet He offered unfathomable grace at all times and still offers it today.

This reminds us that we are to aim to offer this same grace to our accusers and those who misunderstand us. We will be misunderstood when we try to obey and follow God in a culture that runs quite contrary in many ways. Our job is to first accept God's grace and then offer it up to others as lovingly as we can. Like Christ.

———————— ⁊⁊⁊ ————————

*God, help us to continually accept Your grace through
Christ and reflect You by offering that same grace to others. Amen.*

CLEANING THE PANTRY OF YOUR SOUL

Brethren, I count not myself to have apprehended: but this one thing
I do, forgetting those things which are behind, and reaching forth
unto those things which are before, I press toward the mark for the
prize of the high calling of God in Christ Jesus. Let us therefore, as
many as be perfect, be thus minded: and if in any thing ye
be otherwise minded, God shall reveal even this unto you.
PHILIPPIANS 3:13–15

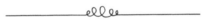

Businessman and minister John G. Lake once said, "Beloved, if any unholiness exists in the nature, it is not there by the consent of the Spirit of God. If unholiness is in your life, it is because your soul is giving consent to it, and you are retaining it. Let it go. Cast it out and let God have His way in your life."

As you grow in Christ, you will find that old thinking has to go to make room for the new understanding of God's desires and plans for your life. It's cleaning the pantry of your soul. Old mind-sets and habits are like junk food or packages with expired dates. As you throw out the old, you find that the new thoughts and habits bring renewed life and strength in Christ.

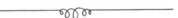

Heavenly Father, I want to think Your thoughts and know Your ways.
Help me to let go of the old ways and live in the new today. Amen.

RUN WITH ENDURANCE

Let us lay aside every weight, and the sin which doth so easily beset us, and let us run with patience the race that is set before us, looking unto Jesus the author and finisher of our faith.

HEBREWS 12:1–2

Running was the first and, for many years, the only event of the ancient Olympic games. So it is no wonder that the New Testament writers use the metaphor to describe the Christian life. The first races were 200-yard sprints. These gradually increased in length as the Olympic games continued to develop. The modern marathon commemorates the legendary run made by a Greek soldier named Pheidippides, who ran from the battlefield outside Marathon, Greece, to Athens to proclaim a single word: *victory!* Then he collapsed and died.

The Christian race lasts a lifetime, with Christ Jesus as our goal, the prize that awaits us at the finish line in heaven. It can't be run all-out as a sprint or no one would last the course. Though there was one race in the ancient games where the runners wore full armor, most of the time the ancient runners ran naked, stripping away anything that would slow them down. Obviously the writer of Hebrews was familiar with the ancient sport of running when he advised believers to run with endurance the race God set before them.

Father, as we run the race You set before us, let us run with endurance, not allowing anything to distract us from the goal of Christ-likeness. Amen.

Day 321

GREAT WORKS

He sent divers sorts of flies among them, which devoured them;
and frogs, which destroyed them. He gave also their increase
unto the caterpiller, and their labour unto the locust.
PSALM 78:45–46

God sent plagues upon the Egyptians, who persecuted the Hebrew people. Through these afflictions, God sent the message that no one could do evil for long and get away unpunished. Our Lord doesn't supersede the laws of nature often, but when He does, it is with good cause. And yet, even in the face of the terrible plagues, the Egyptian pharaoh refused to believe. People who lack the love of God in their lives so often refuse to admit they might be wrong. It is easier to deny God than to do what is necessary to please Him. Christians refuse to deny their hearts, and they continually acknowledge God's great works for what they really are. In our own day, the Lord does not send many plagues to afflict us, but there are definitely enough hardships to make us want to reach out to Him. We need God, and thankfully, we have Him, every step of the way.

My eyes are blind to many of Your great works, Lord.
I miss so much of Your greatness and love. Help me
to see You in new ways each day. Amen.

Day 322

EASY AND LIGHT

For my yoke is easy, and my burden is light.
MATTHEW 11:30

Ever felt like a beast of burden? With all the pressures and expectations of this life, it would be hard not to sometimes. If you had to be such a creature, what kind of master would you choose?

Horses and oxen still plow fields all around the world. They wear yokes across their shoulders, and their burdens are not light. We who feel wearied by the world might sympathize with them as they drag plows through hard, stony ground. They don't get to choose their masters. They can only walk where the reins or the whip make them go. And when their working life is over. . .

So, why would anyone chose to wear a yoke?

Because the one that Christ offers really is light. So light, in fact, that He actually carries our burdens! There is no harness; there is no whip. We get to choose our Master!

All that He asks for a lifetime of companionship followed by an eternity of bliss is that we wear the "yoke" of the love of God. With Jesus guiding our steps, plowing a straight furrow will be our pleasure. And when our working life is over, we'll find the furrow led all the way to heaven.

Father, I am proud to call You Master. You are good and kind to me. You allow me freedom, and when I obey You, You fill my heart with joy. Amen.

Day 323

IN HIS MERCY

*For his merciful kindness is great toward us: and the truth
of the LORD endureth for ever. Praise ye the LORD.*
PSALM 117:2

———————— *elle* ————————

Some people think that God kicked Adam and Eve out of the garden only as a punishment. But just think about it. There were two trees in the garden of special note. One was the tree of the knowledge of good and evil, which the duo ate from, and the other was the tree of eternal life. What could have been more cruel than to allow Adam and Eve access to the tree of eternal life after they had chosen to experience evil? God wanted our eternal existence to be sin free, and so He removed the temptation from the midst of men and women. In His great mercy, He made certain that there was an escape from evil for those who wanted it. God's merciful kindness is truly great toward us. Praise Him always.

———————— *ನಿನ* ————————

*Thank You for making possible an eternity of peace and joy,
free from sin and sorrow. Prepare my heart for
my heavenly home. Amen.*

Day 324

REST DWELLS HERE

This is my rest for ever: here will I dwell; for I have desired it.
PSALM 132:14

The climb was steep and treacherous, and there were no level places to stop. The sun was beating down, and the two climbers were exhausted. Both were beginning to question the wisdom of the climb. Just as they began to despair of ever making it alive, a ledge jutted into the cliff, and both climbers pulled themselves up onto it. There, in the cool shade cast by the rock, the climbers were renewed and strengthened, enabled to finish their ascent.

The Lord provides us with a place to rest in this climb of ours through life. He welcomes us, shades us, protects us, and enables us to go forward strengthened and renewed. We are never far from this rest. All we need to do is turn to the Lord, and He will grant us respite.

Lord, take me into Your loving arms to comfort and energize me.
I get so tired sometimes, and I need a place to escape.
Help me to turn inward, to dwell with Christ,
and to draw upon His power. Amen.

Day 325

LOVE YOUR ENEMIES

But love ye your enemies, and do good, and lend,
hoping for nothing again; and your reward shall be great.
Luke 6:35

These words, spoken by Jesus, are some of the hardest words we have to consider. Love our enemies? Really? The thought of loving those who do us harm just doesn't sit right. The thought of giving kindness in return for malicious intent makes no sense and causes our stomachs to knot up, our shoulders to tighten. Love our enemies? Please, God, no.

Isn't it enough to avoid our enemies and do them no harm?

Sometimes. Maybe. But most of the time God calls us to a love so brave, so intense that it defies logic and turns the world on its side. He calls us to love like He loves. That means we must show patience where others have been short. We must show kindness where others have been cruel. We must look for ways to bless, when others have cursed.

Something about that just doesn't feel right to our human hearts.

But God promises great rewards for those who do this. Oh, the rewards may not be immediate. But when God promises great rewards, we can know without doubt that any present struggle will be repaid with goodness and blessing, many times over.

Dear Father, help me to love those who hate me, bless those who
curse me, and show kindness to those who have been cruel.
Help me to love like You love. Amen.

Day 326

HEED HIS VOICE

Be wise now therefore, O ye kings:
be instructed, ye judges of the earth.
PSALM 2:10

Where is the voice of God in our world today? In times past, God's people were listened to, and the influence of the faithful was amazing. Why isn't that so true today?

Many today may think, "We're too bright for that religious stuff now. We're too advanced." What could be further from the truth? Without the counsel of the Lord, everything is ignorance. In trying to deal with our problems apart from God, we are creating more problems than we can handle. The answer is not in running from the Lord, but in running to Him.

In our own lives, we need to learn to let the Lord rule. Giving God control of our lives is not a sign of weakness, but it is the greatest show of strength we will ever make. Under the guidance of God, we become conquerors in a world that tries hard to break us down.

Oh Lord, be close to me, building me up and keeping me ever in
Your loving care. Do not let me be swayed from the path You have
set me on. Others may fail me, but You never will. Hallelujah! Amen.

Day 327

LOVE WITHOUT LIMITS

Thy mercy, O LORD, is in the heavens;
and thy faithfulness reacheth unto the clouds.
PSALM 36:5

God's love and faithfulness have no bounds. They reach to the heavens. They stretch to the skies and beyond. This is hard for us to understand. As humans, even our very best attempts at love and faithfulness are limited. God's love is limitless. When God created you, knit you together in your mother's womb, and brought you into this world, He loved you. He loves you just as much today as He did when you were an innocent baby. He is incapable of loving you any less or any more than He already does. His love is not based on what you do or don't do. It is not here today and gone tomorrow due to any mistake or failure in your life. He is faithful even when we are faithless. If it seems that you are not as close to God as you once were, He is not the one who moved. Draw close to your heavenly Father. You will find that He is there, faithful and true, ready to receive you back unto Himself. Thank the Lord today for an unfailing, unfathomable sort of love. What a blessing is the love of our faithful God!

Thank You, God, for loving me with a love that reaches to the heavens. You are faithful even when I am not. I love You, Lord. Amen.

ONE NAME

I will make thy name to be remembered in all generations:
therefore shall the people praise thee for ever and ever.
PSALM 45:17

———————— ℓℓℓℓ ————————

The sculptor looked at the piece of stone and thought. His mind whirled at the possibilities the stone presented. He could make anything he wanted. He could carve out great beauty. He could create a monument to himself. He could immortalize a great figure from history. He could sculpt a statement of power and dignity. His mind danced with imagination. He began to dream of the ultimate statement he could make. He looked into the sky and saw the glories there. He looked at the trees and flowers. He watched people walking past. He thought of waterfalls and rainbows and beautiful music. His heart swelled full, then sank. What could he possibly carve into stone that would do justice to the world of wonder he lived in? He set about his carving, working with great care and determination. After days of labor and love, he unveiled the greatest work his life could offer. Three letters, finely shaped, lovingly created. The greatest legacy the artist could give. The name was GOD.

———————— ༒༒ ————————

Make my life a symbol of Your love and a sign of Your grace.
I live my life in Your will, trying to be the best person I can
be. Accept my life as an offering of love. Amen.

PROVIDING IT ALL

For God so loved the world, that he gave his only begotten Son,
that whosoever believeth in him should not perish,
but have everlasting life.
JOHN 3:16

―――――― ⟋⟍⟋⟍ ――――――

Beginning with Adam, God provided for His loved ones: a ram for Abraham to spare his son, manna for the wandering Jewish people. The Bible resonates with the provisions of a mighty God. And the Word says our God is the same today as He was then. So we know He will provide for our needs. True love reflected by His care for us every day.

His provision is not just for our material needs, but more importantly He extends us unmerited favor, grace, when we least deserve it. He provides us with an all-encompassing love once we accept it. And He seals His promises with the gift of the Holy Spirit, making us heirs to the throne. When we realize the depth of care we've received from our heavenly Father, it is breathtaking.

Always a step ahead, He made provision before any need existed. God gave us His all, His best, when He gave us His Son. He provided it all. We serve a glorious and mighty God.

―――――― ⟋⟍⟋⟍ ――――――

Lord, Your encompassing love amazes me. Thank You for all
You have done and will continue to do in my life. Amen.

SEVEN

*Seven times a day do I praise thee
because of thy righteous judgments.*
PSALM 119:164

In the Bible, the number seven symbolizes completeness. God created the world in seven days. Seven days complete a week. Major festivals such as the Passover and Tabernacles and wedding feasts lasted seven days. In Pharaoh's dream, the seven good years followed by seven years of famine represented a complete cycle. In the New Testament, seven churches are mentioned in Revelation.

The psalmist prayed seven times a day. He lifted up praises to God throughout the entire day. He filled the minutes of his life with gratitude and paying attention to God.

The Bible tells us to pray without ceasing. A fixed-hour prayer ritual is called "praying the hours" or the "daily office." Hearts and minds turn toward God at set times. We make an effort to create a space in our busy lives to praise God and express our gratitude throughout the day.

You can create any kind of prayer schedule. Each stoplight you pass, the ring of the alarm on your watch, or a pause during television commercials can all serve as simple reminders to pray. You can be alert during the day for ways God protects and guides you.

Seven moments a day—to thank the Lord for all the moments of our lives.

*Sometimes I forget to pray; busyness gets in the way. But I can
change that! I will set aside specific times throughout
my day to pray and praise You, Lord. Amen.*

Day 331

HEARS ALL, SEES ALL

Understand, ye brutish among the people: and ye fools,
when will ye be wise? He that planted the ear, shall he
not hear? he that formed the eye, shall he not see?
PSALM 94:8–9

There's no fooling God. There is no place we can go where He does not see our every move. Those people who think they have God fooled are only fooling themselves. God sees all things, He hears all things, and nothing escapes His attention. For those who live in sin, that is a very frightening thought. For those who walk in righteousness, there is no problem. Let the Lord watch. It is good to know that He is here.

Lord, be with me this day. Search my life, and help me to correct
the wrong things that I do. Keep me walking in the light,
and prevent me from straying into darkness. Amen.

Day 332

KEEPING QUIET

Hatred stirreth up strifes: but love covereth all sins.
PROVERBS 10:12

⟳

Let's face it. We all enjoy a juicy bit of gossip now and then. As wrong as that seems, most of us are guilty of stirring the pot, at one time or another. It's not the worst thing we can do, right?

But God's Word tells us that gossip is more indicative of hatred than love. Words can do more damage than any amount of physical harm. Gossip hurts. It tears down and wounds our spirits. It causes deep pain, which can take years to heal. And sometimes its wounds never heal, this side of eternity.

Love always protects, always heals, always builds up. Sometimes, it's necessary to reveal hurtful information. But more often, we can just let things go and protect those around us from hurtful comments. We can keep our mouths shut, quit stirring the pot, and let conflicts die before they begin. Or at least, we can choose not to contribute to the conflict.

Hatred fans the flames of controversy and dissension without concern for who is hurt. Love, on the other hand, covers over wrongs. When love is exercised, conflict can be smothered before the damage gets out of control.

⟳

*Dear Father, I want to build others up, not tear them down.
Forgive me for stirring up conflict. Help me to show wisdom
and love by refusing to contribute to gossip,
controversy, and dissension. Amen.*

Day 333

THIS DAY

This is the day which the LORD hath made;
we will rejoice and be glad in it.
PSALM 118:24

Rainy days are loved by farmers. Snowy days are loved by children who can stay home from school. Storms are loved by mystery fanatics. Gray days are loved by romantics. Sunny days are loved by picnickers. Warm days are loved by beachgoers. Cool days are loved by those who stroll. All days have their purposes under heaven. Enjoy the day that the Lord has made. He has many more to share.

Let me appreciate the gift of this day. Help me to use my time wisely,
teach me to rejoice, and fill me with joy that never ends. Amen.

Day 334

BUDGET BREAKER

Then said the LORD unto Moses, Behold, I will rain bread from heaven for you; and the people shall go out and gather a certain rate every day, that I may prove them, whether they will walk in my law, or no.
EXODUS 16:4

———————— ✇ ————————

The month lasted longer than the paycheck. The grocery bill exceeded the budget. Medical expenses surpassed the rent. It's not an easy road to travel, yet one that many of us walk.

Isn't it interesting that we can trust God for eternal life, yet find it harder to trust Him for help with the mortgage?

In the Old Testament, God told the wandering Israelites He would feed them "bread from heaven," but with one caveat: He would only allow them to gather enough food for one day. No storing food away for the dreaded what-ifs of tomorrow. They would simply have to trust their God to faithfully supply their needs.

They didn't always pass the "trust test"—and neither do we. But thankfully, God is faithful in spite of us! He will meet our needs when we come to Him in simple trust. Then we can bask in His faithfulness.

———————— ✇ ————————

Father, Your Word promises to supply all my needs. I trust You in spite of the challenges I see. You are ever faithful. Thank You! Amen.

REJOICING WITH FRIENDS

*And when he cometh home, he calleth together his friends
and neighbours, saying unto them, Rejoice with me;
for I have found my sheep which was lost.*

LUKE 15:6

Gathering with friends and family can be so much fun, especially when you have something to celebrate. Birthday parties, holidays, weddings, and anniversaries are a blast when you're celebrating with people you love. There's just something about being together that adds to the excitement.

God loves a good party, especially one that celebrates family togetherness. Just like the good shepherd in today's verse, He throws a pretty awesome party in heaven whenever a lost child returns to the fold. Celebrating comes naturally to Him, and—since you're created in His image—to you too!

Think of all the reasons you have to celebrate. Are you in good health? Have you overcome a tough obstacle? Are you handling your finances without much grief? Doing well at your job? Bonding with friends or family? If so, then throw yourself a party and invite a friend. Better yet, call your friends and neighbors together, as the scripture indicates. Share your praises with people who will truly appreciate all that the Lord is doing in your life. Let the party begin!

*Lord, thank You that I'm created in the image of a God who knows
how to celebrate. I have so many reasons to rejoice today. Thank You
for Your many blessings. And today I especially want to thank You
for giving me friends to share my joys and sorrows. Amen.*

Day 336

REAL WORK

Again, I considered all travail, and every right work,
that for this a man is envied of his neighbour.
This is also vanity and vexation of spirit.
ECCLESIASTES 4:4

Labor isn't meaningless. Achievement isn't meaningless either. Man's envy of his neighbor is the spoiler. What we do to be like others, what we want because other people have it, those are the meaningless things.

"Keeping up with the Joneses" is all very well in this life, but the Joneses (whoever they might be for you) are mortal, and their example is finite. When they go the way of all mortal things, their works, achievements, and everything we emulated—or wished we were or wished we had because they had it—all of that goes with them, like dust blowing in a good stiff breeze.

For a life's work to be meaningful, its effects should be independent of the life that made it. Great men and women get that for a while—until history forgets them. Humble, faith-filled souls find real meaning not in trying to get what their neighbors have, but by reaching out to those neighbors, and others, in God's name, making their labor the Lord's work. Their achievements will mean something forever.

Lord, remind me that my labor and all that I achieve should bring
You glory. Allow my work to leave Your footprint on
Earth even after I am gone. Amen.

Day 337

I FORGIVE YOU

The discretion of a man deferreth his anger;
and it is his glory to pass over a transgression.
PROVERBS 19:11

Great power comes in these three little words: *I forgive you.* Often they are hard to say, but they are powerful in their ability to heal our own hearts. Jesus taught His disciples to pray, "Forgive us our debts, as we forgive our debtors" (Matthew 6:12). He knew we needed to forgive others to be whole. When we are angry or hold a grudge against someone, our spirits are bound. The release that comes with extending forgiveness enables our spirits to commune with God more closely and love to swell within us.

How do you forgive? Begin with prayer. Recognize the humanity of the person who wronged you, and make a choice to forgive. Ask the Lord to help you forgive the person. Be honest, for the Lord sees your heart. Trust the Holy Spirit to guide you and cleanse you. Then step out and follow His leading in obedience.

By forgiving, we can move forward, knowing that God has good things in store for us. And the heaviness of spirit is lifted and relief washes over us after we've forgiven. A new sense of hope and expectancy rises. *I forgive you.* Do you need to say those words today?

Father, search my heart and show me areas where I might need
to forgive another. Help me let go and begin to heal. Amen.

THE LORD HIMSELF GOES BEFORE YOU

*And the L*ORD*, he it is that doth go before thee; he will be
with thee, he will not fail thee, neither forsake thee:
fear not, neither be dismayed.*

DEUTERONOMY 31:8

How comforting and freeing when we allow God to go before us! Stop and consider that for a moment: You can relinquish control of your life and circumstances to the Lord Himself. Relax! His shoulders are big enough to carry all of your burdens.

The issue that has your stomach in knots right now? Ask the Lord to go before you. The problem that makes you wish you could hide under the covers and sleep until it's all over? Trust that God Himself will never leave you and that He is working everything out.

Joshua 1:9 tells us to "be strong and of a good courage; be not afraid, neither be thou dismayed: for the LORD thy God is with thee whithersoever thou goest." Be encouraged! Even when it feels like it, you are truly never alone. And never without access to God's power.

If you've trusted Christ as your Savior, the Spirit of God Himself is alive and well and working inside you at all times. What an astounding miracle! The Creator of the universe dwells within you and is available to encourage you and help you make right choices on a moment-by-moment basis.

*Thank You, Lord, for the incredible gift of Your presence in each
and every situation I face. Allow me to remember this and
to call upon Your name as I go about each day. Amen.*

Day 339

TRIALS AND WISDOM

My brethren, count it all joy when ye fall into divers temptations;
knowing this, that the trying of your faith worketh patience. But let
patience have her perfect work, that ye may be perfect and entire,
wanting nothing. If any of you lack wisdom, let him ask of God,
that giveth to all men liberally, and upbraideth not;
and it shall be given him.
JAMES 1:2–5

Trials and troubles are an everyday part of living here in a fallen world. Pastor and author Max Lucado says, "Lower your expectations of earth. This isn't heaven, so don't expect it to be."

Things won't be easy and simple until we get to heaven. So how can we lift our chin and head into tomorrow without succumbing to discouragement? We remember that God is good. We trust His faithfulness. We ask for His presence and peace during each moment. We pray for wisdom and believe that the God who holds the universe in His hands is working every single trial and triumph together for our good and for His glory.

This verse in James tells us that when we lack wisdom we should simply ask God for it! We don't have to face our problems alone. We don't have to worry that God will hold our past mistakes against us. Be encouraged that the Lord will give you wisdom generously without finding fault!

Lord Jesus, please give me wisdom. So many troubles are weighing
me down. Help me give You all my burdens and increase
my faith and trust in You. Amen.

Day 340

HE MAKES ALL THINGS NEW

Create in me a clean heart, O God; and renew a right spirit within me. Cast me not away from thy presence; and take not thy holy spirit from me. Restore unto me the joy of thy salvation; and uphold me with thy free spirit.
PSALM 51:10–12

King David committed adultery and had the woman's husband killed in battle (Psalm 51). Talk about guilt! Yet the Bible says David was a man after God's own heart. David loved God, and being a king with power, he messed up royally!

David had faith in God's goodness. He was truly repentant and expected to be restored to God's presence. He could not stand to be separated from God. He recognized that he must become clean again through the power of forgiveness.

Perhaps there have been times when you felt distant from God because of choices you made. There is no sin that is too big for God to cover or too small to bother Him with. He is willing to forgive, and He forgets when you ask Him. He expects you to do the same. If you don't let forgiven sin go, it can become a tool for torture for the enemy to use against you. God sent Jesus to the cross for you to restore you to relationship with Him.

Heavenly Father, thank You for sending Jesus to pay for my sins. Forgive me and make me new. Fill me with Your presence today. Amen.

Day 341

LIKE LITTLE CHILDREN

*And they brought young children to him, that he should touch them:
and his disciples rebuked those that brought them. But when Jesus
saw it, he was much displeased, and said unto them, Suffer the little
children to come unto me, and forbid them not: for of such is the
kingdom of God. Verily I say unto you, Whosoever shall not receive
the kingdom of God as a little child, he shall not enter therein.*
MARK 10:13–15

Have you ever heard a child pray from his heart? Not just a memorized prayer that he repeats before lunch but a real, honest prayer? A four-year-old boy prayed this:

"Dear God, I really don't like all the bad dreams I've been having. Will You please make them stop?"

His prayer was so pure and honest. He prayed, believing that God would listen to his prayer and do something about it. He wasn't afraid to say how he really felt.

This passage in Mark tells us that no matter how old we are, God wants us to come to Him with the faith of a child. He wants us to be open and honest about our feelings. He wants us to trust Him wholeheartedly, just like little kids do.

As adults we sometimes play games with God. We tell God what we think He wants to hear, forgetting that He already knows our hearts! God is big enough to handle your honesty. Tell Him how you really feel.

*Father, help me come to You as a little child and be more
open and honest with You in prayer. Amen.*

Day 342

SLEEP ON IT

It is of the LORD's mercies that we are not consumed,
because his compassions fail not. They are new
every morning: great is thy faithfulness.
LAMENTATIONS 3:22–23

"Sleep on it." Researchers have found that to be sound advice. They believe that sleep helps people sort through facts, thoughts, and memories, providing a clearer look at the big picture upon waking. Sleep also separates reality from emotions like fear and worry, which can cloud our thinking and interfere with rational decision-making.

Scientifically speaking, sleep is good medicine. For Christians, the biological effects of sleep are outweighed by the spiritual benefits of the new day God gives us. At the end of an exhausting day, after the worries and the pressures of life have piled high, we may lie down, feeling as though we can't take another moment of stress. But God's Word tells us that His great mercy will keep our worries and problems from consuming us.

Through the never-ending compassion of God, His faithfulness is revealed afresh each morning. We can rise with renewed vigor. We can eagerly anticipate the new day, leaving behind the concerns of yesterday.

Heavenly Father, thank You for giving me a new measure of Your
mercy and compassion each day so that my concerns don't consume
me. I rest in You and I lay my burdens at Your feet. Amen.

Day 343

INTO HIS PRESENCE

Let us come before his presence with thanksgiving,
and make a joyful noise unto him with psalms.
PSALM 95:2

If God is everywhere, how is it possible to come "before" or "into" His presence? While it's true that God is ever-present, His children are given a special invitation to draw near to Him. Yes, He may be at the banquet, but *we* can occupy the seat of honor right next to Him.

The way we draw near to God is through a beautiful, balanced combination of reverence and excitement. While our respect for God requires a measure of solemnity, God is no fuddy-duddy. He wants us to be happy and joyful in His presence. He longs to hear a simple, sincere, excited thank-You from His children, for all the things He's done in the past. He longs to see us sing and dance in His presence and tell Him how much we love Him.

When God feels distant, we can remember our special invitation to join Him in intimate conversation. He will welcome us into His arms when we fall before Him, give excited thanks, and sing joyful songs of love and praise.

Dear Father, thank You for inviting me into Your presence.
Sometimes I barge right in, spouting off my list of requests,
and I forget to say "thank You." I forget to tell You how
wonderful You are. Forgive me for that. Thank You,
Father, for all You've done for me. I love You. Amen.

Day 344

PRAYING FOR GOD'S WILL

For this cause we also, since the day we heard it, do not cease to pray for you, and to desire that ye might be filled with the knowledge of his will in all wisdom and spiritual understanding.
COLOSSIANS 1:9

The apostle Paul reminded the Colossians that he was continuously praying for them to be filled with the knowledge of God's will. Read the verse above closely. How did Paul ask God to fill them with the knowledge of His will? The only way that we can know His will—*through all the wisdom and understanding that the Spirit gives*. Paul was speaking to believers here. Christians have received the Holy Spirit as their Counselor and Guide. Those who do not have a personal relationship with Christ are lacking the Spirit, and thus, they are not able to discern God's will for their lives. Always take advantage of the wonderful gift that you have been given. If you have accepted Christ as your Savior, you also have the Spirit. One of the greatest things about the Holy Spirit is that He helps us to distinguish God's call on our life from the other voices of the world. Pray that God will reveal His good and perfect will for your life. His Holy Spirit at work in you will never lead you down a wrong path.

God, help me to draw upon the wonderful resource that I have as a Christian. Help me, through the power of the Holy Spirit, to know Your will. Amen.

Day 345

RIGHT WHERE WE SHOULD BE

Be strong and of a good courage; be not afraid,
neither be thou dismayed: for the Lord thy
God is with thee whithersoever thou goest.

JOSHUA 1:9

It's easy to tell others not to worry. It's easy to remind our friends that God is with them and He's got everything under control. And it's easy to remind ourselves of that, when everything's going smoothly.

But when life sails us into rough waters, our natural instinct is to be afraid. We worry and fret. We cry out, not knowing how we will pay the bills or how we will face the cancer or how we will deal with whatever stormy waves crash around us. When life is scary, we get scared.

And believe it or not, that's a good thing. Because when we are afraid, when we are overwhelmed, when we realize that our circumstances are bigger than we are, that's when we're in the perfect place for God to pour out His comfort and assurance on us.

He never leaves us, but sometimes when life is good, we get distracted by other things and don't enjoy His presence as we should. When we feel afraid, we are drawn back to our heavenly Father's arms. And right in His arms is exactly where He wants us to be.

Dear Father, thank You for staying with me and giving me courage.
Help me to stay close to You, in good times and bad. Amen.

Day 346

PERFECT PEACE

Thou wilt keep him in perfect peace, whose mind is stayed on thee:
because he trusteth in thee. Trust ye in the LORD for ever:
for in the LORD JEHOVAH is everlasting strength
ISAIAH 26:3–4

───────── ✦ ─────────

What does perfect peace look like? Is it a life without problems? Is it a smooth ride into the future without any bumps in the road? Not for the Christian. We know life on earth won't ever be easy, but God promises to keep us in perfect peace if our thoughts are fixed on Him.

Perfect peace is only found by having a moment-by-moment relationship with Jesus Christ. It is ongoing faith and trust that God really has it all figured out. It's believing that each setback, heartbreak, problem, and crisis will be made right by God

You can live in peace even during the messy stuff of life. You don't have to have everything figured out on your own. Doesn't that take some pressure off?

And the God of all grace, who called you to His eternal glory in Christ, after you have suffered a little while, will Himself restore you and make you strong, firm, and steadfast (1 Peter 5:10). That's perfect peace.

───────── ✦ ─────────

Heavenly Father, thank You for offering me peace in the midst of the
stress of this life. Thank You that I'm not in charge and that
You have everything already figured out. I trust You. Amen.

THE NEXT STEP

Thy word is a lamp unto my feet, and a light unto my path.
PSALM 119:105

———— *elle* ————

Change is unsettling. It doesn't matter who we are—old or young, rich or poor, married or single. Change can be exciting, but it also brings with it the unknown. And that can be a little unnerving.

When we face changes, the path ahead often looks dark and twisted. We squint and strain to see down the road, but we just can't see clearly. Truth is, we don't always need to see into the distance. We only need to see the step ahead of us. Then another step. Then another step.

When the path ahead is obscure, we can go to God's Word for guidance. His Word will light our way. Oh, it may not tell us exactly what's coming a year from now, or even a month from now. But if we depend on Him and follow the guidance He's given us, His Word will act as a road map for the step ahead. It will light the pathway at our feet, so we know we're not stepping off a cliff.

When we rely on His Word and follow it consistently, we can trust His goodness. Even when the future is unclear, we can move ahead with confidence, knowing He will lead us to the best place for us, and His goodness and love will stay with us every step of the journey.

———— *oooo* ————

Dear Father, thank You for lighting my way. Help me to follow You today and trust You for my future. Amen.

THE WINNING TEAM

If God be for us, who can be against us?
ROMANS 8:31

We always *know* God is for us, but it doesn't always *feel* that way. Even though we know the end of the story, even though we know we are on the winning team, sometimes it feels like we're losing battle after battle. It can feel like cancer is winning. Or the chemo or radiation that goes along with cancer feels like it's whipping us. Sometimes our relationships are difficult, and we feel like we're on the losing team.

We can make sure God really is on our team, in the little battles, when we conduct ourselves in a way that honors Him. If we've been in the wrong, we can't claim that God is on our side in that battle. But when we love God with all our heart, when we serve Him and serve others, when we keep our promises and make the people around us feel loved and valued and cherished, we can know God is pleased. We can know that He will stand behind us, defend us, and support us.

And ultimately, no matter how many battles we may feel like we're losing, if we stand with God, we will stand victorious. The other team may score a few points here and there. But when we're on God's team, we know we're the winners.

Dear Father, thank You for being on my team. Help me to live in a way that represents Your team well. Amen.

Day 349

THE LOVE OF STRANGERS

*But whoso hath this world's good, and seeth his brother have need,
and shutteth up his bowels of compassion from him, how dwelleth
the love of God in him? My little children, let us not love in
word, neither in tongue; but in deed and in truth.*
1 JOHN 3:17–18

When we think of hospitality in the modern sense, we often think about opening our home to friends and family, perhaps bringing a housewarming gift to a new neighbor or a covered dish to a family during an illness. Though all of that is hospitable, the literal meaning of *hospitality* in the Greek means "the love of strangers."

As Christ followers, we are called to give generously and sacrificially to all kinds of people, not just our friends or others that we know. The work of the Holy Spirit transforms our hearts so that we consider others before ourselves, sacrificing our time and resources to give others provision and rest. Exercising true hospitality allows us to use all our gifts for God's kingdom.

*Loving Father, thank You for the many gifts You have given me—time,
talent, and financial resources. Show me how You wish me to use
each gift in a generous and hospitable way for Your kingdom.
I pray that You use me to be a rich blessing to others. Amen.*

Day 350

DEEP ROOTS

*For he shall be as a tree planted by the waters, and that spreadeth
out her roots by the river, and shall not see when heat cometh,
but her leaf shall be green; and shall not be careful in the
year of drought, neither shall cease from yielding fruit.*

JEREMIAH 17:8

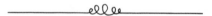

Watering your garden doesn't seem difficult, but did you know you can train a plant to grow incorrectly, just in the way you water it? By pouring water from the hose for only a few moments at each plant, the root systems become very shallow. They start to seek water from the top of the soil, and the roots can easily be burned in the summer sun. By using a soaker hose, the water slowly percolates into the ground, and the plants learn to push their roots deeper into the soil to get water.

Jeremiah talked about a larger plant, a tree. A tree needs deep roots to keep it anchored in the ground, providing stability. The roots synthesize water and minerals for nourishment and then help to store those elements for a later time. Our deep spiritual roots come from reading God's Word, which provides stability, nourishment, and refreshment.

*Father, I do not want to wither in the sun. Help me to immerse
myself in Your Word. When I do, I strike my spiritual roots deeper
into life-giving soil and drink from living water. Help me to be
the fruitful follower of You that I am meant to be. Amen.*

Day 351

A FOREVER PASSWORD

And if children, then heirs; heirs of God,
and joint-heirs with Christ.
ROMANS 8:17

───────── ✢ℓℓℓ ─────────

In today's high-tech society, passwords are required for so many things in our lives: bank ATMs, computer settings, bill paying. These passwords identify the user and are intended to keep others out of our business.

Rejoice. Because God loved us so much, He gave us an eternal password: Jesus. Once we acquire this password through salvation and set our hope in Him, we become heirs of Christ. Children of the King. Precious saints. These are names given to us by the Father to set us apart from the world because of His great love.

Unlike the security passwords for business, this password can never be compromised. We are safe and secure in the Father's arms and able to access His promised gifts. Open your Bible and discover all that is available to you as a believer: eternal life, provision, blessing upon blessing. Then praise Him for His wondrous love. His awesome care. *Jesus.* That's the most important word you'll use. As children of the King, you have rights to so much through your special relationship and kinship. What a blessing it is to know Jesus is the password to the kingdom of God.

───────── ✤✤✤ ─────────

Heavenly Father, thank You for Your everlasting love. I will store the
password You have given me in my heart, for all eternity. Amen.

HE LAUGHS

He that sitteth in the heavens shall laugh.
PSALM 2:4

Ever wonder whether God has a sense of humor? It shouldn't surprise us to find that we who were made in His image laugh as He does. But it's important to read this verse carefully to find out what gives God the chuckles.

Psalm 2 provides a telescope to focus on details in the future. We can see what will happen after Jesus returns to earth: He will set up His kingdom and dole out territories for His faithful servants to rule the world with Him. After a while, though, some people will refuse His rule and plot against Him. Therein lies the humor.

God laughs at the ludicrous. The people secretly plot against a God who reads their very thoughts. They send their strongest to fight the One who holds the universe together single-handedly. They think they can outwit the Creator, whose wisdom and power generated the miles of blood vessels and billions of cells that make up their arrogant beings. It is funny, when you think about it.

No one can outsmart God or outwit His plans for our lives. There's comfort in that thought—and that's no joke.

*Mighty God, I am grateful that You are my Creator,
the one who laughs at vain human attempts to outwit You.
How foolish men are! Always, You will prevail. Amen.*

Day 353

GET ABOVE IT ALL

Set your affection on things above, not on things on the earth.
Colossians 3:2

If you've ever taken a trip by airplane, you know with one glimpse from the window at thirty thousand feet how the world seems small. With your feet on the ground, you may feel small in a big world; and it's easy for the challenges of life and the circumstances from day to day to press in on you. But looking down from above the clouds, things can become clear as you have the opportunity to get above it all.

Sometimes the most difficult challenges you face play out in your head—where a struggle to control the outcome and work out the details of life can consume you. Once removed—far away from the details—you can see things from a higher perspective. Close your eyes and push out the thoughts that try to grab you and keep you tied to the things of the world.

Reach out to God and let your spirit soar. Give your concerns to Him and let Him work out the details. Rest in Him and He'll carry you above it all, every step of the way.

God, You are far above any detail of life that concerns me. Help me to trust You today for answers to those things that seem to bring me down. I purposefully set my heart and mind on You today. Amen.

Day 354

COME ALONGSIDE

Beloved, thou doest faithfully whatsoever
thou doest to the brethren, and to strangers.
3 JOHN 1:5

⸺ ⁀⁀⁀ ⸺

Don't you sometimes wish you were a missionary, devoting yourself completely to God and the Word? All you would do is leave behind everything you've known to risk the ridicule of strangers, the ill-treatment of antagonistic powers, and perhaps, an ignominious death.

No? Don't fancy that? Really?

Those whom God calls (the "beloved" in this verse) get a sense of mission—a willingness to sacrifice and the strength to do the Lord's work. Most of us are never asked to do anything so terribly dramatic.

Before you heave a sigh of relief, though, don't think you have nothing to do. There are Christians risking all for God right now. Some of them will cross our paths; others we'll never meet. Most will be strangers, like the men John thanked Gaius for helping. They are our frontline troops in the battle for souls—and if we aren't fighting alongside them, we can at least support them.

Do what you can to help those called to give their all as missionaries. Never think of them as strangers. Instead, remember this: someone who loves us loves them too.

⸺ ⁀⁀⁀ ⸺

Lord, I pray for Your missionaries serving in the darkest and most
dangerous parts of the world. Protect them. Bless them with the
tools they need, and show me how I can help them. Amen.

Day 355

A CHOICE

Yet I will rejoice in the LORD, I will joy in the God of my salvation.
The LORD God is my strength, and he will make my feet like hinds'
feet, and he will make me to walk upon mine high places.
HABAKKUK 3:18–19

Many days, life seems like an uphill battle, where we are fighting against the current, working hard to maintain our equilibrium. Exhausted from the battle, we often want to throw in the towel. That's when we should realize we have a choice.

What would happen if we followed the advice of the psalmist and turned a cartwheel of joy in our hearts—regardless of the circumstances—then leaned and trusted in God's rule to prevail? Think of the happiness and peace that could be ours with total submission to God's care.

It's a decision to count on God's rule to triumph. And we must realize His Word, His rule, never fails. Never. Then we must want to stand on that Word. Taking a giant step, armed with scriptures and praise and joy, we can surmount any obstacle put before us, running like a deer, climbing the tall mountains. With God at our side, it's possible to be king of the mountain.

Dear Lord, I need Your help. Gently guide me so I might learn
to lean on You and become confident in Your care. Amen.

Day 356

SIMPLY SPEAK

*Be not afraid of them, neither be afraid of their words, though briers
and thorns be with thee, and thou dost dwell among scorpions.*

EZEKIEL 2:6

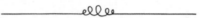

Ezekiel's call was a difficult one. He was to preach judgment to the rebellious, obstinate, and stubborn Israelites (vv. 3–4). Whether they would receive the message was questionable, but for certain they would seek to kill the messenger. Yet God's summons to the prophet was delivered with words of encouragement: "Be not afraid."

Have you ever sensed God prompting you to speak when you preferred to remain silent? As Christians we are called to exhort, encourage, and occasionally rebuke in the spirit of God's love.

Living for Christ is far from a popularity contest. In fact, we are often misunderstood or ridiculed for our spiritual convictions, until we feel as if we are embedded in a field of briers and thorns while venomous scorpions surround every side. But God's mandate is the same as it was in Ezekiel's day, namely, communicate the truth of God's Word with love and without fear.

Just like the prophet of old, we are called to simply speak and leave the rest to God.

*Dear Lord, when I hesitate to speak about the truth of
Your Word, prod me to do so. Remove my fear so
that I can boldly speak out in love. Amen.*

JONAH'S PRAYER

When my soul fainted within me I remembered the LORD:
and my prayer came in unto thee, into thine holy temple.
JONAH 2:7

───────────── ℓℓℓℓ ─────────────

Jonah ran from God. He knew where God had directed him to go, but he refused. He thought he knew better than God. He trusted in his own ways over God's. Where did it get him? He ended up in the belly of a huge fish for three days. This was not a punishment but rather a forced retreat! Jonah needed time to think and pray. He came to the end of himself and remembered his Sovereign God. He describes the depths to which he was cast. This was not just physical but emotional as well. Jonah had been in a deep struggle between God's call and his own will.

In verse 6 of his great prayer from the belly of the fish, we read these words: "Yet hast thou brought up my life from corruption, O LORD my God." When Jonah reached a point of desperation, he realized that God was his only hope. Have you been there? Not in the belly of a huge fish, but in a place where you are made keenly aware that it is time to turn back to God? God loves His children and always stands ready to receive us when we need a second chance.

───────────── ∽∾∽∾ ─────────────

Father, like Jonah I sometimes think my own ways are better
than Yours. Help me to be mindful that Your ways
are always good and right. Amen.

Day 358

FELLOWSHIP

And let us consider one another to provoke unto love and to good works: not forsaking the assembling of ourselves together, as the manner of some is; but exhorting one another.
HEBREWS 10:24–25

Before his conversion, Paul, then known as Saul, was a thug—a mean-spirited man who hated Christians and wanted them killed. Isn't it amazing that this same man became a great apostle who wrote thirteen books of the New Testament?

The Bible says that immediately after his conversion, Paul spent several days with Jesus' disciples. "At once" he began preaching that Jesus was the Messiah. The Bible also says that Paul became increasingly powerful, and he had followers. He traveled with other Christians, and they encouraged one another in their belief and commitment. Paul enjoyed being with other believers. When in prison, he lamented that he couldn't be with them to share encouragement.

Associating with other Christians is more than attending church on Sundays. It is getting to know them on a personal level and discovering what their faith has to offer in fellowship and learning. Paul sought after people whose own gifts would help build his faith. In Romans 1:11–12, he writes, "For I long to see you, that I may impart unto you some spiritual gift, to the end ye may be established; that is, that I may be comforted together with you by the mutual faith both of you and me."

Do you have friends who encourage your faith?

Dear God, thank You for sweet fellowship with Christian friends. Amen.

Day 359

RETURN

For thus saith the Lord G OD *, the Holy One of Israel; In returning
and rest shall ye be saved; in quietness and in confidence
shall be your strength: and ye would not.*
I SAIAH 30:15

Some of the saddest words in the Bible are found at the end of Isaiah
30:15: "And ye would not." Here the Lord sets before His people a
simple formula for the extreme difficulties of life they were experiencing.
By returning to God's ways and resting in Him, they could be safe from
the enemies who sought to destroy them. In quieting their spirits and
trusting in God, they could be strengthened for the battles ahead.
But they were unwilling. Instead they wanted to flee God's presence.

Are we doing the same?

*Father, I'm tired of trying to outrun my problems. May Your peace
flow through me like a mighty river, bringing rest to my soul. Amen.*

Day 360

LOVING FULLY

Jesus said unto him, Thou shalt love the Lord thy God with all thy heart, and with all thy soul, and with all thy mind.
MATTHEW 22:37

When Jesus commanded His followers to love God with all their heart, soul, and mind, He meant that loving God fully means putting aside everything that gets in the way of a relationship with Him. Everything. That's no small order in a world filled with distractions.

So how can today's Christians set aside everything to fully love God? The answer is to shift their desire from serving themselves to serving Him. Love requires action, and the Holy Spirit gives believers power to glorify God with everything they do. Praising Him for His provisions is one way to love Him. Doing selfless acts of service for others as if working for Him is another way. So is loving others as He loves us. Studying the Bible and drawing close to God in prayer is the ultimate act of love toward Him. When Christians center their lives on their passion for God, they learn to love Him fully.

Loving God with heart, soul, and mind takes practice. It means thinking of Him all day and working to glorify Him through every thought and action. It means putting aside one's own desires to serve Someone greater.

Is it possible to love God more than you love anyone or anything else? You can try. That in itself is an act of love.

Dear God, I love You. Help me to love You more through everything I do. Amen.

Day 361

NEVER GIVE UP

And he spake a parable unto them to this end,
that men ought always to pray, and not to faint.
LUKE 18:1

Have you ever felt like you don't have enough energy to utter one more word to anyone, let alone share your feelings with the Lord? Or maybe you've been asking God for the same thing over and over again, and you feel like He's either not listening or decided not to answer.

Jesus gives us a picture of how He wants us to pray in Luke 18. The persistent widow wears down the judge with her constant request until he finally gives in. God wants us to come to Him with everything. He has given us an open door to approach His throne with confidence at all times (Hebrews 4:16).

If an uncaring judge finally responded to the widow's constant pleas, how much more will the God who created us and loves us respond to ours? No matter what you are bringing before the Lord, don't give up! Keep talking to Him. The process will change your heart to be more like His. So when you feel all prayed out, remember that God is listening and working on your behalf.

Heavenly Father, sometimes I feel like the persistent widow
when I come to You over and over again with the same request.
I know You hear my prayer, and I trust that You will do
what is best for me. Help me not to lose heart but to
remember Your love and faithfulness. Amen.

Day 362

COMFORT FOR COMFORT

Wherefore in all things it behoved him to be made like unto his brethren, that he might be a merciful and faithful high priest in things pertaining to God, to make reconciliation for the sins of the people. For in that he himself hath suffered being tempted, he is able to succour them that are tempted.

HEBREWS 2:17–18

God chose to come to earth in human form to be made like us. To understand what it's like to be human. To be able to fully take our place and remove our sins. Because He was fully human while being fully God, He can help. He can comfort. The Bible says that He "comforteth us in all our tribulation, that we may be able to comfort them which are in any trouble, by the comfort wherewith we ourselves are comforted of God" (2 Corinthians 1:4).

It's so encouraging that Jesus was just like us! Our God is not one who wants to remain as a distant high king, out of touch with the commoners. He wants a very personal relationship with each one of us. He lowered Himself to our level so that we could have personal and continual access to Him. His glory knows no bounds, yet He desires to be our Friend. Take great comfort in that.

And then when people around you are troubled, you can step in. You can wrap your arms around someone else who needs a friend because of what Jesus has done for you.

Dear Jesus, thank You for the great gift of Your friendship. Allow me the opportunity to be a friend and comfort to those around me in need. Amen.

Day 363

HAVE THINE OWN WAY

Know ye that the LORD he is God: it is he that hath made us, and not we ourselves; we are his people, and the sheep of his pasture.
PSALM 100:3

"Thou art the potter, I am the clay." Those are ringing words from the song "Have Thine Own Way" that stirs up emotions and a desire to allow God to mold us and make us in His image. But what a hard thing to do. We strive to create our own worlds, to make a plan, to fix it. However, God asks us to allow Him free rein.

Sheep follow their shepherd and trust in him for provision. "As in his presence humbly I bow." Submissive to their masters, they quietly graze the hillsides knowing the shepherd knows best. What a wonderfully relaxing word picture: relying on God's guidance and timing, following His lead.

It is a simple prayer to ask Him to help us give up control, yet not a simple task. In obedience to His word, we can bow our heads and ask for the Holy Spirit's direction and take our hands from the steering wheel. Then wait. Quietly on our hillsides, not chomping at the bit, hearts "yielded and still." We wait for the still, small voice. This day, resolve to listen and follow.

Lord, we humbly bow before You and ask for Your divine guidance. Help us to follow Your plan with yielded hearts, ever ready to give up control to You. Amen.

Day 364

WHAT IS WRITTEN ON YOUR HEART?

And these words, which I command thee this day, shall be
in thine heart. . . . And thou shalt write them upon
the posts of thy house, and on thy gates.
DEUTERONOMY 6:6, 9

In many Jewish homes today, there is a small container attached to the doorway. Inside the box is a tiny scroll containing the words of Deuteronomy 6:9. This is known as a *mezuzah* and serves as a tangible reminder of God's ancient covenant with the Israelites and His desire to have first place in their lives.

In the Old Testament, God's law was written on scrolls and passed down from generation to generation. In the New Testament, we learn that Jesus both fulfilled the old covenant and introduced a new covenant. This new covenant is written on our hearts (Hebrews 10:16). God's Word is our scroll, and it confirms the truths that He has already written on our hearts through the Holy Spirit. In spite of this, we sometimes forget.

What are some practical ways you can remind yourself, each day, of the truth of God's Word? Copy verses on index cards to carry with you, or better yet, commit them to memory. Listen to an audio version of the Bible or to songs composed from scripture. Whatever you do, always be looking for fresh ways to remember the truth that God has written on your heart.

Father, thank You for writing Your truth on my heart.
Help me to look for tangible reminders of Your truth. Amen.

Day 365

PRAISE THE LORD!

Let every thing that hath breath praise
the LORD. Praise ye the LORD.
PSALM 150:6

God looked down upon His creation and saw that it was good. In time, God's creation looked back and saw that God was good. Together they formed a unity of love and devotion. Through their covenant, all creation was brought into harmony. The Lord loves His children, and many of His children love Him back. Praise the Lord with all of your being. With each breath you take, remember that the Lord is God. Nothing you do is done apart from Him. Wherever you go, God is there. He will never leave those who love Him. He gives us new years and new challenges, and He helps us to grow and learn. As we approach each new day, we can enter it confident that God goes with us. Praise the Lord, one and all. The Lord has been very good to His children.

I thank You for the year just past—the challenges and the joys—
and I look forward to the future, asking Your blessing on it.
Be with me, Lord, and with all my loved ones. Keep me in
Your care. Shine Your light upon my path. I praise You! Amen.

SCRIPTURE INDEX

BIBLE ENCOURAGEMENT FOR YOUR HEART

Read through the Bible in a Year Devotional

This lovely devotional features a simple plan for reading through the Bible in one year with an accompanying devotional thought inspired by that day's Bible reading. Each day's devotion will encourage you to read a passage from the Old Testament, New Testament, and Psalms or Proverbs and provides a relevant spiritual takeaway for practical, everyday living.

DiCarta / 978-1-68322-756-4 / $16.99

Daily Devotions for Women Morning and Evening

This charming book features an inspiring reading and prayer twice daily for an entire year, and just-right-sized inspirational readings focus on uplifting topics like Faith, Prayer, Encouragement, Love, Joy, and more— and each speaks directly to a woman's heart, drawing her ever closer to the heavenly Father. As you spend daily quiet time in prayer and study, you'll experience a refreshing blend of biblical truth and encouragement!

Hardback / 978-1-68322-875-2 / $24.99